NOTES ON BAGLEY LINES

A GENEALOGICAL SUMMARY OF NUMEROUS BAGLEY ANCESTORS

VOLUME 2 – 3RD EDITION

By
Timothy W. Bagley

Original Research and Manuscript by
Dr. Norton Russell Bagley

IN MEMORIAM AND DEDICATION

A few years after I first began to research my family history and genealogy in 1988, I was contacted by Dr. Norton Russell Bagley of New Hampshire who was eager to see my research on the Bagleys in Maine and to share his encouragement, insight, wisdom, humor, and guidance. In 1998, when I first printed and shared with him ***The Bagleys and Related Families of Washington County, Maine, and Beyond: A Genealogical Profile of Our Ancestral Families, Volume 1 – In America, Volume 2 – In Europe, and Volume 3 – Ancestral Charts***, Norton was extremely supportive and eagerly discussed the new and expanded Bagley lines I had found or updated.

Norton passed away in 2014 at 94, and while many years and generations removed may have separated us as cousins, he was a dear friend, confidant, mentor, and was always anxious to hear about my latest world travels. He asked me to share and distribute my work, as well as his own, with other researchers to try to ensure that our efforts may be of some use to anyone interested in the Bagley family.

In 2017, Plymouth State University, where Norton was a professor for many years, posted a loving tribute along with some photos at https://library.plymouth.edu/bagley. They note in part that:

> *"Dr. Norton Bagley's philosophy was always "The most important part of teaching is what happens between the teacher and the pupil. That is what makes the child want to learn." Several years ago Dr. Bagley donated property to Plymouth State; the proceeds from its sale established a scholarship endowment. A Plymouth alumnus, Dr. Bagley received his M.Ed. from Boston University and his Ph.D. from the University of Connecticut. In 1972, Dr. Bagley received the Granite State Award for outstanding service to education in the state. "I'll never forget him," noted one alumnus, among the many who remember him fondly. "He is the reason I went to college at all." He retired in 1982.*

The work that Norton and his sister did was an inspiration for many of us and laid the foundation for most of the research done on the Bagleys in America.

- Timothy W. Bagley

TABLE OF CONTENTS

INTRODUCTION BY
DR. NORTON RUSSELL BAGLEY

We first began this work in an effort to create our own connection to Orlando Bagley of Amesbury, MA. The work just grew as we obtained more information and as kind Bagleys and others supplied us with much data. A genealogy is never finished; not only does it need constant up-dating but one discovers more and more branches. One also finds that one has to research other Bagley families to separate them from one's own as, for example, the Samuel Bagley line of Boston. Sometimes branches connect, sometimes they don't – at least not that we can discover in this country.

In 1973 we compiled what material we had on the Orlando line, the Edward Bagley line of New Brunswick and Salt Lake City, and assorted other lines. We sent these to various libraries and historical societies and sold some to others who were interested and who helped us, at cost. We were fortunate in getting a great deal of feed-back. The present edition, the third*, represents the corrections and additions to date. The Samuel Bagley and Edward C. lines have been greatly enlarged and several odds and ends of lines have now been correctly connected.

*__*Note:*__ *No usable, digital files of the original, 4ᵗʰ edition documents still exist. This printing is based on scanned copies of the final manuscripts from Dr. Norton Russell Bagley, which he asked that I continue to add to, work on, and distribute as able. I have made only small, minor corrections to his original text in some of the opening sections for formatting purposes and the rest remains his last manuscript.*

We now have three volumes, the first two are on the Orlando Bagley line; the third is on various other Bagley lines: the Samuel line, the Edward line, Luther of Providence, RI, Samuel of Orange, John of Waterboro, ME, the Stanstead, QUE lines, the Haverhill, MA line, etc. We have not been able to connect these to Orlando or to themselves, although we are reasonably certain of some connections, e.g., the John of Waterboro, ME, probably goes with the Orlando line.

Each Bagley is numbered under parents, together with the dates of his or her birth and death, if known. The same number is carried over into the body of the work in its appropriate place. Each Bagley about whom something is known or who lived to maturity thus appears twice. Once under his or her parents, and again when a more complete description of that Bagley's life is given. Using the number found at the completion of the work, for example, one can find the same number again under that Bagley's parents, and then using the Bagley's parent's number go back to Orlando. There is a complete index of Bagleys by name and by the Bagley number, and a complete index of names other than Bagley together with the number of the Bagley where the name will be found. In some instances, numbers are carried over from volume one to volume two.

No material has been included that we cannot prove from some kind of record, and we cite the record. Where record is lacking, but circumstantial evidence is great, the word probably is used. We have not included material based on mere hunch or wishful thinking. In addition to the material found in these volumes, we have hundreds of file cards on Bagleys whom we cannot prove as to where they go. Wherever evidence is conflicting, we try to cite both sides of the argument.

We thank various people who have supplied information under their numbers in the text or close to the lines they supplied material about. We wish especially to thank our mother, Estella (Floyd) Bagley Maloney for long hours spent on work in vital records and town reports, to Michael Vacca for long hours spent in cemeteries and in searching and filing index cards, to Isabelle Bartholmew of Salt Lake for many hours spent in copy deeds and other records from Salt Lake City archives, to Elizabeth Nichols, a descendant of Orlando through the Mack and Joseph Smith lines; and Paul Anderson, who became an expert in ferreting out information from deeds and wills.

Unfortunately, Mrs. Anderson died in 1987, so that she did not live to see this latest revision. Her work on other families and especially in proving the descent of Anthony Colby, marks her memorial as does this work.

INTRODUCTION TO USING THIS BOOK AND RELATED VOLUMES

Notes on Bagley Lines: A Genealogical Summary of Numerous Bagley Ancestors, Volumes 1 and 2, 3rd Edition, are provided as written and annotated by Dr. Norton Russell Bagley. Norton was unable to provide me with the digital files of his work, so the work is saved from scans of his original prints. While the original prints may not provide the highest quality, they have allowed me to continue to share his work as he requested and at some point, in the future, I hope to be able to complete retyping all of his research to allow for a newer reprint.

Volumes 1 and 2 include:
- Descendants of Samuel Bagley of Weymouth, Massachusetts
- Information on numerous Bagley lines, some of which connect to Orlando of Amesbury or Samuel of Weymouth, and others whose connection remain unconfirmed
- Genealogical lines and details on the Bagleys in England
- Misc. other Bagleys that were found but not yet linked to existing lines

For the Bagley lines in Waldo County and Washington County, Maine, that are descended from Orlando Bagley, and for the ancestral lines of families related to the Bagleys, please see my work in *The Bagleys and Related Families of Washington County, Maine, and Beyond: A Genealogical Profile of Our Ancestral Families, Volume 1 – In America, Volume 2 – In Europe, and Volume 3 – Ancestral Charts.*

Companion works and research done by Norton and/or his sister for *Notes on Bagley Lines* may be found in:
- *Some Descendants of Orlando Bagley of Amesbury, Massachusetts: Volumes 1 and 2, 4th Edition*
- *Families Related to the Bagley and Floyd Families, 2nd Edition*

FORWARD BY DR. NORTON RUSSELL BAGLEY

In 1066, the Sieur de Macei[1] came with William the Conqueror to the conquest of England. Apparently, he was granted lands near the Welsh border, near Chester. One of his younger sons received the manor of Bagley (for low lying). His name is uncertain, but his descendants are all the known Bagleys, whatever the spelling of their names (there are 10 variations). Officials spelled the name according to the way it sounded to them, which depended upon the local dialect. Some of the descendants went to Ireland, apparently with Richard Strongbow[2], and spelled the name 'Begley'. The Bagley book *Notes on Bagley Lines* contains a history of the Bagleys in England.

The tradition is that three Bagley brothers came to Boston; Orlando, Samuel, and Thomas. We have traced the descendants of Orlando and Samuel, but have not been able to find Thomas. For years, the relationship of Orlando to Samuel was uncertain, but recently English records tend to confirm that they were brothers. The Samuel line is found in the *Notes on Bagley Lines* book.

The members of the Orlando line settled in Amesbury, Massachusetts where they were selectmen, sheriffs, and town clerks. Some of Orlando's descendants spread to Kingston and Candia, New Hampshire and then to the Eastern Townships of Canada. Some refused to take allegiance to the King of England and came back into upper New York and ended up in Haverhill, Massachusetts. Another branch went to Maine and settled in Durham, Liberty, and Montville and then on Down East to Jonesport, and Machias. Another branch from New Hampshire went to Vermont, to Hartland, and hence to Durham and Cairo, New York and then to Pennsylvania, Ohio, and to other states of the old Northwest, and from there to the West Coast. A few were found in the South. Like most New England families, the Bagleys scattered widely in their quest for better land and a better life.

The Bagleys were a typical Yankee family, serving in the Revolutionary war, War of 1812, a few in the Mexican War, and a host in the Civil War. They served as officials in their communities and churches, worked to clear the land, went to sea, and did their stint in the mills and factories. A few gained wider fame. Colonel Jonathan Bagley was

---

[1] Sieur is French for 'Sir' as was used as a title of respect. Sieur de Macei. There are several theories of the origin of the name, including:

English (Norman) and French. Habitation name from any of various places in Northern France which get their names from Gallo-Roman personal name of Maccius plus the local suffix- acum.
(Dictionary of Surnames, P. Hanks & F. Hodges, OUP)

A great Cheshire family of whom from their numerousness the proverb, however uncomplimentary, runs "As many Masseys as asses." The founder of the family in England was Harmon Massie, a Norman, who accompanied the Conqueror and acquired Dunham in Cheshire, which has from that circumstance ever since borne the suffix of Massey. From what part of Normandy that personage came is not known, but there are several places in the province from which, with equal claims to probability the name might reasonably be deduced: viz Mace-sur-Orme near Alencon: Macei in the arrondissement of Avranches: Marcei, in that part of Argantan, and Marcei on the Broise near the town of Avranches, the seat of an ancient Barony.
(A Dictionary of Family Names of the United Kingdom, ed M.A. Lower, pub John Russell Smith, London, 1860.

[2] Richard Strongbow was Richard de Clare, Earl of Pembroke, from Wales. He was sent to Ireland in 1168 by King Henry II to restore Dermod MacMorough as King of Leinster.

paymaster of the Massachusetts troops in the French and Indian War. He was a great landholder and died intestate, land poor. The second Orlando's daughter Sarah, married John Mack and they were the maternal ancestors of Joseph Smith, the Prophet of the Church of Latter-day Saints (Mormons). Mary Baker Eddy, a faith healer, stayed at Sarah Bagley's house who took Mary to meet John Greenleaf Whittier, the poet. There was Captain Valentine Bagley who was shipwrecked off the Arabian coast and returned home to dig the Captain's Well in Amesbury. Whittier wrote a poem about that episode. Dr. William Chandler Bagley was developer of the educational philosophy of Essentialism, which has reappeared in the "No Child Left Behind" policy of modern days. John Bagley was governor of Michigan. Further thought will produce others.

My sister, Martha (Bagley) Anderson and her husband Paul, set out o trace the Derry, New Hampshire line of Bagleys. As with all genealogies, the venture grew and grew. I become involved, as did Michael Vacca. All of us became acquainted with multiple graveyards, vital records, probate records, and church records. Too, we heard from Bagleys all over the country and some became good friends. We found we had to research the Samuel Bagley line and other lines to distinguish like-named individuals. We came across the Edward Bagley line of New Brunswick and Salt Lake City from whom many Mormon Bagleys descend. Unfortunately, we have never been able to connect this line to the other lines. We amassed a great file of Bagleys whose place in the known Bagley lines is unknown. We have saved these for other researchers.

More recently, Timothy Bagley, world traveler and currently in government service in Washington, DC, has undertaken to make the Bagley material which he has found, and our material, more available.

Family searching is fun and frustrating. Bagley, wherever and whoever you are, help to enlarge our knowledge of this family.

Good hunting,

Dr. Norton R. Bagley

Sometime teacher, professor, college dean, and author

Note: This was the last forward provided by Dr. Norton Russell Bagley in 2008.

BAGLEY FAMILY ORIGINS

Bagley is from the Saxon, meaning a rising or swelling ground that lies untilled; from boelge, a rising or swelling, and Leagh or ley, plain or pasture ground.

The original spelling appears to have been Baggiley, but it has been, and is, spelled in a variety of ways including Baggley, Bagly, Baggulley, and Bagley.

It appears to have been adopted in England by a man named Macey or Macei, who was seated at Baggiley in the time of William, the Conqueror. William made numerous trips to England, accompanied by small parties of kinsmen and others. There is an account of one of these trips, when he was accompanied by two nephews and eight lesser kinsmen, among the latter, Hama de Macei. Macie is a well-known placed name in Normandy near Avranch.

From Plea Rolls, it appears that John, Lord of Baggiley, in 1170 had sons: Hamon, Howekin, William, Peter, and John. It is not clear if Hamon Massey or John was the first ancestor of the Baggileys in England who came with William and became owners of the Manor of Baggiley from whence the name comes. King in his History of England, dated 1650, states that Baggiley was located in Bulkley Hundred in the Kingdom of March, known as the Vale Royal in England, which reaches from London to the river Mersey which divided Cheshire from Lancashire. When Thomas Bagley of Virginia died in 1672, he mentions his brothers who lived at Macclesfield, Cheshire, England. (See British Bagleys in Notes on Bagley Lines)

About the reign of King John (1213-1216, Hamon of the house of Baggiley was Baron of Dunham-Massey, and during the time "Hamon Massey, and descended from the other Hamon, before named, gave unto Matthew de Bromhal, Duckenfield and two other parts of Baggiley which the father of the said Matthew held of said Hamon, as his inheritance in knight's service to him and his heirs." This Hamon was involved in the rising of the Northern Barons against King John.

In the 15th century, the Baggileys of Cheshire had much interest in Lancashire, the next county, moved over there and changed the name to Baguley. From Cheshire through the several counties going west, the name Bagguley or nearly so is prevalent. But going south the name Bagley is present even in London and other counties; for instance, Ipswich from where the Bagleys first came to America, who were shipwrights and sea captains. Thomas Baggaley of Salt Lake City who had done research on the Bagleys in England here cites the Bagleys who settled in Boston.

Some books say there is one coat of arms for the Bagley family and that it is the same regardless of how the name is spelled or the family's immediate origins. This statement does not seem to be correct for Orlando Bagley. In Worcester, MA Genealogical Society, there is a book containing the coats of arms of early MA families including one for Orlando Bagley, and it is not the one commonly accepted for the Bagleys.

EDWARD BAGLEY OF SALT LAKE CITY, UTAH

Edward Bagley Line - Salt Lake City

1. Richard Bagley possibly father of Edward C. Bagley: m
Esther Puffer. There is no Richard Bagley in the Orlando or
Samuel Bagley lines, now known, who would fit the dates
available, nor does a research of information in New Brunswick
reveal any information about this Richard. A search of early
vital records in CT has revealed nothing. According to Puffer
Genealogy by Charles Nutt, Amos Puffer was b Mar 30, 1757, at
Wrentham, MA, and d Jamaica, VT, Aug 6, 1832. Of his
children, Esther, b Apr 24, 1796, d Oct 6, 1863, m Richard
Bagley. There are several Bagley families in Woodstock, NB
(see Canadian Lines).

2. Edward Cyrenius Bagley 2 Richard 1 (Some family members
say there is no proof his middle name was Cyrenius, but his
middle initial was C. Since he named one son Charles and one
Cyrenius, there is little to go on there). Record held by Hugh
& Ruth Bagley of Montpelier, ID, an authentic record in John
Bagley's handwriting, gives Edward as being b Feb 18, 1815, in
NY, possibly at Border City, Seneca Co; another account gives
him b on same date in Hartford, CT. He m Oct 8, 1833, Julia
Ann Grant, b S Hampton, NB, dau William & Anna Maidstone
(Hillman), Aug 3, 1815, at St John's NB. She d June 4, 1855,
Kansas Territory. Marriage sealed Sept 19, 1894, by M. W.
Merrials with John & Sarah Louise Bagley in proxy. Edward
appears to have been in ship building business and may have
gone from Hartford, CT, and entered the lumber business with
George Phillips because lumber supplies had been exhausted
around Hartford.
     The Diary of George Phillips gives this account of the
conversion of the Bagleys to the Church of Jesus Christ of
Latter Day Saints (from this point, that church will be
referred to as the Church without full name).
     "Jesse W. Crosby and Benjamin Brown were the first two
missionaries ever to preach in our part of the country. They
were robbed and beaten and Brown was left for dead. They were
even required to go before the rulers and magistrates to give
account of the strange doctrine. At last they were brought
before the governor and council and required to leave. They
had organized a branch in the parish of Southampton, and I was
ordained presiding Elder on Oct 5, 1844; this branch numbered
twenty-eight. In a few days the Elders were off for home or
the gathering place of the Saints. From that time on we were
left with very little knowledge concerning the Church until
the first week of Nov, 1852, when we were again visited by
Elder Jesse W. Crosby, who remained with us only a few days on
account of the repeated threats of violence upon his person by
the enemies of the Lord yet he baptized three, John Bagley,
David Jacques and Susannah Jacques, the sixth of Nov, 1852,
and ordained to the office beside myself Thomas Jacques;
Edward Bagley (he and his wife had been baptized in 1850) was
set apart as Teacher and on the same day he left on board the
steamer Reindeer, for home via Fredrickton, St John's and New
York. Our meetings were held regularly on Sunday and
Wednesday in spite of all the opposing friends as many as

there were. On the 25th of Dec I baptized and confirmed Charles Shelton, George Jacques, George Bagley, George and Hannah E. Phillips."

Most of the branch left New Brunswick in May, 1854. Edward Bagley and his family and George Phillips (whose wife had d in Feb 1855) left for great Salt Lake, May 21, 1855. Edward's son, John, had left previously for Utah. They went by boat to Boston and then by rail to St Louis where a steam boat took them to Council Bluffs. From there they went to Salt Lake Valley in the company of Seth Blair. They left June 18, the Phillips and Bagley families traveling together in one wagon, two yoke of oxen, fifteen in number. On June 26, 1855, Julianna Bagley and one of Phillip's daughters died of cholera. Alma Bagley, who was about seven years old at the time remembered his mother got up, cooked breakfast for her family and before sundown she had died and was buried. Seventy years later when he was 82 he described her death. He said the wolves howled and the mourning doves mourned and he cried just like he had when he was seven years old. Julia Ann Bagley was buried about 40 miles from Mormon Grove. June 23, Cyrenius Bagley died. Another son, George Ford, is said to have died on the way. The party arrived at Salt Lake Sept 25, 1855 and were settled at Provo, on the 29th. The next week they were rebaptized by Thomas Jacques in Dry Creek. Bishop Bud presided and Charles Shelton was clerk.

The first winter was especially hard as all Edward owned was one ox and half a tent. He traded the ox for a little cabin and tore up the old tent to make diapers for the baby. The boys slept on a pile of straw in the corner. Edward had bought his wife many pretty dresses to wear when they arrived in Utah, but after her death they were more poverty stricken than ever and had had to sell the dresses one by one to get food for the children. Each time a dress was sold, Edward would sit and cry. Because of their condition, Alma lived with the McClellans and Hyrum was given to the Lant family to raise.

Edward d June 16, 1868, at Payson, Utah, and was buried there (Much of the above material adapted from an account by Alverda de Lange Carson). He is supposed to have m again in 1865, but the records have been burned.

<u>Children:</u> (All b South Hampton, NB except Hyrum)
3.   Ann M. 3, b Dec 23, 1833; d 1845
4.   Charles Stewart 3, b Jan 30, 1835; d Jan 11, 1913
5.   John 3, b Apr 20, 1836; d Feb 10, 1923
6.   George 3, b Apr 26, 1838; d June 1, 1855
7.   David 3, b Nov 12, 1839; d May 4, 1855
8.   William Henry 3, b Oct 8, 1841; d Jan 25, 1923
9.   Cyrenius 3, b Apr 6, 1843; d 1855
10.   Joseph Smith 3, b Apr 9, 1845; d Apr 10, 1897.
11.   Edward Alma 3, b Apr 10, 1847; d May 29, 1929
12.   Cynthia Ann (Libby) 3, b May 13, 1849
13.   Francis M. 3, b Apr 19, 1851; d Aug 26, 1866
14.   Hyrum 3, b Feb 2, 1854, Woodstock, NB; d Apr 4, 1932

<u>4.   Charles Stewart Bagley 3, Edward 2, Richard 1, b 5</u>

Hampton, NB, Jan 20, 1835; d Jan 11, 1915, Big Cottonwood, UT;
m Julia Ann Fredericka Hansen, dau Andress & Anne (Nielson),
Oct 27, 1861, by Bishop David Brinton, b Felser, Denmark, Apr
24, 1845, d Aug 3, 1923. He was in the lumber business with
Feramore Little and Charles Decker. News account of his death
gives children list and says he was survived by brother John
of Montpelier, ID; William of Charleston; Edward A. of Grass
Valley and Hyrum A. of Brinton, UT, and one sister Libby
Bagley of ID.

Children:
15. Alice Olena 4, b Aug 4, 1863, East Mill Creek, UT; d Dec
26, 1868
16. Edward Cyrenius 4, b Jan 2, 1865; d July 9, 1943, Salt
Lake City
17. Andrew H. 4, b East Mill Creek, UT, Apr 28, 1867; d Nov
28, 1931, East Mill Creek
18. Frank E. 4, b Cottonwood, UT, May 6, 1877; d Apr 3, 1936,
Salt Lake City
19. Grant Charles 4, b Cottonwood, UT, Jan 17, 1872; d Sept,
1916
20. Ann Maynetta 4, b East Mill Creek, UT, Nov 19, 1869; d
June 11, 1934
21. Julia 4, b Cottonwood, UT, Sept 23, 1874; d Salt Lake
City, Jan 13, 1946
22. Martin Ensign 4, b Cottonwood, UT, Jan 17, 1880; d June
27, 1894
23. Estella Mabel 4, b July 13, 1883; d Nov 30, 1924
24. Zola Venese 4, b Dec 26, 1886

5. John Bagley 3, Edward 2, Richard 1, b South Hampton, NB,
Apr 30, 1834; baptized Nov 23, 1852, in St John's River by
Elder Jesse W. Crosby; ordained Elder, 1857, by James Cummings
who was ordained by Joseph Smith and Oliver Cowdery; ordained
High Priest, Apr 14, 1875, by William Budge, President, who
was ordained by Brigham Young; m (probably) (1) Sarah Louise;
m (2) Mary J. or Margaret Allen, dau Andrew & Delilah
(Andrews), b Sept 22, 1844, d Sept 2, 1914.   He d Feb 10,
1923.
     His diary written by himself and copied by his
granddaughter tells of his journey across the plains, the
cholera epidemic and his arrival at Salt Lake City where he
went to see the Temple Block which had a rock foundation about
three feet high with a doby wall twelve feet high around it,
containing ten acres of land. In the southwest corner was a
large tabernacle and in front of the east gate was an immense
deep hole with a large rock in each corner of it. He learned
that this was the foundation hole for the temple.
     He tells of being called by Brigham Young to open up and
build mills in Big Cottonwood Canyon. He remained there for
seven years helping to build mills, make roads, and haul
timber, for which his wages were one dollar and a half a day
and board when he used the ax, and fourteen dollars a month
when he drove team and his washing and board.

Children:

25.   John Allen 4, bSalt Lake City, May 16, 1862; d Oct 10,
1941, Montpelier, ID
26.   Martha Ann 4, b Feb 4, 1864; d May 9, 1867, Draper, UT
27.   Cyrenius Jackson 4, b Draper, UT, Mar 16, 1866; d Dec 19,
1935, Fairview, WY
28.   Edward Andrew 4, b Paris, Bear Lake, ID, Feb 22, 1868; d
Oct 27, 1983
29.   William Henry 4, b Mar 23, 1870, Paris, ID; d Sept 19,
1889
30.   Parley 4, b Apr 2, 1872, Paris, ID; d Jan 14, 1889
31.   David 4, b Mar 5, 1874, Montpelier, ID; d Lava Hot
Springs, ID, Nov 26, 1928
32.   Perney 4, b Aug 13, 1876, Montpelier, ID; d Apr 13, 1943
33.   Mary Delilah 4, b July 27, 1878; d Aug 15, 1946
34.   Charles Allen 4, b Montpelier, ID, Nov 19, 1880
35.   George Hugh 4, b Montpelier, ID, July 23, 1883; d Apr 21,
1964
36.   Thomas Coleman 4, b Montpelier, ID, Feb 5, 1886; d there,
Oct 1, 1924
37.   Lawrence 4, b Jan 14, 1888, Montpelier, ID
38.   James Orin 4, b Apr 7, 1896

9.   William Henry Bagley 3, Edward 2, Richard 1, b South
Hampton, NH, Oct 8, 1841; d Jan 25, 1923; settled Charleston,
UT; m Hannah Brunyer, b Liverpool, Eng., Apr 30, 1846, d June
11, 1919, dau Harmon & Lucy (Crich).   He lived on his
homestead in Provo Valley with the exception of one year when
he moved to Midway for protection against Indians. 1865-1875,
he freighted between Salt Lake City and Charleston. Lover of
fine horses.   Member of Capt Joseph W. Carroll's Co of
militia.

Children:
39. William Harmon 4, b Sept 9, 1861; d June 10, 1862
40. Sarah Louise 4, b Dec 5, 1863; d July 17, 1904
41. George Henry 4, b Sept 19, 1865, Charleston, UT; d Sept
15, 1915
42. Lottie Frances 4, b Sept 2, 1867 ?, Park City, UT; d Nov
16, 1931
43. Julia Ann 4, b July 28, 1869 ?, Charleston, UT
44. Lucy 4, b May 20, 1872, Charleston, UT
45. Edward 4, b July 3, 1875, Charleston, UT; d Sept 14, 1921
46. Saddie 4, b Feb 10, 1877, Charleston, UT; d Jan 10, 1878
47. Evelyn 4, b May 18, 1878, Charleston, UT; d Aug 5, 1935
48. Roy 4, b Aug 14, 1880, Charleston, UT
49. Jane 4, b Jan 29, 1884, Charleston, UT; d Mar 23, 1885

10.   Joseph Smith Bagley 3, Edward 2, Richard 1, b Apr 9,
1845, South Hampton, NH; d Apr 10, 1897, Charleston, UT; m Nov
14, 1869, Ann Van Wagoner, b Apr 22, 1852, Council Bluffs, IO,
d Apr 24, 1881, Charleston, UT, dau John Halman & Clarissa
(Tappan); m (2) June 28, 1882, Hannah Jensen, b Drammen,
Norway, Oct 4, 1863, d Mar 3, 1949, dau Lars & Ann (Pederson).

Children: (All b Charleston, UT)
50. Alice Loretta 4, b Apr 5, 1871; d Nov 24, 1871

51.   Joseph Van 4, b 1872; d Mar 2, 1942, Granger, WY
52.   Hyrum 4, b Feb 12, 1875; d Sept 14, 1914
53.   Cynthia Ann Elizabeth 4, b Oct 12, 1876; d Dec 17, 1890
54.   Clarissa or Claracy 4, b June 8, 1878; d Jan 18, 1913
55.   Minerva Ann 4, b Apr 8, 1881; d Dec 20, 1957
56.   Jennie 4, b Sept 4, 1886; d Jan 4, 1962
58.   Mary 4, b Oct 27, 1888
59.   David 4, b June 23, 1891
60.   Pearl 4., b Mar 5, 1894
61.   Delilah 4, bv May 28, 1896; d Mar 5, 1903

11.   Edward Alma Bagley 3, Edward 2, Richard 1, b Feb 10,
1847, South Hampton, NB; d May 28, 1929; baptized at eight
years old in 1855, in St John's River by Thomas Jacques;
called to mission in the northern states, Jan 4, 1868;
ordained a Seventy at Koosharem, Nov 26, 1884, by Francis M.
Lyman, Apostle; ordained High Priest and Bishop of Koosharem,
May 7, 1891, by Apostle Lyman; m (1) Sept 17, 1869, Mary
Almeda McClellan, dau William & Almeda (Day), who d Oct 27,
1889; m (2) Feb 16, 1885, Christine Torgerson, dau Hans & Anne
Guarena (Olsen), b Oct 23, m 1867, Hoxsum, Norway; first eight
children by Mary; others by Christine.

Children:
62.   Mary Adelina 4, b June 12, 1871, Payson, UT; d Oct 21,
1872
63.   Edward Carroll 4, b Feb 28, 1873, Payson, UT; d Aug 25,
1957
64.   Julia Estella Emerette 4, b Apr 14, 1875, Payson, UT; d
Oct 5, 1958
65.   Emma Retta 4, b Mar 10, 1877, Payson, UT; d Feb 20, 1879
66.   James Alvin 4, b Apr 14, 1879, Greenwich, UT; d Jan 27,
1920
67.   Cynthia 4, b Apr 28, 1881, Greenwich, UT; d Oct 17, 1940
68.   Rhoda A. 4, b Aug 24, 1884, Greenwich, UT
69.   George A. 4, b Sept 6, 1886, Greenwich, UT
70.   Cyrenius 4, b Aug 12, 1884, Greenwich, UT
71.   Anna Christine 4, b Aug 27, 1886, Greenwich, UT; d Apr
12, 1888
72.   Mary Allen 4, b Sept 10, 1889, Greenwich, UT; d May 2,
1965
73.   Mettie Alverda 4, b Oct 5, 1891, Greenwich, UT
74.   Hyrum Orson 4, b Jan 22, 1894, Koosharem, UT; d Dec. 1964
75.   Joseph Mortimer 4, b June 13, 1896, Koosharem, UT
76.   Lorenzo Davier 4, b July 11, 1899, Greenwich, UT; d Dec
14, 1915
77.   Owen Roosevelt 4, b Apr 13, 1903, Greenwich, UT
78.   Helen Elfonda 4, b June 21, 1906, Greenwich, UT
79.   Talmage Seymour 4, b Jan 25, 1909, Koosharem, UT

12.   Cynthia Ann (Libby) Bagley 3, Edward 2, Richard 1, b May
13, 1849, South Hampton, NB; m John Ferris.

14.   Hyrum Bagley 3, Edward 2, Richard 1, b Feb 2, 1854,
Woodstock, ME; d Apr 4, 1932, South Cottonwood, UT; m July 1,
1878, Harriet Dilworth Brinton, b Nov 21, 1857, Big

Cottonwood, UT, d Jan 16, 1943, Downey Bannock, ID, dau David
& Harriet (Dilworth).

Children:
80.   Harriet Eliza or Retta 4, b May 18 or Nov 8, 1879, Big
Cottonwood, UT; d Aug 17, 1949
81.   ERliza Dilworth 4, b Aug 29, 1881, Big Cottonwood, UT; d
Dec 31, 1884
82.   Clara Luella 4, b Sept 1, 1883, Big Cottonwood, UT; d May
4, 1909
83.   Caleb Dilworth 4, b Mar 29, 1885, Big Cottonwood, UT; d
July 5, 1951
84.   Eleen 4, b Feb 2, 1887, Big Cottonwood, UT
85.   Ellis Grant 4, b Oct 8, 1888, Big Cottonwood, UT; d Jan
26, 1919
86.   Hyrum Grant 4, b Dec1, 1891, Big Cottonwood, UT
87.   Melba Adele 4, b Nov 30, 1893, Big Cottonwood, UT
88.   Evanageline 4, b July 12, 1897, Big Cottonwood, UT; d
June 24, 1937
89.   David Brinton 4, b Dec 28, 1899, South Cottonwood, UT
90.   Frank Mortimer 4, b July 19, 1904, South Cottonwood, UT

16.   Edward Cyrenius Bagley 4, Charles 3, Edward 2, Richard 1,
b Jan 2, 1865, East Mill Creek, UT; d July 9, 1943, Salt Lake
City; m Dec 17, 1889, Amanda Barr Neff, b Oct 16, 1867, East
Mill Creek, UT, d Jan 28, 1946, Salt Lake City, dau Anne Barr
Neff & Catherine (Thomas).

Children: (All b Murray, UT, except # 94, 95)
91.   Amanda 5, b Sept 29, 1890; d Oct 10, 1890
92.   Cyrene Neff 5, b June 16, 1892
93.   Julia Kathleen 5, b June 30, 1894
94.   Hattie Erma 5, b Sept 14, 1896, Cottonwood, UT
95.   Marie 5, b Jan 22, 1900, Cottonwood, UT
96.   Charles Stuart 5, b June 20, 1902
97.   Amee K. 5, b Sept 19, 1904
98.   Maxime N. 5, b Dec 28, 1906
99.   Isabel N. 5, b Apr 18, 1909
100.   Edward Neff 5, b Jan 13, 1912

17.   Andrew H. Bagley 4, Charles 3, Edward 2, Richard 1, b
East Mill Creek, UT, Apr 28, 1867; d Nov 28, 1931, East Mill
Creek, UT; m Apr 10, 1901, Frances Minerva Stillman, b June
30, 1871, East Mill Creek, d there Nov 6, 1945, dau Charles &
Elizabeth (Neff).

Children:
101.   Andrew Stillman, 5, b Oct 5, 1910, East Mill Creek, UT; d
June 4, 1965
102.   Frances 5, b July 1, 1912, East Mill Creek, UT

18.   Frank Erastus Bagley 4, Charles 3, Edward 2, Richard 1, b
Cottonwood, UT, May 8, 1877; d Apr 3, 1936, Salt Lake City; m
June 3, 1906, Florence Grace Armstrong, b Aug 14, 1879/80,
Salt Lake City, d there Nov 9, 1933, dau Francis & Isabella
(Siddaway).

Child:
103.   Daryl 5, b Nov 23, 1907, Salt Lake City; d Oct 20, 1968,
Los Angeles, CA

19.   Grant Charles Bagley 4, Charles 3, Edward 2, Richard 1, b
Cottonwood, UT, Jan 17, 1872; d Sept, 1916; m   Feb   22,   1899,
Etta Davis.

Children:
104.   Lorna 5, b July 11, 1902, Provo, UT
105.   Julia Etta 5, b Mar 13, 1914, Provo, UT

20.   Ann Maynette Bagley 4, Charles 3, Edward 2, Richard 1,   b
East Mill Creek, UT, Nov 19, 1869; d June 11,   1934;   m   July,
1892, Samuel King, b Fillmore, UT, Jan   9,   1868,   d   Nov   29,
1924, son William & Josephine (Henry).

Children: (All b Provo, UT)
106.   Creighton Grant 5, b Apr 14, 1895;   d   Oct   9,   1930;   m
1924, Alice
107.   Ronan 5, b 1896; m Walter Johnson
108.   Karl Vernon 5, b May, 1910; m Wilhelmina,   dau   Orson   &
Sylvia Olson
109.   Margaret 5, b 1906; m ——–Robinson

21.   Julia Bagley   4,   Charles   3,   Edward   2,   Richard   1,   b
Cottonwood, UT, Sept 23, 1874; d Salt Lake City, Jan 13,   1946;
m Sept 20, 1899, Herbert Thayer Hills, b Nov   12,   1876,   Salt
Lake City, d there Mar 4, 1905, son Lewis S. & Rhoda (Thayer).
He had previously m Theresa Maria Burton.

Children:
110.   Herbert Bagley 5, b Sept 19, 1902,   Salt   Lake   City;   m
Sept 26, 1928, Gladys Granger; seven children, one of whom was
Nancy Jane
11.   Lamar S. 5, b Nov, 1904; d Aug 6, 1968, Salt Lake City; m
Melba Bringhurst, July 31, 1929

23.   Estella Mabel Bagley 4, Charles 3, Edward 2, Richard 1, b
July 13, 1883; d Nov 30, 1924; m June 26, 1906, Herbert   Eliot
Cutler, who d Sept 30, 1924, Salt Lake City.

Children:
112.   Farren Eliot 5, b July 11, 1911, Salt Lake City;   m   Apr
7, 1937, Leola Adeline Booth
113.   Estelle 5, b Feb 23, 1916, Salt   Lake   City;   m   Oct   2,
1937, Grant Eldredge; six children

24.   Zola Venese Bagley 4, Charles 3, Edward 2, Richard   1,   b
Dec 26, 1898; m Sept 27, 1917, Courtney B. Harris, b   Apr   29,
1890, Stewart, IO. d Mar 23, 1968, Van Nuys, CA, son Thomas   &
Emily (Bailey); no children; they brought up children   of   her
sister Estella.

25.   John Allen Bagley 4, John 3, Edward 2, Richard 1, b   Salt

Lake City, May 16, 1862; d Oct 9, 1941, Montpelier, ID; m Aug
3, 1883 (1) Sarah Lawson, b Laki, UT, Mar 23, 1861, d Mar 30,
1885, dau John & Margaret (Vance); m (2) Aug 15, 1888, Mena
Valves Furrow, b Nov 13, 1863, d Nov 11, 1905, Montpelier, ID,
dau John & Amanda (Van Horn); m (3) 1890, Ila Eliza Austin, b
Jan 9, 1865, Morgan, UT, d Mar 28, 1894, dau Edward & Elnora
(Lane); m (4) 1903, Mary Matilda Peterson, b Sept 2, 1876,
Bloomington, ID, d Oct 24, 1918, dau Nils & Margaret
(Sorenson); m (5) Amanda Margaret Anderson, b Dec 14, 1861,
Boone, KY, dau Enoch & Amelia (Riggs). He was a graduate of
Brigham University, Class of 1982: First child by first wife;
next ten by Mena; last five by Mary Peterson.

Children: (All b Montpelier, ID, except # 125, 126, 127, 128,
129)
114.   Lewis Loraine 5, b Mar 7, 1884; d Dec 24, 1959
115.   Mary Juanita 5, b Nov 2, 1889
116.   Cloudsey Furrow 5, b Apr 14, 1890; d Nov 27, 1891
117.   George Brimhall 5, b Jan 2, 1895; d Jan 2, 1893
118.   John Lafayette 5, b Dec 23, 1894; d Jan 22, 1895
119.   Moretta Vivorea 5, b May 22, 1896; d July 10, 1926
120.   Almorean 5, b Mar 9, 1898
121.   Hawley 5, b Nov 2, 1899
122.   Lucille 5, b June 20, 1891
123.   Nina 5, b Jan 8, 1903
124.   Stillborn 5, b Oct 27, 1905
125.   J. Grant 5, b Mar 24, 1907, Seaside, OR
126.   John A. 5, b Sept 15, 1907, Salt Lake City; d June 19,
1941)
127.   Major Harriman 5, b July 19, 1909, Salt Lake City
128.   Virginia Margaret 5, b Dec 27, 1912, Bloomington, ID
129.   Harold 5, b Aug 30, 1913, Bloomington, ID; d same day

27.   Cyrenius Jackson Bagley 4, John 3, Edward 2, Richard 1, b
Draper, UT, Mar 16, 1866; d Dec 18, 1935, Fairview, WY; m (1)
Jan 7, 1890, Celeste Sophie Dalrymple, b Jan 31, 1868, Hyrum,
UT, d Nov 22, 1923, Fairview, WY, dau Oscar & Mary M.
(Potter); m (2) Jessie Whitton.

Children:
130.   Mary Viola 5, b Oct 26, 1890, Montpelier, ID; d Aug.
1962
131.   Pauley Eugene 5, b Jan 10, 1892, Montpelier, ID
132.   Emogene Kizziah 5, b July 19, 1895, Crow Creek, ID
133.   Oliver Arthur 5, b Apr 12, 1897, Crow Creek, ID
134.   Muriel Margaret 5, b Apr 22, 1899, Crow Creek, ID; d Oct
23, 1924
135.   Cyrenius Hugh 5, b Jan 26, 1906, Fairview, WY
136.   Lewis Ward 5, b May 21, 1908, Granger, WY; d June 17,
1966
137.   Ellsworth Allen 5, b June 19, 1910, Fairview, WY

31.   David Bagley 4, John 3, Edward 2, Richard 1, b Mar 5,
1874, Montpelier, ID; d Lava Hot Springs, ID, Nov 26, 1928; m
Mar 6, 1900, Laura Conrad, b Sept 23, 1873, dau Vincent & Mary
Jane (Eigluney). Her other husband was Howard Aldrich.

Children:
138.   John Conrad 5, b Dec 3, 1901, Granger, WY
139.   Elizabeth Irene 5, b May 12, 1903, Granger, WY; d Aug
23, 1903
140.   Laura Lorene 5, b Apr 5, 1905, Montpelier, ID; d July 5,
1935
141.   June 5, b Oct 11, 1907, Montpelier, ID

32.   Perney Bagley 4, John 3, Edward 2, Richard 1, b Aug 13,
1876, Montpelier, ID; d Apr 13, 1943; m 1935, Wilford Clark.

33.   Mary Delilah Bagley 4, John 3, Edward 2, Richard 1, b
July 27, 1878; d Aug 15, 1946; m Apr 2, 1896, James Quayle.

34.   Charles Allen Bagley 4, John 3, Edward 2, Richard 1, b
Montpelier, ID, Nov 1, 1880; m Mar 12, 1903, Beulah Adelia
Dalton, b Mar 17, 1881, Springdale, UT, d Dec 20, 1927, Idaho
Falls, dau John & Adelaide (Chase). Her other husband was
James Tanzer Gurrup.

Children: (b Salt Lake City)
142.   Irene 5, b Oct 10, 1903
143.   Iris 5, b Aug 1, 1906
144.   Mary Audrey 5, b July 15, 1908; d Aug 22, 1933

35.   George Hugh Bagley 4, John 3, Edward 2, Richard 1, b
Montpelier, ID, July 23, 1883; d Apr 21, 1964; m Sept 22,
1906, Ruth May Tubbs, b Sept 22, 1885, Pearson, ID, d Mar 8,
1964, dau Alexander & Ruth (Stewart).

Children:
145.   Hugh Oral 5, b Montpelier, ID, July 23, 1907
146.   Thelma Ruth 5, b Pocatello, ID, Sept 2, 1911
147.   Owen Ellsworth 5, b Montpelier, ID, July 10, 1913
148.   June Margaret 5, b Montpelier, ID, June 12, 1915
149.   Mary 5, b Montpelier, ID, Oct 19, 1917; d same day
150.   Geneil 5, b Montpelier, ID, Nov 23, 1919
151.   Geraldine 5, b Montpelier, ID, July 8, 1924

36.   Thomas Coleman Bagley 4, John 3, Edward 2, Richard 1, b
Montpelier, ID, Feb 5, 1886; d Oct 1, 1924, Montpelier; m June
18, 1913, Sadie Elda Johnson, b Oct 14, 1890, West Jordan, UT,
dau Charles & Annie (Olsen). Her first husband was Luther
William Baldwin.

Children:
152.   Thomas Leland 5, b Smoot, WY, Apr 21, 1914; d Sept 17,
1958
153.   Emo Woodrow 5, b Smoot, WY, Feb 20, 1916
154.   Elmer 5, b Smoot, WY, Feb 20, 1916; d same yr; twin to
Emo

37.   Lawrence Bagley 4, John 3, Edward 2, Richard 1, b Jan 14,
1888, Montpelier, ID; m May 2, 1926, Lillian Priest.

39.   James Orin Bagley 4, John 3, Edward 2, Richard 1. b Apr
2, 1896.

40.   Sarah Louisa Bagley 4, William 3, Edward 2, Richard 1. b
Dec 5, 1863; d July 17, 1904; m George Calvin Murdock.

41.   George Henry Bagley 4, William 3, Edward 2, Richard 1, b
Sept 19, 1865, Charleston, UT; d Sept 15, 1915, Victor, ID; m
Sept 19, 1885, Marie Eliza Edwards, b Jan 6, 1866, Salt Lake
City, d Dec 21, 1907, dau Philip & Mary (Simmons); m (2) Annie
Gnetta Petersen.

Children: (All b Charleston, UT, except #165A)
155.   George Perley 5, b Mar 16, 1886
156.   Eliza Allen 5, b Aug 8, 1887; d June 12, 1955
157.   Frederick 5, b Apr 9, 1889
158.   Mary Hannah 5, b Feb 19, 1891; d Dec 30, 1913
159.   Lona May 5, b May 14, 1893; d July 6, 1926
160.   Lorenzo Edwards 5, b May 12, 1895
161.   Ruby Leona 5, b Mar 12, 1897
162.   Clara Alice 5, b Apr 12, 1899; d Apr 14, 1948
163.   Retta 5, b June 1, 1901
164.   Firl Edwards 5, b July 26, 1903
165.   Sadie Marie 5, b Nov 2, 1908
165A.   Roland 5, b Oct 27, 1911, Victor, ID; d July 23, 1962

42.   Lottie Frances Bagley 4, William 3, Edward 2, Richard 1.
b Sept 2, 1869 ?, Park City, UT; d Nov 16, 1931; m Ephraim
Knowlton.

43.   Julia Ann Bagley 4, William 3, Edward 2, Richard 1, b
July 28, 1869 ?, Charleston, UT; m Heber William Widdison.

44.   Lucy Bagley 4, William 3, Edward 2, Richard 1, b May 20,
1872, Charleston, UT; m William Watson.

45.   Edward Bagley 4, William 3, Edward 2, Richard 1, b July
31, 1875, Charleston, UT; d Sept 11, 1921; m Josephine Gee.

47.   Evelyn Bagley 4, William 3, Edward 2, Richard 1, b May
18, 1878, Charleston, UT; d Aug 5, 1935; m George Summers.

48.   Roy Bagley 4, William 3, Edward 2, Richard 1, b Aug 14,
1880, Charleston, UT; m Elizabeth Sweavel.

51.   Joseph Van Bagley 4, Joseph 3, Edward 2, Richard 1, b
1872, Charleston, UT; d Mar 2, 1942; m Apr 10, 1908, Granger,
WY, Cora Yeoman, b Oct 24, 1884, Rehigh, ND, dau Charles &
Ella (Jones).

Children:
166.   Joseph Loraine 5, b Mar 11, 1909, Salt Lake City
167.   Grant Van 5, b July 7, 1910, Rock Springs, WY; d May 10,
1933
168.   Fremont Yeoman 5, b Oct 13, 1914, Granger, WY; d Oct 25,
1914

169.   Minerva Anne 5, b Mar 30, 1917, Granger, WY
170.   Vera LaVone 5, b Oct 7, 1918, Granger, WY
171.   Harold Eugene 5, b Oct 9, 1921, Granger, WY
172.   Eleanor 5
173.   Earle Dale 5, b May 19, 1924; d Mar 12, 1925

52.   Hyrum Bagley 4, Joseph 3, Edward 2, Richard 1, b Feb 12,
1875, Charleston, UT; d Sept 14, 1914; m Dec 29, 1898,
Isabelle or Arabella Loader, b Dec 20, 1879, d Mar 23, 1958,
dau Harry & Annie (Pierce).

Children:
174.   Burnett 5, b May 13, 1900, Charleston, UT; unm
175.   Nima LaVone 5, b Sept 20, 1901, Charleston, UT; d June
10, 1965

54.   Clarissa Bagley 4, Joseph 3, Edward 2, Richard 1, b June
8, 1878, Charleston, UT; d Jan 18, 1913; m Dec 16, 1898,
Joseph Parley Edwards, b Mar 17, 1875, d Apr 26, 1947, son
Philip & Mary (Simmons).

Children:
176.   Bernell Joseph 5, b Apr 1, 1899, Charleston, UT; d June
30, 1958; m June 6, 1923, Hannah Wadley
177.   Vivian 5, b Jan 3, 1900, Charleston, UT; m Fern Wadley
178.   Oliver 5
179.   Ruth 5, b June 5, 1906; d July 2, 1913

55.   Minerva Ann Bagley 4, Joseph 3, Edward 2, Richard 1, b
Apr 6, 1881, Charleston, UT; d Dec 20, 1957; m Dec 16, 1896,
John Oliver Edwards, son Philip & Mary (Simmons).

Children: (b Charleston, UT)
180.   Clarence 5, b May 26, 1898
181.   Minerva 5, b Oct 11, 1900; m Tony George
182.   Maude 5, b Sept 22, 1904
183.   Viola 5, b Dec 31, 1908
184.   Dana 5, b Aug 26, 1911; m H. C. Champagne

56.   Hilda Bagley 4, Joseph 3, Edward 2, Richard 1, b Apr 10,
1883, Charleston, UT; m Jan 23, 1900, John Harry Loader, b Jan
27, 1878, d Oct 11, 1923, son Harry & Annie (Pierce).

Children:
185.   Harry 5, b Sept 2, 1900, Pleasant Grove, UT; m June,
1931, Merle Curtis
186.   Delilah 5, b Sept 30, 1902, Pleasant Grove, UT; d Dec 5,
1956; m Aug 17, 1922, Howell Davis
187.   Virgil 5, b Nov 24, 1905, Mercer, UT; m Sept 7, 1935,
Zelma Drake
188.   Maurice Grant 5, b Feb 27, 1908, Charleston, UT; m June
11, 1928, Margaret Eids
189.   Lars LaVerle 5, b Nov 18, 1910, Charleston, UT; m Sept
24, 1940, Thelma Steed
190.   Nina 5, b Mar 27, 1913, Charleston, UT; m Eldon Wright

57.   Jennie Bagley 4, Joseph 3, Edward 2, Richard 1, b Sept 4, 1886, Charleston, UT; d Jan 4, 1962; m Dec 21, 1904, Frederick Parker, b Nov 3, 1884, in England, d Apr 7, 1944.

Children: (b Charleston, UT)
191.   Afton 5, b Sept 23, 1905; d Oct 24, 1946; m Sept 7, 1927, Stephen Angus
192.   Frederick 5, b Apr 25, 1908; d Jan 9, 1909
193.   Dwayne 5, b July 17, 1910; m Oct 23, 1932, Sarah Christenson
194.   Marvin 5; b Dec 9, 1912; m Ruth P. Clawson
195.   Dale 5, b Dec 23, 1915; d July 29, 1927

58.   Mary Alice Bagley 4, Joseph 3, Edward 2, Richard 1, b Oct 27, 1889, Charleston, UT; m June 3, 1907, John Alexander Anderson, b May 14, 1886, Heber, UT, son Gustaf Ludwig & Elizabeth Stuart (Avid).

Children: (b Heber, UT)
196.   Evan LeRoy 5, b Mar 1, 1908; m Vera W. Murray
197.   Thelma 5, b July 21, 1909; m Robert M. Knight
198.   Joseph Dean 5, b July 18, 1911; d Nov 2, 1916
199.   Pearl 5, b Jan 13, 1915
200.   Belda 5, b Sept, 1917
201.   Cavon 5, b Dec 24, 1918
202.   Maurine 5, b Aug 15, 1921
203.   John Elwood 5, b Sept 1, 1923; d same day

59.   David Bagley 4, Joseph 3, Edward 2, Richard 1, b June 29, 1891, Charleston, UT; m Aug 16, 1911, Nellie Gabling, b Feb 24, 1891, Wahlsburg, UT, d Dec 18, 1961, dau George & Ada (Glen).

Children:
204.   David Brant 5, b Lund Bannock, ID, Aug 6, 1912; living Dublin, OH, 1961
205.   George Dale 5, b Salt Lake City, Aug 19, 1914; a doctor; living Altadena, CA, 1961
206.   Ruth 5

60.   Pearl Bagley 4, Joseph 3, Edward 2, Richard 1, b Mar 5, 1894, Charleston, UT; m Sept 26, 1917, Worthington Mahoney.

61.   Edward Carroll Bagley 4, Edward 3, Edward 2, Richard 1, b Feb 28, 1873, Payson, UT; d Aug 25, 1957; baptized May 5, 1904, by William Seegmilla, ordained a bishop, Sept 26, 1920, by Hyrum G. Smith. Bishop of Koosharem Ward, Sevier Stake, Sevier Co, UT, from 1920 to 1930; m Pauline Martinsen, Nov 5, 1896, b Roykam, Norway, Jan 11, 1875.

Children:
207.   Edward Merrill 5, b Aug 15, 1897, Greenwich, UT
208.   Ellis Lynn 5, b Oct 20, 1898, Koosharem, UT
209.   Rodney Virginius 5, b Apr 13, 1900, Greenwich, UT
210.   Illa Mary 5, b Apr 3, 1903, Greenwich, UT
211.   Ben Erin 5, b Jan 29, 1908, Koosharem, UT; unm

13

212.   Vonda Idell 5, b May 7, 1911, Koosharem, UT
213.   Donna Pauline 5, b July 12, 1913, Koosharem, UT

64.   Julia Esetlla Emerette Bagley 4, Edward 3, Edward 2,
Richard 1, b Apr 14, 1875, Payson, UT; d Oct 5, 1958; m Sept
25, 1895, Sidney Orlando Rust, b Apr 17, 1877 ?; m (2)
Theodore Anderson, b Feb 7, 1864, Oslo, Norway. d Apr 27,
1922. First two children by Rust.

Children:
214.   Burton 5, b Oct 26, 1896, Greenwich, UT; m May 15, 1918,
Lillian Spark
215.   Eva Loreen 5, b Mar 29, 1901, Greenwich, UT; m June 27,
1921, George Maynard Wright
216.   Lillie Mabel 5, b Sept 10, 1906, Koosharem, UT; m Dec
21, 1941, Donald H. Savage
217.   Mary Este 5, b 1908, Koosharem, UT; m Dec 22, 1932,
Talmage S. Burr
218.   Theodore Alma 5, b Richfield, UT; unm

66.   James Alvin Bagley 4, Edward 3, Edward 2, Richard 1, b
Apr 14, 1879, Payson, UT; d Jan 27, 1920; m May 3, 1899,
Diantha Anderson, b Dec 6, 1875, Salina, UT, dau Jens
Christian & Karen (Jenson).

Children:
219.   Mary Caroline 5, b & d Nov, 1899, Greenwich, UT
220.   Voyle LaRae 5, b Dec 24, 1900, Koosharem, UT; d June,
1960
221.   Grant Lyle 5, b Aug 3, 1903, Annabelle, UT; d Nov 1953
222.   Iola Estella 5, b Jan 6, 1906, Richfield, UT
223.   Maida Julia 5, b Mar 21, 1908, Greenwich, UT; unm
224.   James Carroll 5, b Greenwich, UT, July 20, 1910
225.   Ellen Irene 5, b Nov 23, 1912, Greenwich, UT; d May 18,
1958
226.   Vera Myrtle 5, b Oct 13, 1913, Greenwich, UT

67.   Cynthia Bagley 4, Edward 3, Edward 2, Richard 1, b Apr
28, 1881, Greenwich, UT; d Oct 17, 1940; m June 8, 1899, John
Waldemar Delange, b Mar 26, 1873,

Children:
227.   Vera Luella 5, b May 1, 1900, Koosharem, UT; d June 25,
1904
228.   Orrel 5, b Sept 6, 1901, Koosharem, UT; m Sept 27, 1927,
Arvilla Dennison, b Aug 29, 1906, Casteldale, UT, d May 6,
1959; six children: Gordon, Lyla, Leland, Clark & Cynthia
229.   Thelma 5, b Apr 6, 1903, Koosharem, UT; d Mar 22, 1907
230.   Mary Alverda 5, b Apr 1, 1905, Koosharem, UT; m July 8,
1938, Russell Carson
231.   Edward Owen 5, b Aug 12, 1906, Koosharem, UT; m June 3,
1939, Argentina Cimina
232.   Vernon H. (twin) 5, b Dec 11, 1910, Emery, UT; d Feb 18,
1912
233.   Verdus H. (twin) 5, b Dec 11, 1910, Emery, UT; d Dec 11,
1911

68. Rhoda A. Bagley 4, Edward 3, Edward 2, Richard 1, b Aug 24, 1884, Greenwich, UT; m Dec 17, 1903, Joseph Franklin DeLange, b Mar 26, 1880, Koosharem, UT.

Children:
234. Rhoda 5, b Dec 23, 1904, Greenwich, UT; m Apr 2, 1931, Harold Thompson
235. Alma Leonard 4, b Sept 21, 1906, Greenwich, UT; d May 25, 1906
236. Talmage Young 5, b June 1, 1908, Koosharem, UT; m June 26, 1931, Selene Mae Taylor

237. Mary Burena 5, b Aug 5, 1910, Koosharem, UT; m July 18, 1930, Harold Blake Robinson
238. Winona Christena 5, b Apr 1, 1912, Koosharem, UT; m Feb 26, 1934, Elbert V. Sorensen
239. Elna Lanea 5, b Apr 10, 1914, Koosharem, UT; m Apr 21, 1933, Dennie LeRue Brown
240. Inez Wanda 5, b Oct 20, 1915, Koosharem, UT; d Mar 4, 1929
241. Joseph Leland 5, b Nov 8, 1917, Koosharem, UT; m June 22, 1925, Edna Bowshardt
242. Dorthell 5, b Jan 11, 1920, Koosharem, UT; m June 6, 1925, Lynn Ivan Torgerson
243. Phyllis Pernece 5, b Jan 16, 1922, Koosharem, UT; m May 31, 1940, Ardell Hunt
244. Norma Lou 5, b Mar 15, 1924, Richfield, UT; d Oct 5, 1954
245. Shirley Rae 5, b Aug 13, 1928, Richfield, UT; m Oct 29, 1945, Preston Reeve Jackman

69. George Alma Bagley 4, Edward 3, Edward 2, Richard 1, b Apr 28, 1881, Greenwich, UT; m May 29, 1912, Mary Elizabeth Wingate, b July 8, 1895, Monroe, UT.

Children: (b Greenwich, UT)
246. Dean A. 5, b Feb 17, 1913
247. Lula Venita 5, b Nov 6, 1914
248. Iona 5, b Oct 30, 1916
249. Lynn 5, b Nov 16, 1918
250. Keith 5, b May 15, 1924
251. Ada Aloan 5, b Feb 8, 1925
242. Rolland McKay 5, b Mar 20, 1929
253. Viola 5, b Mar 29, 1932

70. Cyrenius Bagley 4, Edward 3, Edward 2, Richard 1, b Aug 12, 1889; m Sept 30, 1908, Lucille Brindley, b Nov 16, 1891, Angle, UT, dau Howard & Emily.

Children:
254. Emily Almeda 5, b Oct 3, 1910, Greenwich, UT
255. Cyrenius Lazone 5, b Jan 13, 1913, Koosharem, UT
256. Utahna 5, b Apr 11, 1914, Greenwich, UT; d Dec 10, 1945
257. Melba Lucille 5, b May 6, 1918, Greenwich, UT

72. Mary Ellen Bagley 4, Edward 3, Edward 2, Richard 1, b Sept 10, 1889, Greenwich, UT; m Francis Sterling, Aug 27, 1925.

Child:
258. Betty Jean 5

73. Mettie Alverda Bagley 4, Edward 3, Edward 2, Richard 1, b Oct 5, 1891, Greenwich, UT; m Gilbert Hallows, Nov 14, 1917.

74. Hyrum Orson Bagley 4, Edward 3, Edward 2, Richard 1, b Jan 22, 1894, Koosharem, UT; d Dec 23, 1964; m Aug 30, 1916, Salt Lake City, Myrtle Elvira Clark, dau Ferdinand & Hannah (Christensen).

Children:
259. Beth 5, b Dec 24, 1916, Mt Pleasant, UT
260. Louise 5, b Nov 10, 1920, Mt Pleasant, UT
261. Christina LaVerne 5, b Jan 12, 1925, Koosharem, UT
262. Garth Orson 5, b Mar 12, 1930, Koosharem, UT

75. Joseph Mortimer Bagley 4, Edward 3, Edward 2, Richard 1, b June 13, 1896, Koosharem, UT; m Jennie Nay Manwill, dau James & Theresa (Schaugoard), b Feb 21, 1899.

Children: (b Koosharem, UT)
263. Iva 5, b Nov 30, 1919
264. Faun 5, b Mar 2, 1927

77. Owen Roosevelt Bagley 4, Edward 3, Edward 2, Richard 1, b Apr 13, 1903, Greenwich, UT; m June 1, 1923, Richfield, UT, Irene Marie Brown, b Mar 10, 1901, Koosharem, UT, dau William & Amelie (Olsen).

Children: (b Koosharem, UT)
265. Betty 5, b Dec 30, 1923; d Mar 15, 1924
266. Martha Jean 5, b Apr 29, 1925
267. Owen Loraine 5, b Jan 26, 1927
268. Wyonna 5, b Dec 11, 1929
269. Lorenzo 5, b Nov 23, 1931
271. Mildred 5, b Feb 17, 1934
272. Noel Elvin 5, b Sept 27, 1937

78. Helen Alfonda Bagley 4, Edward 3, Edward 2, Richard 1, b June 21, 1906, Greenwich, UT; m Jan 7, 1928, Lynn Wingit.

Child:
273. Marva 5, b Nov 2, 1929, Salina, UT; m Van Chamberlain Esplin, b May 8, 1922, Orderville, UT, son Henry Cox & Lucy (Chamberlain).

79. Talmage Seymour Bagley 4, Edward 3, Edward 2, Richard 1, b Jan 25, 1909, Koosharem, UT; m Lapreal Albrecht, June 6, 1930, Richfield, UT.

80. Harriet Eliza or Hetta Bagley 4, Hyrum 3, Edward 2,

Richard 1, b May 18 or Nov 8, 1879, Big Cottonwood, UT; d Aug 17, 1949; m June 20, 1900, William David Turner, b July 14, 1874, d May 6, 1963, Los Angeles. His mother's name was Jane Howarth.

Children: (All b South Cottonwood, UT)
274. William Kinder 5, b Dec 11, 1901; m May 7, 1926, Verna Stewart
275. Vida J. 5, b Mar 16, 1903; m June 6, 1920, Charles Hoskin McDonald
276. Clara Luella 5, b Oct 16, 1905; m Ray Gardner
277. Amos Bagley 5, b Oct 27, 1907; m Rosalie Lee Fuller
278. Edna Evelyn 5, b Mar 13, 1908; m Hyensley Leffer
279. Harriet Dilworth 5, b Nov 13, 1909; m Mar 5, 1933, John Thomas Blackwell
280. David Bronton 5, b Apr 11, 1912; m Mary Jean Geate
281. Hyrum Alvin 5, b May 3, 1914; m Dorothy Emery
282. Margaret Elizabeth 5, b Aug 31, 1916; m Harvey Johns
283. Robert Howarth 5, b May 8, 1918; m Fay Arriti
284. Barbara Ellis 5, b Mar 26, 1920; m Lewis Harry Verbrugte

82. Clara Luella Bagley 4, Hyrum 3, Edward 2, Richard 1, b Sept 1, 1883, Big Cottonwood, UT; d May 4, 1909; m Jan, 1905, Jacob Weiler Bringhurst, b Oct 17, 1883, son Robert & Elizabeth (Weils).

Children:
285. Melba 5, b Nov 26, 1905, Taylorsville, UT; m July 31, 1928, Larmar Hills
286. Luella 5, b May 31, 1905, Taylorsville, UT; m June 22, 1929, James Cudworth
287. Jacob 5, b Nov 7, 1908, Brigham, UT; m Apr, 1931, Gwendolyn Blair

83. Caleb Dilworth Bagley 4, Hyrum 3, Edward 2, Richard 1, b Mar 30, 1895, Big Cottonwood, UT; d July 5, 1951; m Dec 1, 1909, May Lloyd, dau Henry & Margaret (Graham).

Child:
288. Avis 5, b Apr 30, 1912, Salt Lake City; m Edward W. Fox; they were divorced; no children

84. Eileen Bagley 4, Hyrum 3, Edward 2, Richard 1, b Feb 2, 1887, Big Cottonwood, UT; m May 24, 1910, Thomas Roam, b Feb 26, 1885, d June 7, 1926, son Thomas & Mary (Miller).

Children: (b Downey, ID)
289. Arthur 5, b Apr 29, 1911; m May, 1941, Lucille Hayes
290. Thomas 5, b June 15, 1912; m Nov 7, 1940, Margaret Evans
291. Grant 5, b Sept 26, 1913; m Sept 14, 1936, Rose Gold
292. Merle 5, b Jan 20, 1916; m Feb 11, 1939, Frank Forrest

85. Ellis Grant Bagley 4, Hyrum 3, Edward 2, Richard 1, b Oct 8, 1888, Big Cottonwood, UT; d Jan 26, 1919; m Jan 9, 1907, Milas E. Miller.

86. Hyrum Brant Bagley 4, Hyrum 3, Edward 2, Richard 1, b Dec
1, 1891, Big Cottonwood, UT; m June 28, 1922, Marie
Gustaveson, b Dec 1, 1902, dau Ernest & Mary (Quirt).   They
were divorced.

Children:
293.   Eliot Lamar 5, b Oct 21, 1925, Big Cottonwood, UT
294.   Brant Wilbur 5, b Oct 21, 1923, Big Cottonwood, UT
295.   Clint LaMarr 4, b Feb 20, 1926
296.   Laurence Miles 5, b Jan 19, 1928, Salt Lake City
297.   William 5

87. Melba Adele Bagley 4, Hyrum 3, Edward 2, Richard 1, b Nov
30, 1893, Big Cottonwood, UT; m Apr, 1913, Charles Laurenson.

88. Evangeline Bagley 4, Hyrum 3, Edward 2, Richard 1, b July
12, 1897, Big Cottonwood, UT; d June 24, 1937; m Oct, 1916,
Edward J. Weiss.

89. David Brinton Bagley 4, Hyrum 3, Edward 2, Richard 1, b
Dec 28, 1899, South Cottonwood, UT; m Aug 23, 1933, Estrid
Elenora Fors. No children.

90. Frank Mortimer Bagley 4, Hyrum 3, Edward 2, Richard 1, b
July 19, 1904, South Cottonwood, UT; m Sept 13, 1924, Harriet
B. Ainsworth, dau Benjamin & Harriet (Goff); he apparently m
(2) Constance (Merrill) Van Frank.

Children:
298.   Darwin Mortimer 5, b May 20, 1925, Sandy, UT
299.   Eva L. 5, b Oct 23, 1929, Murray, UT
300.   Noel (Ainsworth), b June 3, 1941, Murray, UT (adopted by
Frank)
301.   Constance (Van Frank) 5, b Feb 23, 1948
302.   Jeffrey (Van Frank) 5, b July 24, 1954
303.   Allen (Van Frank) 5, b Sept 16, 1955
304.   Carole (Van Frank) 5, b Dec 30, 1957
Last four children of Constance (Merrill) Van Frank by
previous m adopted by Frank Mortimer Bagley

92. Cyrene Neff Bagley 5, Edward 4, Charles 3, Edward 2,
Richard 1, b June 16, 1892, Murray, UT; m July, 1917, Martha
Eliza Davidson, at Logan, UT, b July 21, 1893, Logan, d July
22, 1948, Cottonwood, UT, dau Hyrum & Eliza (Hawkes).

Children:
305.   David Cyrene 6, b Oct 16, 1921, Cottonwood, UT
306.   Charles Robert 6, b Feb 20, 1922, Cottonwood, UT; d Apr
26, 1940, Elysian Gardens, UT
307.   Marian Martha 6, b Mar 14, 1925, Murray, UT
308.   Myrtle Jean 6, b Feb 8, 1927, Murray, UT
309.   Catherine Lucille 6, b Mar 18, 1930, Murray, UT
310.   Frank Davidson 6, b Aug 2, 1928, Murray, UT

93. Julia Kathleen Bagley 5, Edward 4, Charles 3, Edward 2,
Richard 1, b June 30, 1894; d Nov 7, 1971, Salt Lake City; m

Sept, 1917, Irwin Nelson, b Apr 11, 1892, son Waldemar & Karen (Jensen).

Children:
311.	Irvin T. 6, b Dec 8, 1918, Milton, UT; d Jan 18, 1933
312.	Kathleen 6, b Dec 6, 1923, Cottonwood, UT; m May 20, 1944, Melvin Hulme
313.	Lila Jay 6, b dec 5, 1925, Cottonwood, UT; m Oct 4, 1945, Daren Blanchard
314.	Waledmar Rene 6, b June 6, 1931, Cottonwood, UT; m June 5, 1957, Audrey Kirton
315.	Andrew T. 6, b Apr 5, 1933, Cottonwood, UT; m Apr 24, 1953, Nadine Rutherford
316.	Frederick Bagley 6, b Mar 12, 1938, Cottonwood, UT; m Dec 31, 1955, Diane Morton

24. Mattie Erma Bagley 5, Edward 4, Charles 3, Edward 2, Richard 1, b Sept 14, 1896, Cottonwood, UT; m Aug 31, 1924, Joseph Howard Maugham.

Children:
317.	Mary 6, m Ross Sargent
318.	Walter Leon 6, b Feb 14, 1930, Madison, WS; m Shirley Alice Jensen, b June 29, 1932, dau LeRoy & Alice (Lee)
319.	Kathleen 6, b Jan 28, 1932; m Don Leslie Lind, Murray, UT, b May 18, 1930, son Leslie & Elizabeth (Whitmore)

26. Charles Stuart Bagley 5, Edward 4, Charles 3, Edward 2, Richard 1, b June 20, 1902, Murray, UT; m June 12, 1929, Miriam Gwendolyn Granger, b Aug 1, 1905, Salt Lake City, dau Harry Corydon & Florence Violar (Plomteau).

Children:
320.	Florence Amanda 6, b Jan 11, 1930, Salt Lake City; d Dec 24, 1939
321.	Miriam Gwendolyn 6, b Jan 10, 1931, Salt Lake City
322.	Corydon Stewart 6, b May 14, 1932, Murray, UT
323.	Henry Granger 6, b Sept 2, 1933, Murray, UT
324.	Martin Works 6, b Mar 21, 1936, Murray, UT

27. Gibbs K. Bagley 5, Edward 4, Charles 3, Edward 2, Richard 1, b Sept 19, 1904, Murray, UT; m Nov 27, 1936, Lucy Bringhurst, b July 27, 1914, Murray, UT, dau Samuel & Lenora (Kemp).

Children:
325.	Richard Ames 6, b Apr 16, 1938, Salt Lake City
326.	Lawrence Samuel 6, b Sept 2, 1946, Salt Lake City
327.	James 6, b Oct 7, 1948

28. Maxine N. Bagley 5, Edward 4, Charles 3, Edward 2, Richard 1, b Dec 8, 1906, Murray, UT; m June 30, 1936, Arthur E. Lind.

Child:
328.	Karl Edward 6, m Suzanne Richards

99. Isabel N. Bagley 5, Edward 4, Charles 3, Edward 2,
Richard 1, b Apr 18, 1909, Murray, UT; m Aug 16, 1951, Hugh M.
Bartholemew. She died late 1980's. She spent many hours of
correspondence and research on the various Bagley lines.   No
children.

100. Edward Neff Bagley 5, Edward 4, Charles 3, Edward 2,
Richard 1, b Jan 13, 1912, Murray, UT; m Jan 24, 1936, Helen
Young.

Children:
329. Edward Dallin 6, b Aug 27, 1938, Salt Lake City
330. Bonnie Marsha 6

101. Andrew Stillman Bagley 5, Andrew 4, Charles 3, Edward 2,
Richard 1, b Oct 27, 1910, East Mill Creek, UT ; d there June
4, 1965; m June 4, 1935, Faye Wiseman, b Sept 19, 1909, Salt
Lake City, dau William Logan & Lucy (Morris).

Children: (b Salt Lake City)

331. Pamela 6, b Aug 9, 1936
332. Sheila 6, b June 26, 1937
333. Sharolyn 6, b Dec 20, 1940
334. Logan Andrew 6, b Oct 5, 1944

102. Frances Bagley 5, Andrew 4, Charles 3, Edward 2, Richard
1, b July 1, 1912, East Mill Creek, UT; m Sept 14, 1936,
William P. Thorn, b Nov 3, 1903, son Alfred & Mary (Pyper).
Supposed to have three children.

Child:
335. Linda 6, b June 1, 1941; m Donald Lee Jensen, b dec 18,
1936, son John C. & Evelyn (Hanson)

103. Daryl Bagley 5, Frank 4, Charles 3, Edward 2, Richard 1,
b Nov 23, 1907, Salt Lake City; d Oct 20, 1968, Los Angeles; m
(1) Richard Badger, b July 31, 1906, Salt Lake City, d Mar 27,
1951, son Jesse & Mary (Swain); m (2) Douglas Burton, b Apr
12, 1909, Salt Lake City, son D. H. & Evelyn (Eldridge).

Child:
336. Dixie Daryl 6, b Apr 3, 1937, Salt Lake City

104. Lorna Bagley 5, Grant 4, Charles 3, Edward 2, Richard 1,
b July 11, 1902, Provo, UT; m George Winder, b Aug 20, 1902,
Salt Lake City, son William & Rose (Taylor).

105. Julia Etta Bagley 5, Grant 4, Charles 3, Edward 2,
Richard 1, b Mar 13, 1914, Provo, UT; m Frank Christophe
Jensen, b Nov 4, 1911, Revallas, NY, son Christophe & Marion
(Choate).

Children:
337. Frank 6, b Dec 21, 1940, Salt Lake City; d Dec 31, 1955
338. Grant Bagley 6, b Dec 12, 1942, Salt Lake City; m Julia

Ann Jensen, b Nov 2, 1944, Salt Lake City

114.   Lewis Loraine Bagley 5, John 4, John 3, Edward 2, Richard 1, b May 7, 1884, Montpelier, ID; d Dec 21, 1959; m Laurence Elaine Neff, b May 24, 1886, East Mill Creek, UT, dau John & Ann Eliza (Benedict) June 18, 1909; m (2) Mena Valve Furrow, b Aug 15, 1888.

Children:
339.   John Alan 6, b Sept 3, 1911, East Mill Creek, UT
340.   Louis Neff 6, b Apr 30, 1910, Salt Lake City; d there Mar 26, 1963
341.   Stewart Loraine 6, b July 12, 1913, Salt Lake City
342.   Benedict 6, b Apr 11, 1915, East Mill Creek, UT
343.   Sarah Louise 6, b Jan 25, 1919, East Mill Creek, UT; d June 21, 1919
344.   Charles 6, b Feb 8, 1920, East Mill Creek, UT
345.   Marjorie 6, b June 24, 1921, East Mill Creek, UT
346.   Donald Neff 6, b July 18, 1927, East Mill Creek, UT

115.   Mary Juanita Bagley 5, John 4, John 3, Edward 2, Richard 1, b Nov 2, 1889, Montpelier, ID; m May 1, 1907, William Arch Whitely.

118.   Moretta Vavores Bagley 5, John 4, John 3, Edward 2, Richard 1, b May 22, 1896, Montpelier, ID; d July 10, 1926; m May 6, 1917, J. O. Ira C. Stone.

120.   Gladrean Bagley 5, John 4, John 3, Edward 2, Richard 1, b Mar 9, 1898, Montpelier, ID; d Sept 4, 1969; m (1) Yvonne Peterson, b Jan 12, 1906, dau Angus & Rose (Evans). They were divorced. He m (2) June 5, 1937, Ilene N. Schick, b Sept 4, 1906, dau Frederick & Minnie (Schnitt).

Children:
347.   Delene 6, b Mar 9, 1940, Salt Lake City
348.   Ann 6, b Jan 7, 1943, Salt Lake City

121.   Hawley Bagley 5, John 4, John 3, Edward 2, Richard 1, b Nov 2, 1899, Montpelier, ID; m June 7, 1918, Adelilah Hogensen, b Apr 16, 1897, dau Charles & Mary (Anderson).

Children:
349.   Charles Allen 6, b Dec 3, 1920, Montpelier, ID; d Feb 11, 1939
350.   Gerald Hawley 6, b Jan 10, 1922, Montpelier, ID
351.   Melvin J. 6, b Jan 1, 1924, Green River, WY
352.   Elna Jean 6, b Feb 27, 1927, Green River, WY
353.   Lila Marie 6, b Aug 24, 1928, Salt Lake City

123.   Nina Bagley 5, John 4, John 3, Edward 2, Richard 1, b Jan 3, 1903, Montpelier, ID; m Nov, 1924, Henry Erickson.

125.   J. Grant Bagley 5, John 4, John 3, Edward 2, Richard 1, b Mar 24, 1906, Seaside, OR; m Mary Barnhill.

126. John A. Bagley 5, John 4, John 3, Edward 2, Richard 1, b Sept 15, 1907, Salt Lake City; d June 19, 1941; m May 10, 1940, Illa Hoops.

127. Major Harriman Bagley 5, John 4, John 3, Edward 2, Richard 1, b July 19, 1907, Salt Lake City; m July 26, 1930, Selma Gerrord.

129. Virginia Margaret Bagley 5, John 4, John 3, Edward 2, Richard 1, b Dec 27, 1912, Bloomington, ID; m Feb 4, 1930, Dave Olen.

130. Mary Viola Bagley 5, Cyrenius 4, John 3, Edward 2, Richard 1, b Oct 26, 1890; d Aug, 1962; m Thomas Quayle, June 30, 1910.

131. Pawley Eugene Bagley 5, Cyrenius 4, John 3, Edward 2, Richard 1, b Jan 10, 1892, Montpelier, ID; d 1954; m June 7,. 1916, Bertha Howell.

132. Emogene Kizziah Bagley 5, Cyrenius 4, John 3, Edward 2, Richard 1, b July 19, 1895, Crow Creek, ID; m Oct 9, 1917, Samuel E. Roberts, son Arthur & Maytha (Reese), b May 8, 1895, d Nov 16, 1941.

Children: (b Afton, WY)
354. Samuel 6, b June 2, 1918; m Mar 22, 1940, Rebecca Bastian
355. Russell 6, b Jan 22, 1920; m Oct 5, 1941, Nellie Dayton
356. Lelath 6, b Jan 26, 1922; m July 16, 1942, Arlene Hill
357. Bernice 6,, b Feb 18, 1924; m Mar 18, 1942, Dick Letensor
358. Emogene 6, b Aug 18, 1926; m July 31, 1945, Vernon Edgren
359. Ramola 6, b Feb 19, 1931; m Mar 18, 1947, Dan Welch
360. Betty 6, b Mar 6, 1938; m Feb 13, 1966, Jesse Perry
361. Kathleen 6, b Apr 27,----; m Leonard Young

133. Oliver Arthur Bagley 5, Cyrenius 4, John 3, Edward 2, Richard 1, b Apr 12, 1897, Crow Creek, ID; m Apr 3, 1918, Leah Howells.

134. Muriel Margaret Bagley 5, Cyrenius 4, John 3, Edward 2, Richard 1, b Apr 22, 1899, Crow Creek, ID; d Oct 23, 1924; m June 16, 1919, Mondel Tolman.

135. Cyrenius Hugh Bagley 5, Cyrenius 4, John 3, Edward 2, Richard 1, b Jan 26, 1906, Fairview, WY; m June, 1965, Goldie Jackson.

136. Lewis Ward Bagley 5, Cyrenius 4, John 3, Edward 2, Richard 1, b May 21, 1908, Granger, WY; d June 17, 1966; m Apr 3, 1929, Eleone Davis.

137. Ellsworth Allen Bagley 5, Cyrenius 4, John 3, Edward 2, Richard 1, b June 18, 1910, Fairview, WY; m 1936, Bonnie Jean

Stevens.

139.   John Conrad Bagley 5, David 4, John 3, Edward 2, Richard
1, b Dec 3, 1901, Granger, WY; m Nov 18, 1922, Mary Elizabeth
Hutchins, b Aug 31, 1902, Rock Springs, WY.   His mother was
Mary Ann Schenck.

Children:
362.   Betty Irene 6, b Jan 6, 1924, Rock Springs, WY
363.   Dorothy Jean 6, b July 24, 1925, Rock Springs, WY
364.   David 6, b Sept 30, 1928, Granger, WY
365.   Robert Conrad 6, b July 6, 1931, Salt Lake City
366.   George 6

140.   Laura Lorene Bagley 5, David 4, John 3, Edward 2,
Richard 1, b Apr 5, 1905, Montpelier, ID; d July 8, 1935; m
May 2, 1925, Kenneth Brown.

141.   June Bagley 5, David 4, John 3, Edward 2, Richard 1,   b
Oct 11, 1907, Montpelier, ID; m John David Groff.

142.   Irene Bagley 5, Charles 4, John 3, Edward 2, Richard 1,
b Oct 10, 1903, Salt Lake City; m Paul Martin, May 19, 1933.

143.   Iris Bagley 5, Charles 4, John 3, Edward 2, Richard 1, b
Aug 1, 1906, Salt Lake City; m (1) Nov 27, 1927, John Malcolm
O'Halle; m (2) May 18, 1935, John Moore Collect.

144. Mary Audrey Bagley 5, Charles 4, John 3, Edward 2,
Richard 1, b July 15, 1908, Salt Lake City; d Aug 22, 1953; m
Mar 2, 1939, Leonard Jordan.

145.   Hugh Oral Bagley 5, George 4, John 3, Edward 2, Richard
1, b July 23, 1907, Montpelier, ID; m Aug 4, 1928, Nada B.
Whitcher, dau Ralph & Vena (Goodwin), b Jan 19, 1906, Quenemo,
KS.

Children:
367.   Ruby Jean 6, b July 9, 1935, Montpelier, ID; d Nov 25,
1935
368.   Donald H. 6, b Apr 24, 1933, Orlando, CA
369.   Charles R. 6, b Feb 2, 1938, Orlando, CA
370.   Kenneth D. 6, b June 17, 1940, Artoria, CA
371.   Dennis M. 6, b June 6, 1948, Chico, CA

146.   Thelma Ruth Bagley 5, George 4, John 3, Edward 2,
Richard 1, b Sept 2, 1911, Pocatello, ID; m Sept 12, 1930,
Newern Glenn, son Alexander, b Apr 13, 1907.

Children:
372.   Roger 6, b Nov 15, 1931, Montpelier, ID; m Joan
Cattersle, b Eng; six children
373.   Kay 6, b July 19, 1936, Montpelier, ID; d Dec 14, 1936
374.   Jerry 6, b May 24, 1938, Roby, ID
375.   Ronny 6, b Apr 30, 1942, Montpelier, ID
376.   Beth 6, b May 7, 1944, Ontario, OR

377.   Garth 6, b Aug 7, 1951, Ontario, OR

147.   Owen Ellsworth Bagley 5, George 4, John 3, Edward 2,
Richard 1, b July 10, 1913, Montpelier, ID; m July 25, 1933,
Evelyn Tuescher, dau Frederick & Cora (Cordan).

Children:
378.   Owen M. 6, b July 15, 1934, Montpelier, ID; d Mar 30,
1936
379.   Marlene Joyce 6, b Feb 18, 1936, Montpelier, ID
380.   Rulon DeOrr 6, b Apr 1, 1937, Montpelier, ID
381.   Melvin LeRoy 6, b Aug 17, 1938, Artois, CA
382.   Ruth Arlene 6, b May 16, 1940, Montpelier, ID
383.   Arthur Allen 6, b Feb 28, 1942, Montpelier, ID
384.   Milton Cordan 6, b Feb 28, 1944, Portland, OR

148.   June Margaret Bagley 5, George 4, John 3, Edward 2,
Richard 1, b June 12, 1915, Montpelier, ID; m (1) July 3,
1934, Louis D. Booth, b July 5, 1908, Montpelier, ID. d Dec
29, 1935, Soda Springs, ID, son Lewis & Laura (Sorenson); m
(2) Mar 16, 1937, Bruce Beck, son David & Margaret (Love).
June & Louis were divorced July, 1936. She m (3) Arthur Van
Orman, Aug 3, 1962.

Child:
385.   Bruce, Jr., 6, b Dec 29, 1937, Montpelier, ID; m Janet
T. Shimoda, dau George & Hede (Terazawa); b Jan 26, 1933,
Pasadena, CA; had a child Janlin, b June 10, 1963, Murray, UT

150.   Seneil Bagley 5, George 4, John 3, Edward 2, Richard 1,
b Nov 23, 1919, Montpelier, ID; m Mar 23, 1936, Leslie Lamont
Burbank, b Oct 27, 1915, son Chester & Hannah (Larsen).

Children:
386.   Clarence Reed 6, b Jan 3, 1937, Montpelier, ID; d May
27, 1938
387.   Leslie Lamont 6, b Oct 3, 1940, Nyssa Malheur, OR
388.   Ruth Ann 6, b Aug 13, 1944, Caldwell Canyon, ID; m May
5, 1963, Alvin Allen
389.   Stewart Craig 6, b Apr 17, 1947, Nyssa Malheur, OR

151.   Geraldine Bagley 5, George 4, John 3, Edward 2, Richard
1, b July 8, 1924, Montpelier, ID; m July 13, 1940, LeRoy
Joseph Schirm, who d & she m (2) Lamont Norton.

Child:
390.   Larry LeRoy (Schirm) 6, b Aug 14, 1941, Montpelier, ID;
married; at least one child

152.   Thomas Leland Bagley 5, Thomas 4, John 3, Edward 2,
Richard 1, b Apr 21, 1914, Smoot, WY; d Sept 17, 1954; m July
15, 1942, Ida Gwendolyn Jones, b July 9, 1921, dau Fred H. &
Laura (Brown). She m 92) Archibald Rees Morgan.

Children: (b Salt Lake City)
391.   Sharon Ann 6, b Mar 5, 1943

392. Thomas Richard 6, b May 14, 1945

133. Emo Woodrow Bagley 5, Thomas 4, John 3, Edward 2, Richard 1, b Feb 20, 1886, Smoot, WY; m Sept 13, 1935, Cora Jones.

134. George Perley Bagley 5, George 4, William 3, Edward 2, Richard 1, b Mar 16, 1886, Charleston, UT; m May 29, 1908, Heda Rozilla Johnson.

135. Eliza Ellen Bagley 5, George 4, William 3, Edward 2, Richard 1, b Aug 8, 1887, Charleston, UT; d June 12, 1955; m Oct 5, 1908, William Henry Murdock.

136. Frederick Bagley 5, George 4, William 3, Edward 2, Richard 1, b Apr 9, 1889, Charleston, UT; m (1) Florence Lucia Peterson; m (2) Sept 22, 1934, Melrhea Shelton, b Jan 18, 1916, dau George & Orba Gertrude (Stephen).

Children: (b Salem, OR)
393. Jack Ray 6, b Dec 14, 1935
394. Loyle F. 6, b Jan 11, 1939

137. Lona May Bagley 5, George 4, William 3, Edward 2, Richard 1, b Mar 14, 1893, Charleston, UT; d July 6, 1926; m Dec 14, 1910, James H. Peterson.

140. Lorenzo Edwards Bagley 5, George 4, William 3, Edward 2, Richard 1, b May 12, 1895, Charleston, UT; m Jan 1, 1917, Ethel Eliza Jensen, b Dec 25, 1894, Salem, ID.

Children: (b Salem, ID).
395. Eddric 6, b Nov 25, 1917; m Apr 25, 1919
396. Dale Jensen 6, b Jan 27, 1919
397. Vaughan Lorenzo 6, b Apr 9, 1921; m Aug 1, 1948
398. Vivian Jensen 6, b Aug 30, 1923
399. Loa 6, b Oct 23, 1925
400. Ruth 6, b Feb 3, 1929
401. Vesta 6, b Apr 7, 1930
402. Ethel Maurice 6, b May 13, 1932
404. Quinton Jensen 6, b July 30, 1934
404. Myron Jensen 6, b Apr 17, 1937
405. Clay Jensen 6, b July 24, 1941

141. Ruby Leona Bagley 5, George 4, William 3, Edward 2, Richard 1, b Mar 12, 1897, Charleston, UT; m Nov 21, 1917, Heber Frederick Price.

142. Clara Alice Bagley 5, George 4, William 3, Edward 2, Richard 1, b Apr 12, 1899, Charleston, UT; d Apr 14, 1948; m Aug 20, 1924, Wilford Mendenhall.

143. Retta Bagley 5, George 4, William 3, Edward 2, Richard 1, b June 1, 1901, Charleston, UT; m Sept 14, 1920, George Marbler Poulsen.

164. Firl Edwards Bagley 5, George 4, William 3, Edward 2, Richard 1, b July 26, 1903, Charleston, UT; m Feb 23, 1921, Howard Tonks; children, one of whom was

Child:
406. Evelyn 6, b May 12, 1924; m Mark Ricks; son Peter & Emily (Arnold), b July 4, 1924; 9 children

165. Sadie Marie Bagley 5, George 4, William 3, Edward 2, Richard 1, b Nov 2, 1905, Charleston, UT; m Apr 26, 1930, Ivan Lake Nelson.

165A. Roland Bagley 5, George 4, William 3, Edward 2, Richard 1, b Oct 27, 1911, Victor, ID; d July 23, 1982, Yakima, WA; m (1), Monabell; they were divorced, and he m (2) Apr 29, 1946, Yakima, WA, Ruby Jane Prine, b May 6, 1926, Emporia, KS, d July 15, 1982, at Yakima, WA, dau Frank & Mary (Strown).

Children: (b Yakima, WA)
406A. Audrey Christine 6, stillborn, Jan 28, 1950
406B. John Robert 6, b July 5, 1952

166. Joseph Loraine Bagley 5, Joseph 4, Joseph 3, Edward 2, Richard 1, b Mar 11, 1909, Salt Lake City; m Hazel N. Stewart.

Child:
407. Clarence Hirum 6, b May 11, 1930, Granger, WY

167. Grant Van Bagley 5, Joseph 4, Joseph 3, Edward 2, Richard 1, b July 7, 1910, Rock Springs, WY; d May 10, 1933; m Veda Weeks, Dec 17, 1931, dau James & Huldah (Erickson).

Child:
408. Vance 6, b Dec 18, 1932, Granger, WY; d same day

169. Minerva Anne Bagley 5, Joseph 4, Joseph 3, Edward 2, Richard 1, b Mar 30, 1917, Granger, WY; m Elmer Butler.

172. Vera LaVone Bagley 5, Joseph 4, Joseph 3, Edward 2, Richard 1, b Oct 7, 1918, Granger, WY; m Howard Jackson.

175. Mima LaVone Bagley 5, Hyrum 4, Joseph 3, Edward 2, Richard 1, b Sept 30, 1901; d June 10, 1965; m Dec 8, 1921, Raymond P. Larsen, son Daniel & Sarah (Farmer).

Children:
409. Jena Lee 6, b Aug 21, 1922, Sandy, UT; m Ross Palmer
410. Lois LaVon 6, b June 30, 1923, Brigham Canyon, UT
411. Colleen 6, b July 26, 1937, Copperton, UT; m Arnold Percy

204. David Grant Bagley 5, David 4, Joseph 3, Edward 2, Richard 1, b Aug 6, 1913, Lund Bannock, ID; living Dublin, CA, 1961.

205. George Dale Bagley 5, David 4, Joseph 3, Edward 2,

Richard 1, b Aug 19, 1914, Salt Lake City; lived Altadena, CA, 1961; medical doctor.

206.   Ruth Bagley 5, David 4, Joseph 3, Edward 2, Richard 1, m ----Robinson; living Salt Lake City, 1961.

207.   Edward Merrill Bagley 5, Edward 4, Edward 3, Edward 2, Richard 1, b Aug 15, 1897, Greenwich, UT; m Sept 8, 1920, Ruby Arminta Olsen, b July 7, 1899, Koosharem, UT, dau Peter & Melva (Schaugaard).

Children: (b Koosharem, UT)
412.   Elaine 6, b June 10, 1921
413.   Melva Pauline 6, b Aug 27, 1922
414.   Lowell Edward 6, b Apr 16, 1924
415.   Jay Merrill 6, b Oct 14, 1925
416.   Lell Olsen 6, b Aug 27, 1927
417.   Carolyn 6, b July 18, 1932
418.   Fern Jeanette 6, b Nov 27, 1934

208.   Ellis Lynn Bagley 5, Edward 4, Edward 3, Edward 2, Richard 1, b Oct 20, 1898, Koosharem, UT; m Feb 3, o926, Bella Elmina Anderson, b Aug 2, 1900, Koosharem, UT, dau Orson Hyde & Hannah R.

Children:
419.   Lorna 6, b Jan 3, 1927, Salina, UT; d Jan 31, 1927
420.   Don Ferrell 6, b Jan 7, 1928, Salina, UT
421.   Colleen 6, b July 12, 1929, Salina, UT
422.   Covnell McKay 6, b Apr 28, 1932, Salina, UT
423.   Barta 6, b July 7, 1935, Koosharem, UT
424.   Wills LeRon 6, b Oct 10, 1941, Salina, UT

209.   Rodney Virginius Bagley 5, Edward 4, Edward 3, Edward 2, Richard 1, b Apr 13, 1900, Greenwich, UT; m Vivian Jensen, Jan 9, 1929. He d Apr 21, 1963, Ogden, UT.

Children:
425.   Rodney D. 6, b Oct 20, 1934, Ogden, UT
426.   Morris R. 6, b Feb 11, 1939
427.   Marilyn L. 6, b Sept 6, 1945

210.   Illa Mary Bagley 5, Edward 4, Edward 3, Edward 2, Richard 1, b Apr 3, 1903, Greenwich, UT; m July 22, 1938, Clifford Alfred Magleby.

Children:
428.   Myva A. 6, b July 5, 1939, Salina, UT; m Nov 25, 1959, Harold K. Moon
429.   Marvin C. 6, b Apr 23, 1941, Salina, UT

212.   Vonda Idell Bagley 5, Edward 4, Edward 3, Edward 2, Richard 1, b May 7, 1911, Koosharem, UT; m July 2, 1931, Rolland LaRue Anderson.

Children:

430.   Marlow R. 6, b May 13, 1934, Salina, UT; m Jennie Asay
431.   Armand M. 6, b Dec 2, 1936; d Feb 9, 1938
432.   Carmen 6, b Dec 26, 1740
433.   Kathleen 6, b Sept 30, 1943
434.   Jan C. 6, b Jan 16, 1949
435.   Kerry D. 6, b July 23, 1950

213.   Donna Pauline Bagley 5, Edward 4, Edward 3, Edward 2,
Richard 1, b July 12, 1913, Koosharem, UT; m Mar 21, 1934,
Royal Thomas Harwood, b Nov 15, 1910.

Children:
436.   Donna C. 6, b July 11, 1935, Aurora, UT; m Dwight
Williams
437.   Earvel R. 6, b Feb 27, 1941, Richfield, UT
438.   Robald V. 6, b Feb 23, 1943, Salina, UT
439.   Newell E. 6, b Mar 1, 1946, Salina, UT
440.   Thomas K. 6, b Sept 24, 1947, Salina, UT
441.   Layne B. 6, b Apr 13, 1949, Salina, UT

220.   Voyle LaRae Bagley 5, James 4, Edward 3, Edward 2,
Richard 1, b Dec 24, 1900, Koosharem, UT; d June 14, 1980; m
Oct 13, 1920, Emma Irene Torgensen.

Children:
442.   Royona (Petersen) 6, adopted, b Oct 9, 1927, Mapleton,
WY
443.   Wilda D. (Petersen) 6, adopted, b June 17, 1931 Salt
Lake City
444.   Baby dau 6, b & d Jan 7, 1935
445.   Emma L. 6, b Feb 28, 1938, Salina, UT
446.   Clell V. 6, b May 11, 1941, Salina, UT

221.   Grant Lyle Bagley 5, James 4, Edward 3, Edward 2,
Richard 1, b Aug 3, 1903, Annabelle, UT; d Nov, 1943; m Aug
15, 1928, Nellie Cartwright, b Sept 2, 1903, Staffordshire,
Eng.

Children:
447.   Nellie L. 6, b June 21, 1929, Richmond, UT
448.   Grant Richard 6, b Sept 22, 1920, Richmond, UT
449.   Lu Ann 6, b Feb 9, 1945, Logan, UT

222.   Zola Estella Bagley 5, James 4, Edward 3, Edward 2,
Richard 1, b Jan 16, 1906, Richfield, UT; m June 10, 1927,
Forrrut Luther Barlow, b Dec 15, 1895, Warwick, WV, d Jan 21,
1943, Lordsburg, NM.

Children:
450.   Floyd 6, b Nov 29, 1920, Provo, UT; m Feb 13, 1953,
Verona Chavex
451.   Bruce 6, b Aug 24, 1931, Provo, UT

224.   James Carroll Bagley 5, James 4, Edward 3, Edward 2,
Richard 1, b July 20, 1910, Greenwich, UT; m June 6, 1934,
Pearl Amelia Olsen, b Mar 20, 1911, Provo, UT, dau Parley &

Eliza (Beal).

Children:
452.   Carol Jean 6, b June 25, 1935, Provo, UT
453.   Glenna 6, b Mar 4, 1938, Provo, UT
454.   James K. 6, b Jan 1, 1941, Provo, UT
455.   Lynette 6, b Apr 16, 1942, Provo, UT
456.   Jay W. 6, b June 19, 1946, Yakoma, WA
457.   Grant A. 6, b Aug 22, 1947, Sunnyside, WA
458.   Kathleen 6, b Apr 6, 1950, Sunnyside, WA
459.   Shannon L. 6, b Aug 17, 1951, Sunnyside, WA

225.   Ellen Irene Bagley 5, James 4, Edward 3, Edward 2, Richard 1, b Nov 23, 1912; d May 18, 1958; m Glen A. Olsen; no children.

226.   Nora Myrtle Bagley 5, James 4, Edward 3, Edward 2, Richard 1, b Oct 13, 1913, Greenwich, UT; m (1) Oct 13, 1941, Byron Woodland, who d Feb 4, 1944; m (2) Sept 12, 1952, Leland Nielson.

Children: (b Provo, UT)
460.   Kathleen 6, b Feb 25, 1942; m June 1, 1958, Thomas Parris
461.   Mammes 6, b Jan 1, 1958

236.   Dean A. Bagley 5, George 4, Edward 3, Edward 2, Richard 1, b Feb 12, 1914, Greenwich, UT; m Nov 10, 1937, Ada Sorenson, b Dec 17, 1912, dau Ole & Alta (Brown).

Children: (b Salina, UT)
462.   Gloria 6, b Oct 10, 1938
463.   Roger Dean 6, b Dec 4, 1940
464.   Richard V. 6, b Oct 11, 1943
465.   Bobby Rae 6, b Oct 14, 1948

247.   Lulu Venita Bagley 5, George 4, Edward 3, Edward 2, Richard 1, b Nov 6, 1914, Greenwich, UT; m Dec 14, 1938, Reed Payne.

Children:
466.   Patsy A. 6, b Dec 24, 1939, Salina, UT; m July 21, 1962, Wendall Heston
467.   Mary Lou 6, b Oct 28, 1941, Elsinore, UT; m Nov 5, 1960, Warren Harward
468.   Wanda L. 6, b Jan 4, 1945, Glenwood, UT
469.   Reed J. 6, b Apr 4, 194-, Salina, UT
470.   Terry R. 6, b Dec 13, 1954, Richfield, UT
471.   Robert B. 6, b Nov 2, 1957

248.   Iona Bagley 5, George 4, Edward 3, Edward 2, Richard 1, b Oct 30, 1916, Greenwich, UT; m Feb 4, 1942, Raymond Frank Black.

Children:
472.   Owen R. 6, b May 16, 1945, Cedar City, UT

473.   Earl B. 6, b Aug 26, 1947
474.   Frankie B. 6, b May 22, 1956, Provo, UT

249.   Lynn Bagley 5, George 4, Edward 3, Edward 2, Richard 1,
b Nov 16, 1918, Greenwich, UT; m Mary Glenmona DeLange, June
29, 1943.

Children:
475.   Verl L. 6, b July 11, 1944, Salina, UT
476.   Mary Ann 6, b Jan 4, 1947, Salina, UT
477.   LaRell A. 6, b June 17, 1951, Saliona, UT
478.   Sherry L. 6, b Feb 20, 1954, Salina, UT
479.   Marvin D. 6, b Oct 19, 1958, Richfield, UT

250.   Keith Bagley 5, George 4, Edward 3, Edward 2, Richard 1,
b May 13, 1924, Greenwich, UT; m Fern Egbert, July 7, 1945.

Children:
480.   Barbara 6, b July 27, 1946, Ogden, UT
481.   Patricia 6, b Sept 27, 1954, Ogden, UT
482.   Susan 6, b May 13, 1957, Monterey, CA
483.   David 6, b Apr 4, 1958, Ogden, UT (twin)
484.   Darlene 6, b Apr 4, 1958, Ogden, UT (twin)

251.   Ada Alean Bagley 5, George 4, Edward 3, Edward 2,
Richard 1, b Feb 8, 1925, Greenwich, UT; m Dec 28, 1944,
George Leland Savey.

Children:
485.   George 6, b Feb 1, 1946, Salina, UT
486.   Susan 6, b Dec 26, 1947, Salina, UT
487.   Alma 6, b & d Feb 1, 1949, Provo, UT
488.   Kenneth 6, b Aug 29, 1951, Provo, UT
489.   Elden 6, b Aug 31, 1956, Provo, UT
490.   David 6, b Nov 7, 1958, Panguitch, UT

252.   Rolland McKay Bagley 5, George 4, Edward 3, Edward 2,
Richard 1, b Mar 20, 1929, Greenwich, UT; m Elsie LaVerda
Chappel.

Children: (b Salina, UT)
491.   Jessie C. 6, b June 20, 1949
492.   Rolland G. 6, b Sept 21, 1950, Salt Lake City
493.   Rex M. 6, b Jan 5, 1954
494.   Gale J. 6, b Sept 21, 1955
495.   Steven S. 6, b Oct 27, 1957
496.   Charlene 6, b July 11, 1962

253.   Viola Bagley 5, George 4, Edward 3, Edward 2, Richard 1,
b Mar 29, 1932, Greenwich, UT; m Donald Lowork Herzog.

Children: (b Salt Lake City)
497.   Ross D. 6, b Jan 29, 1955
498.   Randy J. 6, b May 12, 1956
499.   Judy K. 6, b Nov 9, 1958
500.   Donald G. 6, b Dec 27, 1960

254. Emily Almeda Bagley 5, Cyrenius 4, Edward 3, Edward 2, Richard 1, b Oct 3, 1910, Greenwich, UT; m July 27, 1932, Victor Magleby.

Children:
501. Carvel V. 6, b July 14, 1934, Salina, UT; m Apr 18, 1958, Jerry Turner
502. Carol L. 6, b Dec 10, 1937, Salina, UT

255. Cyrenius Lazono Bagley 5, Cyrenius 4, Edward 3, Edward 2, Richard 1, b Jan 13, 1913, Koosharem, UT; d July 21, 1964; m Aug 30, 1939, Edna LaRue Thorpe.

Children: (b Salina, UT)
503. William 6, b June 13, 1940
504. Richard L. 6, b Aug 12, 1947
505. Marilyn L. 6, b Mar 24, 1949

256. Utahna Bagley 5, Cyrenius 4, Edward 3, Edward 2, Richard 1, b Apr 11, 1914, Greenwich, UT; d dec 10, 1945; m Jan 30, 1934, Miles Grant Anderson.

257. Melba Lucille Bagley 5, Cyrenius 4, Edward 3, Edward 2, Richard 1, b May 6, 1918, Greenwich, UT; m July 27, 1944, Ronald F. Jensen.

Children: (b Salina, UT)
506. Melba V. 6, b June 12, 1945
507. Merrill R. 6, b Feb 11, 1949
508. Randall J. 6, b May 14, 1951
509. Utahna V. 6, b Apr 26, 1952
510. Janet 6, b Oct 14, 1955

259. Beth Bagley 5, Hyrum 4, Edward 3, Edward 2, Richard 1, b Dec 24, 1916, Mt Pleasant, UT; m Apr 16, 1940, Proctor Bohman.

260. Louise Bagley 5, Hyrum 4, Edward 3, Edward 2, Richard 1, b Nov 10, 1920, Mt Pleasant, UT; m Oct 24, 1941, Grant Johansen.

261. Christena LaVerne Bagley 5, Hyrum 4, Edward 3, Edward 2, Richard 1, b Jan 12, 1925; m May 24, 1943, Chad Sorenson.

262. Garth Orson Bagley 5, Hyrum 4, Edward 3, Edward 2, Richard 1, b Mar 12, 1930, Koosharem, UT; m May 1, 1953, Evelyn Brown.

263. Iva Bagley 5, Joseph 4, Edward 3, Edward 2, Richard 1, b Nov 30, 1919, Koosharem, UT; m June 8, 1941, June Powell.

264. Keun Bagley 5, Joseph 4, Edward 3, Edward 2, Richard 1, b Mar 2, 1927, Koosharem, UT; m July 11, 1944, Bastian Mace.

267. Owen Loraine Bagley 5, Owen 4, Edward 3, Edward 2, Richard 1, b Jan 25, 1927, Koosharem, UT; m Dorothy Valence

Bench, b June 22, 1931, Salina, UT, dau Samuel & Lenora J. (Brunholt).

Children:
511. Jacques Owen 6, b Apr 4, 1952, Burbank, CA
512. Lamont Jay 6, b Nov 28, 1953, Richfield, UT
513. Kenneth Loraine 6, b Oct 5, 1955, Salt Lake City
514. Lark Ann 6, b July 12, 1958, Salt Lake City
515. Jan 6, b & d Jan 25, 1960
516. Robin Marie 6, b Aug 6, 1962, Salt Lake City

269. Lorenzo Bagley 5, Owen 4, Edward 3, Edward 2, Richard 1, b Nov 23, 1931, Koosharem, UT.

272. Noel Elvin Bagley 5, Owen 4, Edward 3, Edward 2, Richard 1, b Sept 27, 1937, Koosharem, UT.

293. Eliot Lamar Bagley 5, Hyrum 4, Hyrum 3, Edward 2, Richard 1, b Oct 21, 1925, Big Cottonwood, UT.

294. Grant Wilbur Bagley 5, Hyrum 4, Hyrum 3, Edward 2, Richard 1, b Oct 21, 1923, Big Cottonwood, UT; supposed to have m & had two sons.

295. Clinton Lamar Bagley 5, Hyrum 4, Hyrum 3, Edward 2, Richard 1, b Feb 20, 1925; m Jane Lane, dau John & Della (Dunyon).

Children:
517. Barry Lamar 6, b Sept 11, 1950, Dallas, TX
518. Robert Allan 6, b Feb 10, 1957, San Diego, CA

296. Laurence Miles Bagley 5, Hyrum 4, Hyrum 3, Edward 2, Richard 1, b Jan 19, 1928, Salt Lake City; m Cassandra A. Bailey, b Sept 16, 1928, dau William & Cassandra (Debenham).

Children:
519. Kevin Miles 6, b Sept 8, 1952, Salt Lake City
520. Patrick Francis 6, b Feb 10, 1956, East Mill Creek, UT
521. Lisa Cassandra 6, b Aug 4, 1959, Oceanside, CA
522. William Grant 6, b May 27, 1960, Salt Lake City

297. William Bagley 5, Hyrum 4, Hyrum 3, Edward 2, Richard 1

298. Darwin Mortimer Bagley 5, Frank 4, Hyrum 3, Edward 2, Richard 1, b May 20, 1925, Sandy, UT; m Deon Smith, b Feb 14, 1926, dau Parley & Leona (Allan).

Children:
523. Merridy 6, b May 19, 1954, Salt Lake City
524. Jeff 6, b Jan 13, 1961

299. Eva L. Bagley 5, Frank 4, Hyrum 3, Edward 2, Richard 1, b Oct 23, 1929, Murray, UT; m Sept 22, 1948, Quinton Casperon.

300. Noel Bagley 5, Frank 4, Hyrum 3, Edward 2, Richard 1, b

June 3, 1941, Murray, UT; m Bonnie Olsen.

302. Jeffrey Bagley 5, Frank 4, Hyrum 3, Edward 2, Richard 1,
b July 24, 1954.

303. Allen Bagley 5, Frank 4, Hyrum 3, Edward 2, Richard 1, b
Sept 16, 1955.

305. David Cyrene Bagley 6, Cyrene 5, Edward 4, Charles 3,
Edward 2, Richard 1, b Oct 16, 1921, Cottonwood, UT; m Oct 10,
1944, Salt Lake City, Reuvo Chamberlain, b June 210, 1920, dau
Justin & Helen Mar (Bunker).

Children: (b Murray, UT)
525. Stillborn 7, b Oct 1, 1945
526. Amy Marie 7, b June 27, 1948
527. Charles 7, b Dec 14, 1949
528. Nancy 7, b Oct 13, 1951
529. Ruth 7, b Dec 26, 1953
530. Beth 7, b Oct 28, 1958

307. Marian Martha Bagley 6, Cyrene 5, Edward 4, Charles 3,
Edward 2, Richard 1, b Mar 14, 1925, Murray, UT; m Aug 11,
1950, Logan, UT, Deney Leon Woodward, b June 2, 1927,
Franklin, ID, son Ivan & Ordell (Doney).

Children:
531. DeAnn 7, b Dec 27, 1951, Logan, UT
532. Marilyn 7, b Oct 24 1952, El Paso, TX
533. Renee 7, b Aug 23, 1954, Salt Lake City
534. Stanley Ross 7, b Dec 28, 1955, Salt Lake City
535. Brent Alan 7, b Nov 11, 1957, Salt Lake City
536. Carol Carnie 7, b Apr 18, 1959, Salt Lake City
537. Ralph Bagley 7, b Mar 21, 1959, Salt Lake City

308. Myrtle Jean Bagley 6, Cyrene 5, Edward 4, Charles 3,
Edward 2, Richard 1, b Feb 8, 1927, Murray, UT; m Harvey
Lloyd, b Aug 15, 1924, Central, ID, son Ellis & Mary
(Sorenson).

Children:
538. Robert Harvey 7, b Oct 5, 1953, Logan, UT
539. Marian 7, b Oct 18, 1955, Logan, UT
540. Jennifer 7, m July 3, 1958, Grace, ID
541. Paul Alan 7, b Sept 16, 1964, Salt Lake City

309. Catherine Lucille Bagley 6, Cyrene 5, Edward 4, Charles
3, Edward 2, Richard 1, b Mar 18, 1930, Murray, UT; m May 12,
1950, Murray, UT, Frank Pond Reese, b Mar 10, 1927, Benson,
UT, son Frank & Jenney (Pond).

Children:
542. Dale 7, b Sept 15, 1951, Richmond, VA
543. Martha 7, b Nov 20, 1952, Richmond, VA
544. Lucille 7, b Dec 4, 1954, Hampton, VA
545. Daughter 7, b July 24, 1956, Hampton, VA; d July 26,

1956
546. Elaine 7, b Feb 12, 1958, Hampton, VA
547. David Wayne 7, b July 19, 1959, Murray, UT
548. Richard Alan 7, b Dec 1, 1960, Murray, UT
549. Stephen Bagley 7, b Nov 6, 1962, South Cottonwood
Heights, UT
550. Anne 7, b Mar 24, 1964, Murray, UT
551. John Edward 7, b July 3, 1965, Murray, UT

110. Frank Davidson Bagley 6, Cyrene 5, Edward 4, Charles 3,
Edward 2, Richard 1, b Aug 2, 1928, Murray, UT; m Sept 9,
1955, Marlene Larson.

Children:
552. Calvin Frank 7
553. Paul Harold 6
554. Laura Marlene 7
555. Carolyn 7
556. Cynthia 7
557. Susan 7

321. Miriam Gwendolyn Bagley 6, Charles 5, Edward 4, Charles
3, Edward 2, Richard 1, b Jan 10, 1931, Salt Lake City; m Mar
22, 1958, Delbert Grant Eccles, son John, b Dec 6, 1920.

Children:
558. David Stuart 7, b Nov 21, 1958, Almogordo, NM
559. Miriam G. 7, b Oct 28, 1960, Los Angeles

322. Corydon Stewart Bagley 6, Charles 5, Edward 4, Charles
3, Edward 2, Richard 1, b May 14, 1932, Murray, UT; m June 7,
1957, Gloria Randall, b Mar 26, 1934, dau Jack & Stella
(Hansen).

Children:
560. Corydon Randall 7, b Nov 16, 1958, Murray, UT
561. Darrell Stewart 7, b Feb 12, 1960
562. Joane 7, b Jan 15, 1962
563. Susan 7, b Mar 19, 1963
564. Lani 7, b Oct 21, 1964, Murray, UT; d Sept 7, 1965

323. Henry Granger Bagley 6, Charles 5, Edward 4, Charles 3,
Edward 2, Richard 1, b Sept 2, 1933, Murray, UT; m Dec 13,
1956, Bertelle Beaverson.

324. Martin Works Bagley 6, Charles 5, Edward 4, Charles 3,
Edward 2, Richard 1, b Mar 21, 1936, Murray, UT; unm, 1960.

325. Richard Ames Bagley 6, Ames 5, Edward 4, Charles 3,
Edward 2, Richard 1, b Apr 16, 1938, Salt Lake City; m Nov 30,
1957, Terry Head; no children.

326. Lawrence Samuel Bagley 6, Ames 5, Edward 4, Charles 3,
Edward 2, Richard 1, b Sept 2, 1941, Salt Lake City; m Nov 22,
1961, Salt Lake City, Sandra Lee Mason, b 1943, dau John.

Children:
565.   Lawrence 7, b June 15, 1962, Salt Lake Cty
566.   Joseph Ames 7, b May 20, 1963, Salt Lake City

327.   James Bagley 6, Ames 5, Edward 4, Charles 3, Edward 2,
Richard 1, b Oct 7, 1948.

329.   Edward Dallin Bagley 6, Edward 5, Edward 4, Charles 3,
Edward 2, Richard 1, b Aug 27, 1938, Salt Lake City; m Dec 18,
1961, Carolyn Creamer, b Dec 17, 1950, Boise, ID, dau Charles
& Mary (Taylor).

Child:
567.   Edward Bryan 7, b Mar 22, 1964, Salt Lake City

330.   Bonnie Marsha Bagley 6, Edward 5, Edward 4, Charles 3,
Edward 2, Richard 1, m Aug 19, 1963, Bruce Stowell.

Child:
568.   Bagley 7, b Aug 27, 1965

331.   Pamela Bagley 6, Andrew 5, Andrew 4, Charles 3, Edward
2, Richard 1, b Aug 9, 1936, Salt Lake City; m Sept 1, 1955,
John Harold Stagg, Jr.

Children:
569.   Lynell 7, b Aug 1, 1956, Salt Lake City
570.   Lance 7, b Sept 23, 1957
571.   Jon Drew 7, b Jan 29, 1959

332.   Sheila Bagley 6, Andrew 5, Andrew 4, Charles 3, Edward
2, Richard 1, b June 26, 1937, Salt Lake City; m June 26,
1937, Boyd Alonzo Lindquist.

Children:
572.   Darlena Boyd 7, b May 11, 1960, Salt Lake City
573.   Kathryn 7, b Aug 17, 1962

333.   Sharolyn Bagley 6, Andrew 5, Andrew 4, Charles 3, Edward
2, Richard 1, b Dec 20, 1940, Salt Lake City; m June 13, 1962,
Peter Warren McKeller.

Child:
574.   Melaney 7, b Apr 17, 1963, Salt Lake City

334.   Logan Andrew Bagley 6, Lewis 5, John 4, John 3, Edward
2, Richard 1, b Sept 3, 1911, East Mill Creek, UT; m May 15,
1932, Phebe Snarr, b May 6, 1911, Morelos, Mex., d Oct 20,
1941, dau Daniel & Phoebus (McCarroll). he m (2) Sarah Lois
Jex, Sept 20, 1952, dau Heber & Sarah (Bird).

Children: (b Salt Lake City)
575.   Laurence Snarr 7, b Oct 7, 1933
576.   John Craig 7, b dec 3, 1953
577.   Susan Elizabeth 7
578.   Lynne 7, b Dec 16, 1936

340. Louis Neff Bagley 6, Lewis 5, John 4, John 3, Edward 2, Richard 1, b Apr 30, 1910; d Mar 27, 1963; m Jan 5, 1934, Frances Swan, b Feb 26, 1907, Los Angeles, dau Charles Durton & Agnes (Brant).

Children: (b Salt Lake City)
579. Roy 7, b 1936; dead by 1963
580. Barbara Lou 7, b Aug 28, 1940
581. Katharine 7, b Feb 9, 1942
582. Charles Loraine 7, b Nov 25, 1934; d Nov 25, 1936
583. Douglas Eugene 7, b Aug 21, 1945

341. Stewart Loraine Bagley 6, Lewis 5, John 4, John 3, Edward 2, Richard 1, b July 12, 1913, Salt Lake City; m Nov 20, 1936, Lucille Carter Kreuger, b May 15, 1914, Nephi, UT, dau Algeon McKay Carter & Margaretta (Norton). She was adopted by a Mr. Kreuger.

Children: (b Salt Lake City)
584. Kent 7, b Oct 18, 1938
585. orna Lucille 7, b May 27, 1941
586. Steven Stuart 7, b Sept 27, 1945
587. Nancy Ann 7, b May 20, 1952

342. Benedict Bagley 6, Lewis 5, John 4, John 3, Edward 2, Richard 1, b Apr 11, 1915, East Mill Creek, UT; m Aug 1, 1936, Marie Pehrson, b May 11, 1917, Salt Lake City, dau Ernest William & Agnes Isabel (Gabrielson).

Children:
588. Jo Anne 7, b Aug 4, 1937, Salt Lake City
589. Grant Pierce 7, b Apr 20, 1941, Salt Lake City
590. John Neff 7, b Apr 21, 1944, Murray, UT
591. Donna Marie 7, b Dec 30, 1947, Murray, UT

344. Charles Bagley 6, Lewis 5, John 4, John 3, Edward 2, Richard 1, b Feb 8, 1920, East Mill Creek, UT.

345. Marjorie Bagley 6, Lewis 5, John 4, John 3, Edward 2, Richard 1, b June 24, 1921, East Mill Creek, UT; m Oct 8, 1941, East Mill Creek, Charles Robert Turner, b Jan 8, 1918, son Albert & Laura (Brown).

Children: (b Grand Junction, CO)
592. Laura Elaine 7, b July 30, 1942
593. Janet Lorraine 7, b Dec 14, 1945
594. Margaret Louise 7, b Jan 4, 1949
595. Nancy Charlotte 7, b Dec 21, 1951
596. Barbara Joan 7, b July 29, 1954

346. Donald Neff Bagley 6, Lewis 5, John 4, John 3, Edward 2, Richard 1, b July 18, 1927, East Mill Creek, UT; m Aug 29, 1951, Toledo, OH, Mima Ericson (Carolyn Doreen Packham), b Nov 12, 1929, Los Angeles, dau Harold Parkman & Edythe Louise (Stone).

597. Tiffani 7, b Apr 1, 1953, San Bernadino, CA

347. Delene Bagley 6, Almorean 5, John 4, John 3, Edward 2, Richard 1, b Mar 9, 1940, Salt Lake City; m Robert Stone.

350. Gerald Hawley Bagley 6, Hawley 5, John 4, John 3, Edward 2, Richard 1, b Jan 10, 1922, Montpelier, ID; m Apr 1, 1944, June Luindgren.

351. Melvin J. Bagley 6, Hawley 5, John 4, John 3, Edward 2, Richard 1, b Jan 1, 1924, Green River, WY.

364. David Bagley 6, John 5, David 4, John 3, Edward 2, Richard 1, b Sept 30, 1928, Granger, WY.

365. Robert Conrad Bagley 6, John 5, David 4, John 3, Edward 2, Richard 1, b July 6, 1931, Salt Lake City.

366. George Bagley 6, Hugh 5, David 4, John 3, Edward 2, Richard 1.

368. Donald H. Bagley 6, Hugh 5, George 4, John 3, Edward 2, Richard 1, b Apr 24, 1933, Orlando, CA.

369. Charles F. Bagley 6, Hugh 5, George 4, John 3, Edward 2, Richard 1, b Feb 2, 1938, Orlando, CA.

370. Kenneth D. Bagley 6, Hugh 5, George 4, John 3, Edward 2, Richard 1, b June 17, 1940, Artoris, CA.

371. Dennis M. Bagley 6, Hugh 5, George 4, John 3, Edward 2, Richard 1, b June 4, 1948, Chico, CA.

379. Marlene Joyce Bagley 6, Owen 5, George 4, John 3, Edward 2, Richard 1, b Feb 18, 1936, Montpelier, ID; m Dec 7, 1955, Dwight Hemmort.

380. Rulon DeOrr Bagley 6, Owen 5, George 4, John 3, Edward 2, Richard 1, b Apr 1, 1937, Montpelier, ID; m Aug 24, 1956, Sylvia Warner.

381. Melvin LeRoy Bagley 6, Owen 5, George 4, John 3, Edward 2, Richard 1, b Aug 17, 1939; m May 26, 1961, Frankie Sue Sorensen.

382. Ruth Arlene Bagley 6, Owen 5, George 4, John 3, Edward 2, Richard 1, b May 15, 1941, Montpelier, ID; m May 24, 1956, LeVon Hemmert.

383. Arthur Allen Bagley 6, Owen 5, George 4, John 3, Edward 2, Richard 1, b Feb 23, 1942, Montpelier, ID; married.

384. Milton Gordan Bagley 6, Owen 5, George 4, John 3, Edward 2, Richard 1, b Feb 28, 1944, Portland, OR; married.

392. Thomas Richard Bagley 6, Thomas 5, Thomas 4, John 3,
Edward 2, Richard 1, b May 14, 1945, Salt Lake City.

393. Jack Ray Bagley 6, Frederick 5, George 4, William 3,
Edward 2, Richard 1, b Dec 14, 1933, Salem, ID.

394. Loyle F. Bagley 6, Frederick 5, George 4, William 3,
Edward 2, Richard 1, b Jan 11, 1939, Salem, ID.

396. Dale Jensen Bagley 6, Lorenzo 5, George 4, William 3,
Edward 2, Richard 1, b Jan 27, 1919, Salem, ID; m June 4,
1947, Helen Campbell.

397. Vaughan Lorenzo Bagley 6, Lorenzo 5, George 4, William
3, Edward 2, Richard 1, b Apr 9, 1921, Salem, ID; d Aug 1,
1945.

399. Loa Bagley 6, Lorenzo 5, George 4, William 3, Edward 2,
Richard 1, b Oct 23, 1925, Salem, ID; m Sept 3, 1946, Elmo
Cheney Davis.

400. Beth Bagley 6, Lorenzo 5, George 4, William 3, Edward 2,
Richard 1, b Feb 3, 1929, Salem, ID; m June 25, 1953, Mark
LeRoy Hall.

402. Ethel Maurine Bagley 6, Lorenzo 5, George 4, William 3,
Edward 2, Richard 1, b May 13, 1932, Salem, ID; m June 16,
1955, Argus Andrian Clinger.

403. Quinton Jensen Bagley 6, Lorenzo 5, George 4, William 3,
Edward 2, Richard 1, b July 30, 1934, Salem, ID.

404. Myron Jensen Bagley 6, Lorenzo 5, George 4, William 3,
Edward 2, Richard 1, b Apr 17, 1937, Salem, ID; m Mar 22,
1957, Rose Irene Chandler.

405. Clay Jensen Bagley 6, Lorenzo 5, George 4, William 3,
Edward 2, Richard 1, b July 24, 1941, Salem, ID.

406A. John Robert Bagley 6, Roland 5, George 4, William 3,
Edward 2, Richard 1, b July 5, 1952, Yakima, WA.

407. Clarence Hyrum Bagley 6, Joseph 5, Joseph 4, Joseph 3,
Edward 2, Richard 1, b May 11, 1930, Granger, WY.

413. Melva Pauline Bagley 6, Edward 5, Edward 4, Edward 3,
Edward 2, Richard 1, b Aug 27, 1922, Koosharem, UT; m Vermont
Clements Harward.

Children:
598. Stanley Vermont 7, b Sept 7, 1950
599. Richard Merrill 7, b Aug 29, 1951 (twin)
600. Randall Thomas 7, b Aug 29, 1951 (twin)
601. Susan Jeanette 7, b Apr 19, 1956
602. Calvin Edward 7, b July 31, 1958

603.   Cheryl Elaine 7, b Mar 23, 1962

414. Lowell Edward Bagley 6, Edward 5, Edward 4, Edward 3,
Edward 2, Richard 1, b Apr 16, 1924, Koosharem, UT; m Aleith
Anderson, b Dec 1, 1923.

Children:
604.   John Edward 7, b Feb 5, 1947
605.   Aleith Anne 7, b Jan 3, 1948
606.   Renee 7, b Nov 9, 1949
607.   Marilyn Mignon 7, b Mar 4, 1953
608.   Marian 7, b Mar 18, 1955

415.   Jay Merrill Bagley 6, Edward 5, Edward 4, Edward 3,
Edward 2, Richard 1, b Oct 14, 1928, Koosharem, UT; m
Elizabeth Whittenburgh, b Mar 5, 1926, dau David & Lei (Ivell).

Children:
609.   David Jay 7, b Nov 20, 1947, Richfield, UT
610.   Margaret 7, b May 7, 1949, Logan, UT
611.   Becky Carrol 7, b Feb 23, 1953, Denver, CO
612.   Jeanette 7, b July 25,. 1956, Logan, UT
613.   Marilyn 7, b Oct 26, 1960

416.   Loli Olsen Bagley 6, Edward 5, Edward 4, Edward 3,
Edward 2, Richard 1, b Aug 27, 1927, Koosharem, UT; m Carole
Dianne Baker, b May 8, 1928.

Children:
614.   James Baker 7, b June 12, 1955
615.   Robert Loli 7, b Oct 24, 1956
616.   Elizabeth Carole 7, b Oct 1, 1960
617.   Edward Kent 7, b Feb 26, 1962

417.   Carolyn Bagley 6, Edward 5, Edward 4, Edward 3, Edward
2, Richard 1, b July 18, 1932, Koosharem, UT; m Howard Lee
Edwards, b June 10, 1931.

Children:
618.   Bryant Bagley 7, b Dec 12, 1954
619.   Howard McKay 7, b Nov 6, 1956
620.   Mitchell Lee 7, b Oct 10, 1958

418.   Fern Jeanette Bagley 6, Edward 5, Edward 4, Edward 3,
Edward 2, Richard 1, b Nov 27, 1934, Koosharem, UT; m Donald
Robert Johnson, b Mar 4, 1933.

Child:
621.   Constance Jeanette 7, b Apr 12, 1961

420.   Don Ferrell Bagley 6, Edward 5, Edward 4, Edward 3,
Edward 2, Richard 1, b Jan 7, 1929, Saline, UT; d June 15,
1961; m June 6, 1953, Margaret S. King.

421.   Colleen Bagley 6, Edward 5, Edward 4, Edward 3, Edward
2, Richard 1, b July 12, 1929, Salina, UT; m June 6, 1952,

Robert Hugh Gehrig.

<u>422.   Coynell McKay Bagley 6, Edward 5, Edward 4, Edward 3,</u>
<u>Edward 2, Richard 1,</u> b Apr 28, 1932, Salina, UT; m June 6,
1957, Faun De Leeuw, dau Hyrum & Ann (Torgerson).

Children:
622.   Douglas K. 7, b Aug 9, 1958, Richfield, UT
625.   Ann 7, b Aug 13, 1960, Salt Lake City

<u>423.   Barta Bagley 6, Edward 5, Edward 4, Edward 3, Edward 2,</u>
<u>Richard 1,</u> b July 7, 1933, Koosharem, UT; m Sept 2, 1953, Paul
Rickenbach.

<u>424.   Wills LeRon Bagley 6, Edward 5, Edward 4, Edward 3,</u>
<u>Edward 2, Richard 1,</u> b Oct 10, 1941, Salina, UT; m Nov 21,
1964, Salina. Coleen Torgerson.

<u>425.   Rodney D. Bagley 6, Rodney 5, Edward 4, Edward 3, Edward</u>
<u>2, Richard 1,</u> b Oct 20, 1934, Ogden, UT; m Sept 1, 1960, Alice
Grover.

<u>426.   Morris R. Bagley 6, Rodney 5, Edward 4, Edward 3, Edward</u>
<u>2, Richard 1,</u> b Feb 11, 1939.

<u>442.   Rovona Bagley 6, Voyle 5, James 4, Edward 3, Edward 2,</u>
<u>Richard 1,</u> b Oct 9, 1927, Mapleton, WY; m Nov 14, 1945, Anton
N. Casto.

<u>443.   Wilda D. Bagley 6, Voyle 5, James 4, Edward 3, Edward 2,</u>
<u>Richard 1,</u> b June 17, 1931, Salt Lake City; m Sept 5, 1950,
Rhoda Brown.

<u>445.   Emma L. Bagley 6, Voyle 5, James 4, Edward 3, Edward 2,</u>
<u>Richard 1,</u> b Feb 28, 1938, Salina, UT; m Dec 17, 1960, Larry
Higgins.

<u>446.   Clell V. Bagley 6, Voyle 5, James 4, Edward 3, Edward 2,</u>
<u>Richard 1,</u> b May 11, 1941, Salina, UT; m July 30, 1965,
Virginia.

<u>447.   Nellie L. Bagley 6, Grant 5, James 4, Edward 3, Edward</u>
<u>2, Richard 1,</u> b June 21, 1929, Richmond, UT; m Sept 2, 1947,
Neldon L. Robinson.

<u>448.   Grant Richard Bagley 6, Grant 5, James 4, Edward 3,</u>
<u>Edward 2, Richard 1,</u> b Sept 22, 1920, Richmond, UT; m Sept 14,
1951, Billie Done.

<u>452.   Carol Jean Bagley 6, James 5, James 4, Edward 3, Edward</u>
<u>2, Richard 1,</u> b June 25, 1935, Provo, UT; m Sept 2, 1955,
Harvey Underwood.

<u>453.   Glenna Bagley 6, James 5, James 4, Edward 3, Edward 2,</u>
<u>Richard 1,</u> b Mar 6, 1938, Provo, UT; m May 17, 1958, Lowell
Davenport.

454. James K. Bagley 6, James 5, James 4, Edward 3, Edward 2, Richard 1, b Jan 1, 1941, Provo, UT; m Dec 19, 1963, Shirley Drum.

455. Lynette Bagley 6, James 5, James 4, Edward 3, Edward 2, Richard 1, b Apr 16, 1942, Provo, UT; m Dec 19, 1962, Danny Elder.

456. Jay W. Bagley 6, James 5, James 4, Edward 3, Edward 2, Richard 1, b June 19, 1946, Yakima, WA; m June 14, 1968, Kathleen Sargent.

Child:
624. Shawn David 7, b Mar 24, 1970, Provo, UT

457. Grant A. Bagley 6, James 5, James 4, Edward 3, Edward 2, Richard 1, b Aug 22, 1947, Sunnyside, WA; m May 31, 1969, Joan Garrett.

458. Kathleen Bagley 6, James 5, James 4, Edward 3, Edward 2, Richard 1, b Apr 6, 1950, Sunnyside, WA; m Sept 6, 1969, Fred P. Anderson.

459. Shannon L. Bagley 6, James 5, James 4, Edward 3, Edward 2, Richard 1, b Aug 17, 1951, Sunnyside, WA; m Aug 30, 1969, Charles Schwartz.

462. Gloria Bagley 6, Jean 5, George 4, Edward 3, Edward 2, Richard 1, b Oct 10, 1938, Salina, UT; m June 3, 1957, James Larsen.

Children:
625. Lamra 7, b May 16, 1958, Salina, UT
626. Trudy 7, b July 26, 1960; d Oct 31, 1960
627. Gary James 7, b July 22, 1962, Salina, UT

580. Barbara Lou Bagley 7, Louis 6, Lewis 5, John 4, John 3, Edward 2, Richard 1, b Aug 29, 1940, Salt Lake City; m May 24, 1963, Edward Rogers, son Willard.

581. Katherine Bagley 7, Louis 6, Lewis 5, John 4, John 3, Edward 2, Richard 1, b Feb 9, 1942, Salt Lake City; m Apr 10, 1965, Robert Garff, son Kendall.

583. Douglas Eugene Bagley 7, Louis 6, Lewis 5, John 4, John 3, Edward 2, Richard 1, b Aug 21, 1945, Salt Lake City.

584. Kent Bagley 7, Stewart 6, Lewis 5, John 4, John 3, Edward 2, Richard 1, b Oct 18, 1939, Salt Lake City; m Mar 15, 1963, Zola Player.

Child:
628. Lois Kaye 8, b Feb, 1964

585. Lorna Lucille Bagley 7, Stewart 6, Lewis 5, John 4, John

3, Edward 2, Richard 1, b May 27, 1941, Salt Lake City; m Mar 26, 1964, Roy Blaine Moore.

588.   Jo Anne Bagley 7, Benedict 6, Lewis 5, John 4, John 3, Edward 2, Richard 1, b Aug 4, 1937, Salt Lake City; m Sept 17, 1956, William Gregg Calkins, b Nov 4, 1934, Los Angeles; son Ernest & Mary (Reed). She m (2) Robert Lewis Seghim.

Child:
629. Stephen John 8, b 1964, NYC

589. Grant Pierce Bagley 7, Benedict 6, Lewis 5, John 4, John 3, Edward 2, Richard 1, b Apr 20, 1941, Salt Lake City; m June 8, 1961, Margaret Holther, dau David.

Child:
630. Susan 8, b Apr 27, 1963, Baltimore, MD

EDWARD BAGLEY: BAGLEY INDEX

The number refers to the descent from Richard who is #1.
Usually, the name will be found in two places: under the name
of the Bagley father or mother when the name, date of birth,
date of death, etc, is given (where known), and later on in
the work where the same data is repeated and other
information, if any, given. The exceptions to this are when
the Bagley died young or d unm in which case all information
is given in the original citation. Bagley boys who are known
to have lived to child-bearing age but for whom we have no
marriages are carried over. Bagley girls who are known to
have married are given under the parents and again in a later
section. Their children are listed and given a number. This
index does not index Bagley women by married names, but under
Bagleys.

Ada 251
Alexth 605
Alice S, 50
Allen 303
Almorean 120
Amanda 91
Amy 526
Andrew 17, 101
Amos, 97
Ann 3, 20, 71, 348, 623
Arthur 383
Audrey 406A
Avis 238

Barbara 480, 580
Barry 517
Barta 423
Becky 611
Ben 211
Benedict 342
Beth 259, 400, 530
Betty 265, 362
Bobby 465
Bonnie 530
Burnett 174

Caleb 83
Calvin 522
Carol 452
Carole 364
Carolyn 417, 585
Catherine 309
Charlene 496
Charles 4, 34, 96, 306, 344, 349, 569, 527, 582
Christena 74
Clara 82, 162
Clarissa 407
Clay 405
Clell 446

EDWARD BAGLEY: NAMES OTHER THAN BAGLEY INDEX

Number denotes Bagley connected with another person. To find
the person, find the number of Bagley.   Children of Bagley
women have their own number.

Ainsworth, Benjamin 90
Ainsworth, Harriet 90
Ainsworth, Harriet (Goff) 90
Albrecht, Lapreal 79
Alich, Howard 81
Allen, Alvin 388
Allen, Andrew 5
Allen, Delilah (Andrews) 5
Allen, Margaret or May 5
Anderson, Aleith 414
Anderson, Amanda 25
Anderson, Amelia (Riggs) 25
Anderson, Armand 431
Anderson, Bela 200
Anderson, Carmen 432
Anderson, Cavon 201
Anderson, Della 208
Anderson, Diantha 66
Anderson, Elizabeth (Avid) 58
Anderson, Enoch 25
Anderson, Evan 196
Anderson, Fred 458
Anderson, Gustaf 59
Anderson, Hannah 208
Anderson, Jan 434
Anderson, Jens 66
Anderson, John 58, 203
Anderson, Joseph 193
Anderson, Karen (Jensen) 66
Anderson, Kathleen 433
Anderson, Kerry 435
Anderson, Lillie 216
Anderson, Marlow 430
Anderson, Mary 217
Anderson, Maurine 202
Anderson, Milos 256
Anderson, Orson 208
Anderson, Pearl 199
Anderson, Rolland 212
Anderson, Thelma 197
Anderson, Theodore 64, 218
Anjum, Stephen 191
Armstrong, Florence 18
Armstrong, Francis 18
Armstrong, Isabella (Siddway) 18
Arrian, Fay 383
Asay, Pennie 430
Austin, Edward 25
Austin, Elnora (Lane) 25
Austin, Ila 25

BRITISH BAGLEYS

The following is material that has been found on Bagleys in England. It is by no means inclusive. It is offered merely to put what material we know in one place for reference. This material is indexed by page numbers.

The main body of the work was sent to Dr Bagley by Mrs Mel Brefferth of Lake Charles, Louisiana, who is a descendant of Samuel of Boston (See Notes on Bagley Lines in this volumes). Other material was supplied by Thomas Baguley of Salt Lake City. Family work sheets from records of the Church of Jesus Christ of Latter Day Saints have been included as well as odds and ends of materials we have found in our research.

Bagley is from the Saxon, meaning a rising or swelling ground that lies untilled; from boelge, a rising or swelling and Leagh or ley, plain or pasture land. The original spelling appears to have been Baggiley, but it has been, and is, spelled in a variety of ways including Baggley, Bagly, Baggulley, Bagley, and in Ireland, Begley. In the 15th century the Baggileys of Cheshire had much interest in Lancashire and changed to the name to Baguley. From Cheshire through the several counties going west, the name Bagguley is prevalent, but going south the name Bagley is used even in London; e. g., in Ipswich from which many of the first Bagleys came to America who were shipwrights and sea captains. The Irish use Begley, but most families changed to name to Bagley, or had it changed for them by immigration officials. This variety of names and the influx of the Irsh Bagleys into America in the 1840's make tracing specific families very difficult in the British Isles.

It appears the name was adopted in England by a man named Macey or Macei who was seated at Baggiley in the time of William the Conqueror. William made numerous trips to England, accompanied by small parties of kinsmen and others. There is an account of one of these trips, when he was accompanied by two nephews and eight lesser kinsmen, among the latter, Hama de Macei. Macie is a well-known place name in Normandy near Avranch.

From Pea Rolls, it appears that John, Lord of Baggiley in 1170, had sons: Hamon, Howekin, William, Peter and John. It is not clear if Hamon Massey or John was the first ancestor of the Baggileys in England who came with William and became the owners of the Manor of Bagguley from whence the name comes. King in his History of England, dated 1650, states that Baggiley was located in Bulkley Hundred in the Kingdom of March, known as the Vale Royal in England, which reaches from London to the river Mersey which divides Cheshire from Lancashire. When Thomas Bagley of Virginia died in 1672, he mentions his brothers who lived at Macclesfield, Cheshire, England in his will.

About the reign of King John (1213-1216), Hamon of the house of Baggiley was Baron of Dunham-Massey, and during the time "Hamon Massey, and descended from the other Hamon, before named gave unto Matthew de Bromhal, Duckenfield and two others parts of Baggiley which the father of the said Matthew held of the said Hamon, as his inheritance in knight's service to him and his heirs." This Hamon was involved in the rising of the Northern Barons against King John.

Descendants of Orlando Bagley of Amesbury, MA, may claim to descent from the royal family of Plantagenet in England, to six signers of the Magna Carta, and to the Emperor Charlemagne through the Anthony Colby line. The first Orlando m Sarah, dau of Anthony Colby and Susanna (Haddon). This Colby connection to above historical personages has been proven and accepted by the Royal Society of Heralds in England.

Jonathan Bagley, b 1604, Martins in the Field, Suffolk, Eng., m Elizabeth Haddon, b 1607, Sussex, Eng. Two children are known from the records: (1) Elizabeth, b July 31, 1633, Martins in the Field, and (2) Jonathan, b June 14, 1635. Some have supposed that Jonathan was the father of Orlando of Boston and Amesbury, MA, through the coincidence of the names Haddon and the dates, but there has not been definite proof found.

Agnes Bagley, wife of Nicholas, buried May 30, 1580, St James, Clerkenwell

Alexander Bagley either b or d, 1597, Bishop Bott, London

Alice Bagley m Robert Towsy, 1673, Knightsbridge

Alice Bagley m John Townsend, 1760, Marylebone

Ann Bagley m Anthony Blasy, Wetheringsett, Suffolk, 1605

Ann Bagley m John Bruff, Enfield, 1771

Ann Bagley & Increase Crosse m 1734, Mary Mgd. Fish.

Alice Bagley of Alberbury, Shropshire, Eng., b abt 1753, had a son John, b Dec 4, 1773 at Alberbury, Shropshire, Eng. Apparently she was not m. (Alberbury Par Register by Shropshire Par. Reg. Society. Vol 7, Pt 2, p 533)

Anthony Bagley of Leckhampstead, Bucks, Eng., b abt 1610, buried Dec 18, 1637, m Apr 27, 1635, at Leckhampstead, Eng., Mary Whitaker, b abt 1614, of Leckhampstead, Bucks, Eng. (Bucks, L 1, Vol 1, p 10, Leckhampstead, Par. Reg.)

Arthur Bagley of Kinnerley, Shropshire, Eng., b abt 1671, m 1694, at Kinnerley, Shropshire, Eng., Martha Lloyd, b abt 1675, of Kinnerley, Shropshire, Eng.

Benjamin Bagley of St Stepney, London, Eng., b abt 1720, m 1745, at St Stepney, London, Eng., Elizabeth Betts of St Stepney, London, Eng., b abt 1724. (Lond., 12, Vol 1, p 90)

Cecilie Bagley m John Fazekerly. St Sepulcre, London, 1704

Charles Frederick Bagley of St Marylebone, London, Eng., b abt 1825, son of Charles. m June 27, 1850, at St Marylebone, London, Eng., Eleanor Ann Buckwell of St Marylebone, London, Eng., b abt 1829. (St Marylebone reg, by W. E. C. Cotton)

Dorothy Bagley, chr June 19, 1614, St Martin in Field

Edmond Bagley either b or d, 1563, Cornhill

Edward Bagley m Mary Ram, Gregory, London, 1747

Edward Bagley d 1625, ae 60, Bpsgate Bot

Edward Bagley m Frances Bellard, All Hallows, 1665

Elizabeth Bagley, an infant, buried May 4, 1790, at workhouse, St Paul, Covent Garden

Elizabeth Bagley m Richard Walter, 1659, St James, Dukes Place

Elizabeth Bagley m Samuel Hunt, Berking, Suffolk, 1613

Elizabeth Bagley m John Cook, Marylebone, 1692

Francis Bagley of East Stokes, Notts, Eng., b abt 1654, m Elizabeth, b abt 1658, had the following children at East Stoke, Notts, Eng.: (1) Hannah, christened Mar 25, 1680, (2) James, christened Apr 11, 1684, and (3) Thomas, christened June 7, 1687. (F Notts 1)

Francis Bagley m Ailles Hudson, both of St Mary's, Aldermary and had (1) Susanna, b Oct 14, 1628; and (2) Frances, dau Francis, petticoat maker in Walting Street, Dec 8, 1629

Francis Bagley either b or d, 1689, Bpsgate Bot

For descent of George and William Bagley family of Montpelier, IO, see, that family in another part of this volume.

George Bagley of Cardeston, Shropshire, Eng, b abt 1698, m at Cardeston, Eng., Elizabeth of Cardeston, Eng., b abt 1702, and had the following children, b at Cardeston, Eng.: (1) Elizabeth, christened Nov 16, 1723, and (2) Bridgett, christened Dec 17, 1727 (H 1, Vol 5, Shropshire, Eng.)

George Bagley of Wensley, Yorkshire, Eng., b abt 1648, m Sept 2, 1673, at Wensley, Eng., Elizabeth Furniss of Preston, Yorkshire, Eng., b abt 1652. (Reg of Wensley, Vol 1, 1538-17, or p 83)

George Bagley of Thornton, Yorkshire, Eng., b abt 1726, m
Jan 5, 1751, at Thornton, Eng., Mary Marshall of Thornton,
Yorkshire, Eng., b abt 1730. (church of Bentham, Eng.)

George Bagley of Pontesbury, Shropshire, Eng., b abt
1735, m Jan 24, 1758, at Pontesbury, Eng., Elizabeth Davies of
Pontesbury, Shropshire, Eng., b abt 1737, and had the
following children, b at Pontesbury, Eng.:
(1)   George, chr, Jan 4, 1759
(2)   Thomas, chr, May 11, 1761
(3)   Thomas, chr, Jan 3, 1762
(4)   Elizabeth, chr, Feb 13, 1764
(5)   Mary, chr, June 17, 1766
(6)   Sarah, chr, Nov 25, 1768
(7)   Ann, chr Jan 3, 1772

George Bagley of Rowley Regis, Staffs., Eng., b abt 1771,
m Ann or Nancy of Rowley Regis, Staffs., Eng., b abt 1775, and
had the following children,, christened at Rowley Regis,
Staffs., Eng.:
(1)   Mary Ann, Oct 29, 1797
(2)   Maria, May 19, 1799
(3)   Sarah, July 8, 1804
(4)   Thomas, Nov 29, 1812

George Bagley, a butcher, of Pocklington, Yorkshire,
Eng., b abt 1766, m July 25, 1791, Elizabeth Jackson of Holy
Trinity, Kings Court, Yorkshire, Eng., b abt 1779. (Par.
Reg., Holy Trinity, Kings Court, p 171)

George Bagley of Llandrinio, Montgomery, Eng., b abt
1757, m Elizabeth Heeken of Ford, Shropshire, Eng., b abt
1761, and had a son George, b Oct 27, 1782, Ford, Shropshire,
Eng. (Ford Par. Reg., Vol 1, pt 2, p 38, 45)

George Bagley of Buildwas, Shropshire, Eng., b abt 1771,
m July 11, 1796, at Buildwas, Eng., Sarah Harris, b abt 1775,
Buildwas, Shropshire, Eng. (L I, Vol L, Shropshire, Eng.)

George Bagley either b or d, 1625, Cripplegate

George Bagley & Ellen, had dau Ann, b Dec 12, 1641, bur
Mar 28, 1642, St Mitchell , Cornhill

George Bagley & Ellen had stillborn child, Jan 1, 1635,
St Mitchell, Cornhill

George Bagley & Ellen had a dau Elizabeth, chr, June 18,
1637, bur Apr 10, 1639

George Bagley's wife, Elinor, bur Dec 31, 1665, St
Mitchel
l, Cornhill
George Bagley either b or d 1665, Cornhill

George Bagley m Elizabeth Siggins, 1619, St Martin in

Giles Bagley of New Castle, Northumberland, Eng., b abt 1754, m 1779, at New Castle, Elizabeth Swaintrom, of New Castle, b abt 1758. (Boyd Marriages Index, North, 12, Vol 22, p 157)

Giles Bagley of Bolton cum Redmire, Yorkshire, Eng., m ------- of Bolton cum Redmire, b abt 1653, Bolton cum Redmire, and had a son, William, chr May 9, 1681 at Bolton cum Redmire, Yorkshire, Eng.

Gurlielm Bagley, chr June 22, 1600, Clerkenwell

Gyles Bagley of Bolton cum Redmire, Yorkshire, Eng., b abt 1718, m -------, of Bolton cum Redmire, b abt 1722, and had a dau, Elizabeth, chr Oct 1, 1759, at Bolton cum Redmire.

Hannah Bagley m James Brest, Stepney, London, 1708

Hannah Bagley m William Jrel, Marylebone, 1680

Hannah Bagley m Derby Langely, 1677, Knightsbridge

Henrico, son Thomas Bagley b July 2, 1609, St James, Clerkenwell

Henry Bagley, either b or d, 1603, Bermondsey

Henry Bagley, vicar of Iver, Bucks, m Helen Welber, (or Weller), June 12, 1619, Benet Pauls Wharf

Henry Bagley either b or d, 1609, Martin in the Field

Humphrey Bagley either b or d 1642, Westm Mgt

Humphrey Bagley, buried July 3, 1642, St James, Clerkenwell

Humphrey Bagley, stillborn child, buried Mar 8, 1636/7, St James, Clerkenwell

Isabelle Bagley m Jonathan Shipman, 1660, St Mary, Wool.

James Bagley, d 1799, ae 53, Camberwell

James Bagley and Sarah, had son, Edward, chr Apr 8, 1792, Covent Garden

James Bagley of Wolverhampton, Staffs., Eng., b abt 1715, m May 29, 1740, at Wolverhampton, Eng., Elizabeth Perry, of Wolverhampton, Eng., b abt 1719. (Par. Reg., Wolverhampton, Staffs., W 1 d, p 97)

James Bagley, cotton spinner, of Ulverston, Lancashire, Eng., b abt 1772, m June 10, 1797, Ulverston, Eng., Jane

Dennison, of Ulverston, Eng., b abt 1776. (Lancs. U1, Ulvertson, p 442)

James Bagley of London, Eng., b abt 1630; buried Aug 1, 1656, m ——————, of London, Eng., b abt 1634, and had a son John, b abt 1656; buried Mar 6, 1658, London, Eng. (St Paul, Covent Garden, London)

James Bagley from St Clement Danes, buried Jan 15, 1800, ae 33 yrs, St Paul, Covent Garden

James Bagley m Elizabeth Morden, Edmonton, 1834 (Boyd Marr Index)

Jane Bagley m Thomas Walker, 1740, Helen

Jane Bagley m Roger Kellet, Mayfair, 1757

Jane Bagley m Richard Willis, 1662, Stepney

Jane Bagley, widow, buried Jan 1, 1677, St Paul, Covent Garden

Joanes Bagley m Judocia Pheaser, Aug 30, 1591, Clerkenwell

Johanna Bagley, dau John, blacksmith, deceased, m Richard Fyssler, taylor of St Martin in the Field, Dec 26, 1586

John Bagley of London, draper m Emma Smith of St Leonard, Shoreditch, widow of Henry Smith, late of Stepney, Sept 1, 1593

John Bagley m Elizabeth Ralph, Oct 14, 1761, St James, Clerkenwell

John Baglee and Mary Willingham m 1755, East Suffolk

John Bagley m Margaret Doe, George Hanover, 1805 (Boyd Marr Index)

John Bagley m Susan Huchesen, All Hall, 1807 (Boyd MArr Index)

John Bagley & Mary had a dau, Mary Ann, chr, May 30, 1787, St Martin in Field

John Baglee m Ann Crewe, Jan 18, 1785, St George, Hanover Square

John, son Humphrey Bagley, buried Aug 16, 1641, St James, Clerkenwell

John Bagley m Sarah Walker; they had a dau Philippi, chr Aug 3, 1673, Newgate St

John Bagley m Margaret Polter, 1618, St Olave

John Bagley m Isabelle Boswell, Mayfair, London, 1746

John Bagley m Sara Lions, Mayfair, London, 1746

John Bagley either b or d, 1641, Clerkenwell

John Bagley m Rebecca Dukesbury, Marylebone, London 1686

John Bagley m Alice Windham, St Sepulcre, London, 1697

John Bagley either b or d, 1596, Martin in Fields

John Bagley bur ? Sept 7, 1672, Newgate St, London

John Bagley m Judocea Pheaser, 1598, St Martin in Field

John Bagley m Sarah Alcox, Marylebone, 1667

John Bagley m Elizabeth Carman, St Benet, 1674

Jonathan Bagley either b or d 1672, Newgate

Jonathan Bagley m Alice Evans, St Martin in Field, 1560

Jonathan Bagley m Elizabeth Weston, 1642, Suffolk

Jonathan Bagley m Mary Muttet, Ipswich M L, 1622

Jonathan Bagley either b or d 1657, Clerkenwell

Joseph Bagley m Susan Skinner, Helen, London, 1750

Joseph Bagley m Sarah Morley, Marylebone, London, 1693

Joseph Bagley m Mary Pointer, Gregory, London, 1690

Joseph Bagley m Cecile Collins, St James, Dukes Place, London, 1698

Joseph Bagley either b or d, 1656, Covent Garden

Judithea Bagley, either b or d Apr 26, 1618, St Martin in Field

Leonard Bagley of Southill, Bedford, Eng., b abt 1595, m May 8, 1620, Southill, Bedford, Eng., Joan Ward of Southill, Eng., b abt 1599; buried Aug 30, 1642, Southill, Bedford, Eng. (Southill Par. Reg., Bed., 2 Vol 12 - A 61)

Maria Bagley m Johnes Spratt, June 29, 1618, St Martin in Field

Martha Bagley m William Allibone, 1731, Bot Bphgate

Martha Bagley m Jonathan Pinkney, All Hallows, 1763

Mary Bagley m Daniel Cadet, Stepney, London, 1708

Mary Bagley m Thomas Martin, Marylebone, 1710

Mary Bagley m Henry Younger, Benet Wharf, St Paul, 1720

Mary Bagley m Robert Carr, 1728, Benet Pauls Wharf

Mary Bagley m John Goldicutt, Mary in Strand, 1746

Mary Bagley m Joseph Deer, 1744, Lake Old St

Mary Bagley m Henry Burder, 1742, Mary ab Church

Mary Bagley m William Langley, St James, Dukes Place, London, 1715

Mary Bagley m Michael Dorset, Stanwell, 1695

Mary Bagley m Thomas Vantner, St James, Dukes, 1697

Matthew Bagley m Judith Sprig, St Bot Bpsgate, London, 1681

Michael Bagley m Sarah Cute, St James, Dukes, 1666

Nicholas Bagley either b or d, 1610, Clerkenwell

Nicholas Bagley m Agnes Milner, 1609, Clerkenwell; another record says m Agnes Miller, Dec 21, 1609

Mrs. Nicholas Bagley buried Sept 6, 1609, St James, Clerkenwell

Nicholas Bagley buried at Chauncell, Clerkenwell, May 30, 1610

Olive Bagley m William Billington, Grays Inn, 1722

Paul Bagley m Rebecca Bar, St Bot, Bpgate, 1655

Peter Bagley either b or d, 1593, Martin in the Field

Philip Bagley , bur Feb 10, 1673, Newgate

Philip Bagley, son Philip & Joane Bagley, chr Oct 24, 1673, Newgate

Ralph Bagley m Joan White, Enfield, 1590

Rebecca Bagley m Samuel French, Mary in Strand, 1717

Richard Bagley of Sedgeley, Stafford, Eng., chr Nov 26, 1564, son of Robert Bagley, m ———, of Sedgeley, Eng., b abt

1570, and had a dau, b 1613, Sedgeley, Stafford, Eng., ;
buried Mar 20, 1613. (Sedgerley Par. Reg.)

Richard Bagley of East Stokes, Notts.. Eng., b abt 1571,
m --------.of East Stokes, b abt 1575, and had the following
children, christened East Stokes, Eng.:
(1) Robert, July 30, 1597
(2) Katherine, Mar 2, 1599
(3) Richard, Nov 28, 1602
(4) William, Nov 10, 1604/05

Richard Bagley of Pitchford, Shropshire, Eng., b abt
1623; buried Aug 8, 1681, Pitchford, Eng., m Margery of
Pitchford, Eng., b abt 1627, and had the following children,
christened Pitchford, Eng.:
(1) Thomas, Oct 23, 1649
(2) Edward, Jan 14, 1651
(L 1, Vol 1, Pitchford, Shropshire, Eng.)

Richard Bagley of Hopton Castle, Shropshire, Eng., b abt
1625, m Eleanor of Hopton Castle, Eng., b abt 1629, and had
Richard, b July 1, 1657, Hopton Castle, Shropshire, Eng.
(Hopton Castle Par. Reg., Vol 2, pt 2, p 21)

Richard Bagley of Pitchford, Shropshire, Eng., b abt
1665, m 1690, Pitchford, Eng., Anne Davies of Pitchford, b abt
1669; buried Mar 14, 1693, Pitchford, Eng., and had Mary,
christened Nov 26, 1690, Pitchford, Shropshire, Eng. (L 1,
Vol 1, Pitchford, Shropshire, Eng.)

Richard Bagley, buried church yard, Feb 5, 1664, St Paul,
Covent Garden

Richard Bagley either b or d, 1661, Covent Garden

Richard Bagley m Margaret Oleyville, Knightsbridge, 1658

Richard Bagley, buried Jan 2, 1661, poore man, St James,
Clerkenwell

Richard Bagley either b or d, 1664, Cornhill

Richard Bagley either b or d, Dec 3, 1612, St Martin in
Field

Richard Bagley, Jr., of Berks, Gt, son Richard, Sr., Gt,
m Margaret Reddidge, or Beddidge, ae 17, spinster, dau Thomas,
late of Waltham, Berks.. Gt, deceased, m Nov 4, 1632

Robert Bagley m Mary Brookes, Dionis. Beckchurch, London,
1734

Robert Bagley m Elizabeth Hill, Westminster, London, 1747

Robert Bagley, yeoman, bachelor, m Anne Wootton, at St
James, Clerkenwell, Midlesex, Jan 11, 1622

Robert Bagley either b or d, 1645, Westm Mgt

Robert Bagley m Deborah Wale, 1623, St Giles

Robert Bagley m Ellen Hall, 1625, St Mary Woolnoth

Ruth Bagley m Abra Adams, Knightsbride, 1679

Samuel Bagley, m Elizabeth Padnell, Blakenham, East Suffolk

Sarah Bagley, ae 51, buried Dec 14, 1804, St Paul, Covant Garden

Sarah Bagley m Jonathan Blaxdell, Mayfair, 1752

Susan Bagley m John Rowe, Barking, Suffolk, 1613

Susan Bagley m Richard Herine, 1673, St Mary in Strand

Thomas Bagley and Joan Adkins, m Wethersett, Suffolk , m 1603

Thomas Bagley m Joan Parson, St Peter's, Cornhill, 1548

Thomas Bagley m Catherine Berriman, St Michael's, Brook Lane, 1569

Thomas Bagley and Elizabeth Hadwyn, spinster, of St Botolph, Aldergate, m Oct 11, 1576

Thomas Bagley m Susan Vallance, 1603, St Martin in Fields

Thomas Bagley m Sarah Sandall, Apr 4, 1780, St James, Clerkenwell

Thomas Bagley m Margaret Truman, 1611, St Mary in Strand

Thomas Bagley m Ann Dowle, All Hallows, 1662

Thomas Bagley of Acton Burnell, Shropshire, Eng., b abt 1649, m Aug 6, 1674, at Wroxeter, Shropshire, Eng., Anne Rowley of Acton Burnell, Shropshire, Eng., b abt 1653. (Shropshire L I, Vol II, p 40)

Thomas Bagley m Elizabeth Phillips, Clerkenwell, London, Apr 21, 1731

Thomas Bagley m Octavia Carpenter, Marylebone, 1808 (Boyd Marr Index)

Thomas Bagley m Elizabeth Burns, St Paul, Cov. Garden (Boyd Marr Index)

Thomas Bagley of Cardeston, Shropshire, Eng., b abt
1692; buried July 27, 1743, Cardeston, Eng.. m Alice of
Cardeston, Eng., b abt 1696; buried July 20, 1743, Cardeston,
Eng., and had the following children, christened Cardeston,
Eng.:
(1) Anne, June 3, 1718
(2) Mary, 1721, d June 30, 1743
(3) John, Jan 27, 1726
(4) Sarah, Jan 1, 1733
(H 1, Vol 5, Cardeston, Shropshire, Eng.)

Thomas Bagley of Cardeston, Shropshire, Eng., b abt 1671,
m Cardeston, Eng.. Jane, of Hereford, Hereford, Eng., b abt
1675, and had the following children, christened Hereford,
Hereford, Eng.:
(1) George, Aug 24, 1697
(2) John, June 26, 1704
(3) Jane, May 22, 1707
(4) Martha, Sept 5, 1708
(H 1, Vol 5, Cardeston, Shropshire, Eng.)

Thomas Bagley of Oswestry, Shropshire, Eng., b abt 1720,
had an illegitimate child by Katherine Wem of Oswestry,
Shropshire, Eng., christened Oct 28, 1722, Oswestry, Eng., dau
Francis and Katherine Wem, had William Wem, chr Feb 23, 1746,
Oswestry, Eng.; d Mar 10, 1747. (Oswestry, Shropshire, Eng.
printed Par. Reg.)

Thomas Bagley of parish of Fulham, bachelor, m Elizabeth
Amelia Burns, Feb 22, 1825

Thomas Bagley either b or d, 1678, Camberwell

Thomas Bagley either b or d, 1640, Clerkenwell

Thomas Bagley either b or d, 1634, Martin in Field

A stillborn child of Thomas Bagley, bur June 9, 1662, St
Benet, Paul Wharf

Thomas Bagley either b or d, 1594, Apostle, London

Walter Bagley m Elner Henley, Knightsbridge, 1659 (Boyd
Marr Index)

Warwick Bagley m Mary Brown, George Hanover, 1814 (Boyd
Marr Index)

William Bagley and Elizabeth Morgan, Marylebone, London,
m 1693

William Bagley m Margaret Powell, Marylebone, London,
1685

William Bagley of Ludlow, Shropshire, Eng., b abt 1616, m
Anne, of Ludlow, Eng., b abt 1614, and had the following

children christened Ludlow, Shropshire, Eng.:
(1)   Thomas Bagguley, 7 Aug 1636
(2)   Susan Bagley, Apr 21, 1638; buried Apr 22, 1638
(3)   Joan Bagnell, May 4, 1640; buried Aug 24, 1641
(Shrops. H I. vol 13, 14, p 195, 200, 204, 362, 370)

     William Bagley m Mary Crew, Stanwell, 1664 (Boyd Marr
Index)

     William Bagley of Chalcomb, Norths., Eng., b abt 1659, m
May 31, 1684, St Peter's Northampton, Norths., Eng., Elizabeth
Ward of St Peter's, Northampton, Eng., b abt 1663. (Norths 7,
Vol 2, p 27)

     William Bagley of Horseheath, Cambs., Eng., b abt 1614, m
Nov 1, 1639, Horseheath, Eng., Annabel Jackson of Horseheath,
Eng., b abt 1618. (F Cambrs. 1 Eng. 13833379, Horseheath Par.
Reg., p 8)

     William Bagley of Winsted, Yorkshire, Eng., b abt 1696, m
May 4, 1721, Winsted, Eng., Joan Noble of Winsted, Eng., b abt
1700. (Noble Gen.)

     William Bagley of Dingley, Northants, Eng., b abt 1688, m
July 9, 1713, Dingley, Eng., Elizabeth Dane of Corby,
Northants, Eng., b abt 1692. (Northants, Par. Reg., copied by
Cotton)

     William Bagley of Billingsley, Shropshire, Eng., b abt
1706, m Billingsley, Eng., Ann of Billingsley, Eng., b abt
1710, and had a dau, Mary, christened Jan 1,   1732,
Billingsley, Eng. (H 1, Vol 3, Shropshire, Eng.)

     William Bagley of Billingsley, Shropshire, Eng., b abt
1699, m at Billingsley, Eng., Joyce of Billingsley, Eng., b
abt 1703, and had a dau Elizabeth, christened Apr 1, 1725,
Billingsley, Eng. (H 1, Vol 3, Shropshire, Eng.)

     William Bagley either b or d, 1603, Apostle

     William Bagley either b or d, 1625, Cripplegate

     William Bagley either b or d, 1687, Westm James

     William Bagley either b or d, 1687, Westm Mgt

     William Bagley, d 1725, ae 34, Minories

     William Bagley either b or d , 1773, Covent Garden

     William Bagley m Frances Jones, Dunstan West, 1826 (Boyd
Marr Index)

     William Bagley m Elizabeth Savage, George Hanover, (Boyd
Marr Index) (no date in my notes)

     William Bagley m Mabel Towne, Mkt West, 1557 (Boyd Marr
Index)

This record was sent me by the Utah Society of Charlemagne Descendants with references: Americans of Royal Descent by Browning; Royal Lines, by Adams; American Genealogical Compendium by Virkus; Printed Family Histories; records of Genealogical Society

Charlemagne; Pippin, b 1773; Louis the Pious, b 1778; Berhard, b 1797; Karl 2; Judith; Herjbert of Vermandois, b 840; Beatrix of Vermandois; Hugh the Great, d 956; Robert 2, b 970; Henry 1, b 1008; Hugh The Great, b 1027; Isbale of Vermandois; Balduin of Flanders, d 918; Arnulf of Flanders, b 964; Balduin of Flanders, b 940; Arnulf of Flanders, b 961; Balduin of Flanders, b 980; Balduin of Flanders, b 1012; Mathilde of Flanders m 1053 William the Conqueror; Gundred, William of Warren; Ada of Waren; Margaret of Scotland; Henry Bohun; Humphrey Bohun; Humphrey Bohum; Humprey Bohum, William Bohun; Elizabeth Bohun; Elizabeth Fitzalan; Elizabeth Goushill; Elizabeth Wingfield; Elizabeth Brandon; Thomas Garnon; August Garnon; Richard Garnon; Mary Garnon, Beatrix Felton; Anthony Colby; Sarah Colby; Orlando Bagley.

BRITISH BAGLEYS AND OTHER FAMILIES

    The following on the Bagley and Other Families was sent
by Mrs. Mel Brefferth of Lake Charles, LA, and is copied as
she sent the material.

<u>Origin</u>
    Rev. C. Bardsley, an authority on surnames, in his <u>Our</u>
<u>English Surnames</u> says that "Baguley, Bagley, Baggalley,
Baggerley are derived from Baguley, a township near
Northenden, county Chester, England."
    H. Harrison, in his <u>Surnames</u>, says that "Baggallay,
Baggally, Baggarley, Bagley, Baguley are derived from Bagley
or Baguley, i. e., Baga's Lea (Anglo-Saxon Bagan - leak --
Bagab, geniive of Baga"

    It is interesting to note, in passing, that while British
authors agree on the origin of this surname, American writers
occasionally find the name Bagley corrupted from Bigelow and
Beckley.
    This can be ascribed solely to the ignorance of scribes,
just as one sometimes finds the name written Bayley when the
family of Bagley is clearly referred to, e. g., in the
Weymnouth, MA, Vital Records under
*Bagley (see Bayley)
*Bayley (see Bailey, Baily, Bayley, Bayle):
....Samuel (Bagly), dup & 2nd dup Samuel Bayley, son of Samuel
(dup Samuel) and Mary, born Sept 7, 1658.
while in the Boston records, marriages as well as births, the
names are given as Bagley only.

    "Richard Beggarly", who according to Winthrop's Journal,
ii.344, had remained in England, while his wife "had been here
six years" in 1636, when she endeavored to obtain a divorce,
"but the Court ordered he should remain separate from her toll
she might send into England for further proof, and appointed
him 20 shillings from her to set him to work" is again
referred to at the Court of Assistants, June 5, 1638, as
"Baggerly".
    On March 27, 1638, Mrs. Daniell pl against Richard
Beckley, deft, occurs, and the wife seems to have been known
at the same time by the names of Baggerly (Beckley) and Mrs.
Daniels or Daniell (Records of Quarter Court at Salem, MA.)

    In the Conqueror's time Cislebertus et Randulphus et
Hamo, held Sunderland and Baggiley, Cheshire: which at the
coming of the Normans were held by Edward and Suga and Udeman,
and Pet, for four manors, and were gentlemen: wasta est tota,
as it says in the <u>Domesday Book</u>:
    "Gislebertus & Ranulf & Hamo tenant Sundreland &
Bageilei. Eluuard & Suga & Vdeman & Pat tenuerunt, p IIII
(Maneris) & liberi homines fuerunt. Ibi.l. hida geliabilis.
Terra est una caruca & dimidia. Wasta est tota: Tempore Regis
Eduwardi valebat IIII. solidos."
    The three first, says Ormerod, in his <u>History of</u>
<u>Cheshire</u>, "I take to be Gilbert Venables, Baron of Kinderton;
Ranulfus, supposed to be the ancestor of Wainwarings: and
Hamon Massy, Baron of Dunham Massey. Sunderland is locus

cognitus within the town of Dunham Massey.

About the reign of King John, Hamon Massey (then lord of Dunham Massy and descended from the above named Hamon), gave unto Matthew de Bromhal, Bromhale, Duckenfield and two parts of Baggiley, which the father of said Matthew held of said Hamon, as his inheritance in knight's service, to him and his heirs: faciendo praedicto Hamoni et heredibus suis liberum servitum feodi unius locricae: quitting all other service de aratro et hosterio (an instrument of husbandry to break up the earth), et segibus secandis, feu (fire) colligendo, et homagio faciendo de averiis, et de pannagio, et salicher (carrying salt from the Wich, a service very usual in those days), et de omnibus aliis consuetudinibus, etc (Lib. C. Fo. 258 C.)

Certain it is that this town gave name to the family of Baggileys, who were seated here as early as 18 Henry III . 1233 AD.

The township is situated about seven miles south of Manchester, on low ground near the banks of the Mersey. One side of the quadrangle of Baggiley Hall ramains, in the centre of which is the great hall, much dilapidated, but exhibiting an excellent specimen of ancient domestic architecture. The sides are formed of huge beams of oak, the interstices of which are filled up with wicker work. In these are four large square-headed bay windows. At one end is a passage through the building from the exterior to the inner court, the doors of which are concealed from the hall by screens of oak, ornamented with pointed arches of oak. The uprights of these screens ascend until they mix with the roof, which is supported by immense arched beams.

In the great hall rests the effigy of Sir William de Baguley, referred to in Randle Holme's Cheshire Church Notes (Har. MS, 2, 151), taken circa 1633, among other monuments in Bowdon Church.

"In the body of the church, in the south side, this monument cut in freestone for Sir Will. Baguley, Kt, and in the head of the south ile in old glasse, very aunciente, this coate", i. e., on a shield of three lozenges, azure." (The crest of the Bagleys is: On a wreath a a ram's head azure attird, or, charged with three lozenges of the 2d.)

The figure, which is attached to a solid stone slab, which had been removed from Bowdon Church and thrown aside as worthless, while some repairs were being made, is sculptured in full relief, and represents a knight, life-size, and habited in full military costume, in the attitude of repose, with the hands conjoined upon the breast as if in supplication " that men might know that while he died he prayed".

The features are very rudely delineated, says Croston in his short description of this "monumental effigy at Baguley Hall", but in other respects the composition is boldly executed; and excepting that the lower extremities have been mutilated, it is in a fair state of preservation.

The general treatment and the characteristics of the figure, coupled with the fact that, with the exception of the genouillieres, protecting the knees, there is a total absence of plate defences, leads to the supposition that the date of this interesting piece of monumental sculpture is as early as the reign of Edward II, and probably about the year 1320, after which time plate armour began to form a more prominent feature in defensive equipment. The effigy, says Croston, would appear to be that of Sir William Baggalegh, son of Ralph Baggalegh of Baguley. From a Plea Roll of 44 Hen III, 1259, it would appear as if Sir William's father was Peter and not Ralph: "Will., fil Petr' de Baggeleg", grants to John, son of Hamoni de Baggeleg that assart in Bagguley called Enesebrolocis, whihc Will. de Baggeleg by his charter gave to the said Peter, the said John to pay yearly 12d for all services, saving yearly to the said William, John's third "best pig when the pig could find mast for itself."

In the <u>Visitation of Chester, 1580</u>, William de Baguley miles (p 150) and Sir William (p 148) in the Pedigrees of the Leighs of Baguley, is given as the "son of Sir John Baguley, de Baguley in com. Cestriae miles."

The above mentioned Pea Roll, being a legal document, is to be preferred however.

In the Harl. MS. 2074, fo 80b and 2079, fo 16, we find a charter of 1233-6 to the Knights of the Order of St John of Jerusalem, in which William de Baggeley ocurs as a witness.

In 1270, William de Bagguley and Johannes de Legh granted to the latter's son Robert all his possesions in Middlewich (Trans. Lanc. & Chs. Soc. XV 51).

In an inquisition of 1246, Wilmslow parish, Northcliff, village of Cheshire, after Ric. de Orreby, we find William de Baggelegh as one of the jury.

The name occurs in 1303 with one William de Baggelegh, apparently a son of the above, in a chamberlain's account of Cheshire, on Tuesday next after the Feast of St Michael's 1303/4, m. 6, "for license.. 20d." In the same year, after the Feast of St Barnebas, we find another chamberlain's account for the name Ralph de Baggelegh for acknowldging himself " p r c 12 d. and because he did not prosecute 6d."

In a Close Roll of July 20, 1311, 5 ED II m 30, dated at Berwick on Tweed, to the escheater beyond Trent, we find an order to permit John Heyward to mow the corn sown by him at Gillingham... Amice, wife of William de Bageleye and daughter of John Goce, nearest heir of said John, who held land in Gillingham as late escheater beyond Trent."

On Aug 2, 1316, a charter was granted to William de Baggeley of a parcel of land in Wyhtemshawe, Northenden parish, lying in a Middel Eye near the land of said William.

Nov 30, 1318, Sir Nicholas de Eton and his wife, Joan, concede to Sir William de Baggelegh, Kt, and his heirs one hamlet with appurtenances in the village of Echelen, Cheshire county, Northenden parish, called Ryhul, with enclosure called Alvehey, which William de Baggelegh, Jr., held for the term of the life of Lady Cecilia de Stokeport. Thomas de Baggelegh was a witness.

In 10 Edw. II, 1316, Geoffrey, son of William de Baggelegh, occurs in a Plea Roll vs Roger de Platte, relating to fine of tenements in Norsworth and Kenworthy.

Sir William de Baggiley occurs as Lord of Bagguley, 13 Edw II, 1319, and John Baggiley, his son, made a feoffment of the manor of Baggiley in Cheshire, and of his manors ot Hyde and Leveshulme in Lancashire, unto Sir John Legh pf Booths, nigh Knotsford, covenanting that Sir John shall settle them on the said John Baggiley and the heirs male of his body: and for default of such, then to settle the manor of Hyde on Sir John Hyde and his heirs; and to settle tha manor of Baggiley and of Leveshulme upon William, John and Geoffrey, son of the said Sir John Legh, and to the heirs males of their bodies, in order, one after another; the remainder to Thomas, son of Richard Massey: then to John, son of Robert Legh: then to William, son of Piers Legh; then to Robert, son of Robert Massey of Kelsall (Lib C, fo 270). The original instrument, written in French, now with the Legh family of Baggiley, has a seal with the Baggiley arms: three lozenges, with a bear's head for a crest.

William de Baggelegh and Amery, ux. e jus (his wife) occur in a Plea Roll, 1321 v, Hugh de Norworthy, chaplain, touching a fine of tenements in Baggelegh, Kchsles and Hyde.

In a Close Roll of 16 Ed. II. 1322, Oct 24, dated York, to the keeper of land of rebels in County Stafford, we find an order to restore to Neil de Langeford, Kt, his land there, when among his "mainpenors for his good behavious" we find William de Baggelegh, Kt., of Chester (m 24).

In another Close Roll of 19 Ed II. 1325, Nov 26 (m 21), we find an order to the justices of peace not to permit William de Baggeleghe and others to be molested .... by reason of the goods of the rebels.....taken by them whilst in the king's company in the pursuit of the rebels.

In a Close Roll of 1326, Aug 31 (m), to the Sheriff of Lancaster, among the king's servants, we find William de Baggelegh.

In a Patent Roll of the same year, Jan 24 (m 3), we find William de Baggele as a Justice of Peace for Chester.

In a Plea Roll of 1335, we find Will. de Baggelegh, Senr., and Rosia, ux. ej (his wife) vs John Mareschall, relating to fine of tenements in Norworthy, Kenworthy, Sydindon, Somerford and Neuton in Longedenedale.

Isabell, daughter of Sir William Baggiley, and sister and co-heir of John Baggiley of Bagguley, second wife of Sir John Legh of Boothes nigh Knuteford, had a son, Sir William Leghs of Baggiley, Kt. with whom the pedegree of the Leghs of Baggiley begins. The male line of the Leghs of Baguley terminated in one Edward Legh. Afterwards Baggiley was the property of the viscounts Allen, in whom it remained vested to the middle of the eighteenth century when it passed, by purchase, to Joseph Jackson of Rostherns.

Ormerod calls the daughter of Sir William, Isabell, while the Visitation of Cester, 1580, correctly names her Ellen. Isabell married John Hyde of Hyde and Norbury, as his second wife, whose descendants used the heraldic coat of Baguley, inverting the tinctures and adding a chevron.

John Baguley, son of Sir William, is said in the Visitation of Chester, to have dine sine probe (without issue). There was, as we have seen, another son Geoffrey Baguley, who is not referred to further in the records of the time.

Thomas de Baggeley in 1376, Oct 9, presented to James de

Baggeley, the vicarage of Stockport, Chester, on the death of John de Massey.

William de Baggeley was mayor of Stockport, Chester,m in 1382-1384.

Both Thomas and William are supposed to have left issue that perpetuated the line, but the baptismal names of their children are unknown. The probability is that Nicholas who follows was a son but no proof to that effect so that the direct line will, therefore, begin with Nicholas.

The township of Bagguley is situated about seven miles south of Manchester, as has been stated, and in Manchester we find the family residing for some time. The last persons mentioned of the name on the preceding pages, were residents of Stockport in Cheshire, owning land in Marple, situated partly in Cheshire and partly in Berbushire (Marple Bridge).

A few miles east hereof, at Brampton, in county Derby, we now find the first reference to

I. Nicholas Baguley

in the year 1459, as of Mancheswter, a witness, and in the year 1473, on October 27, in a Patent Roll of 13 Edward IV, i.m.4 a "pardon was issued to John Asshe of Brampton Co, Derby, for outlawry in the county of Derby, and for not appearing to satisfy Nichlas Baguley and Joan, his wife, of 33s 4d which they had recovered against him."

Inasmuch as the outlawry comprized the whole of the county of Derby, it is probable that the depreciation must have occurred in or around Marple Bridge, where the Baguley family possessed land. Nicholas does not appear to have been a resident of Brampton, and the proximity to Manchester, Heaton Noris and Stockport, would lead one to infer that Nicholas Baguley was closely related to the Baguleys of Bagiley, Heaton Norris, Stockport and Manchester, which at that time embraced a large number of villages.

Joan, wife of Nicholas Baggulegh, was daughter of Sir William Legh of Baggiley, Kt., a son of Sir John Legh of Boothes nigh Knotsford, and his second wife, a daughter of Sir William Baggiley. Sir William Legh had married Joane, a daughter of William Manwaring of Over Pevee, (33 Edw III. 1359), when he was underage, and Joane only five years old (Lib. B., p 11 x). The child marriages of Chester are notorious and the reader will find much of interest on the subject in Child Marriages, Divorces, and Ratifications, and in the Diocese of Chester, Early English Text Society, Or. ser. No 108. They had no children, however, and Sir William Legh of Baggiley married Joyce, the widow of Sir Ralph Davenport, of Davenport, in Cheshire.

Sir William Legh of Baggiley and Joyce, his wife, leased to Piers de Legh of Lyme, and John, his brother, for six years, all the office of the serjeancy of the hundred of Maxfield, which appertained to the said Joyce during the minority of Reufe Davenport, son and heir of Reufe Davenport lately deceased, rendering to the said Sir William and Joyce 12 marks yearly. Maxfield, 1382. All Saints Day. (Lib. A. fo 150 1). Sir William Legh died leaving issue: two sons, Thomas and Lawrence; the former continuing the line. The widow, Joyce, married Sir John Knightley. (Lib. A. fo 151 W).

This, the most ancient family of the name in England, traces its pedigree through Hamon de Leigh, son of Gilbert de Venables, Baron of Kinderon, and great grandson of Gilbert de Venables, who accompanied the Conqueror to England and was the younger brother of Thibault III, Count of Blois, and a descendant of Thibault, brother of Rollo the Viking, the first Duke of Normandy.

From Hamon are descended the Leighs of Boothes, Baguley, Stoneley, Warw.. Hartwell, Bucks, Birch, Lanc.. and many other families of this name. Sir Walter of Lee, of Lee Hall, parish of Wibenbury, Cheshire, was of this family and father of Johan nes Lee, de Lee, in com. Cestr., who married Isabel, filia Dutton, miles.

From him descended in the fourth generation, Benedict Lee, of Quarendon, Bucks., who made his will, Sept 7, 1476 (P.C.C. Wattyns 26; Archdeaconry of St Albans). His son, Richard, made his will, Nov 20, 1490, and his son Robert Lee, made his will, Oct 8, 1537 (P.C.C. Dinsley, 27); his wife, 1547, June 26 (P.C.C. Nooden 26). Anthony Lee, their son, a member of Parliament for Bucks (H.M. 1 553, fo 78), is buried in St Peter's Quarendon, with an inscription on his tomb. He made his will July 10, 1549 (P.C.C. Goode 23). Of his children, Sir Henry Lee, who made his will, Oct 6, 1609 (P.C.C. Wood 41), was master of the Ordinance to Queen Elizabeth, and became enamored with her new maid of honor, Anne Vavaseur, " our new mayd Mrs. Vavaseur floriseth like the lylly and the rose" (Letter from Sir John Stanhope to Lord Talbot, 1590). She became Sir Henry's mistress, hence the rhyming couplet:

> "Here lyes the old K't good Sir Harry
> By her he loved, but n'er would marry"

Benedict Lee, above mentioned, had a son, John, mentioned in his father's will, 1476, who married Jane, daughter of Henry Wise of Banbury, Oxford. Of his children, we shall refer to Henry presently. Robert Lee, a second son, who made his will, of Vintree parish, London, Aug 7, 1643 "to be buried If I chance to dys in England. If beyond the seas, then to stand to the courtesye of somme well minded Christian.... brother of Henry Lea, of St Martin, London, whether abroad or att home" (P.C.C. Alchin, 125), probated in Barbadoes; also, Aug 23, 1654 (Barbadoes Reg. Wills, Rg. i, fo 186). Robert Lea had emigrated to Barbadoes and is there called "planter".

Henry Lee, of St Martin, London, citizen and draper, made his will, May 31, 1637 (P.C.C.Harvey 106). His son, William Lee, married, in St Mary Le Strand, London, Dec 16, 1618, Jane Catlin, and made his will of Leckonfield, County York, a butcher, Oct 4, 1656 (P.C.C. Ruthen 13).

William Lee, son of William, born Nov 11, 1627, married at Hornsea, York., Feb 8, 1689, Helen Kenith. William Lee of Leckonfield, Sr., was buried May 16, 1720. Widow Ellenor Leigh, made her will, Nov 2, 1724 (York Probate Court, 78:165), in which she refers to Anne, wife of William Rand, as a daughter; sons, William and John, daughter Eleanor, wife of Ph. Bla(s)dell. She was buried Nov 30, 1724.

William Rand, above, a son of James Rand, an apothecary

of London, who in his will, June 20, 1685, refers to "debt owing me from one William Banks now or later resident at Virginia, in the parts beyond the seas....son-in-law Christopher Gould....". A cousin of William Rand, Robert Rand emigrated to Charleston, MA (History of Charleston, 782)

William Lee, the son, emigrated to Bucks Co., PA, 1725, and became a Friend, settling in Upper Wakefield township.

II. Ambrose Baguley

"Fil Nichol. Bagguley et Joan, ux.e.j." occurs in a Plea Roll of the Palatine of Lancaster, 1471. 38 m 2D).

"Sir John Ashton complaineth that Ambrose Baguley of Manchester hath trespasseth on his turbary at Ashton (Salford Hundred)." (Turbary was in English law the right to dig turf, an easement).

Ambrose Baguley appears with Alice, his wife, and William Bagley, their son, Nov 15, 1503 vs Johannes Marshall and Alice, his wife, et al., for improper conveyances of manors and messuages in the counties of Chester and Lancashire, of which William Marshall, father of the said Alice, was seized in fee (Henry VII. 19). Ambrose Baggeley and Alice, his wife, again appear against his "brother-in-law Johannes Marshall, Sept 11, 1509, deft, to protect his wife's interest in the estate of her father, said William Marshall, of Heaton Norris (1 Henry VIII).

The surname, Marshall, occurs as early as 1256, in a Patent Roll. 41. Hen. III., when there is a grant by Ralph Marshal and Matilda, his wife, to Stephen de Windene, clerk, of 24s land with the house in St Botolph's parish, London. William Marshall was father of Richard Marshall of Cockwood, County York, mentioned in the Harl. MSS. 1561. Vis. of Surrey, 1530, 1572, and 1623., as the progenitor of his line, and father of William Marshall of Stamford, County Lincoln, who married Margaret Shepe, and who made his will, July 11, 1545 (Lin. Prob. rec), in which he refers to wife, children, and daughter Elizabeth, wife of William Baggatt. Of this family was Sir Charles Bagot, for some time Secretary of State for Foreign Affairs and Minister Plenopotentiary to the United States, Ambassador to St Petersburg, The Hague and Vienna, and Governor-General of Canada.

Richard Marshall, son of William and Margaret Shepe Marshall, of Stamford, County Lincoln, and of Merton, married Anne, daughter of Thomas Beckwith (of whose family were Capt Wm M. Beckwith, who married Murial, daughter of the Duke of Richmond, and William Beckwith, who emigrated to Barbodoes in the ship Bonaventure). Richard Marshall, who made his will, proved 1571, was buried in All Hallows Church, Stamford, Lincolnshire, Apr 26, 1571.

Of his children, Henry, the eldest son of Southwark, Surrey, married Margaret Courtney of London, and had, with other issue, a daughter Eleanor, who married Robert Bryant. Margaret Courtney's nephew, John Courtney, born in 1602, emigrated with his wife Sybill, to Virginia in 1635, July vj in the ship Paul.

William Marshall, the youngest son, bapt. Oct 17, 1568, married Margaret, daughter of Thomas Chalfont, and Margaret

81

(Harris) Cornwallis, and had Edward Marshall, who emigrated to Virginia, "living in Virginia, at Bucks Row, Feb 16, 1635", and died in 1668, when administration was granted to his brother, John, in the Prerogative Court of England, the latter's brother, Edward and Thomas Marshall having died in "parts beyond the seas."

Thomas Marshall, son of William, emigrated to Barbadoes, and died there in 1670, when administration was granted in England to his brother, John.

(It is interesting to note that Robert Bryant, above-mentioned, had a brother Thomas Bryant, who married Sarah, daughter of Joseph Sherman of Ipswich, Suffolk, as appears from a marriage contract of Mar 1, 1587, and sister of Samuel Sherman, who married Maria Ward and had a son, William Sherman, who emigrated to Duxbury, MA, 1637. He married Prudence Hill, 1638, and removed to Marshfield.

Henry Sherman of Colchester, Essex, in his will, 1638, gave to cousin Johanna Sherman of Ipswich, Suffolk, a messuage, formerly in possession of her brother, Samuel, and his eldest son, William Sherman, now across the seas. Richard Sherman of Boston, 1635, was of this family, as appears from various wills. They were also related to the Philip and Nathaniel Bacon of Barnstaple, MA, referred to in the will of thier father, Sir Nicholas Bacon of Shrubland, Suffolk, 1658 "my two sons, Philip and Nathaniel have willfully left me in my ould age and are beyond the seas without my leave...." For additional data about the Chalfont-Harris-Bryant connections and familie, see further on.

John Marshall, second son of Richard Marshall, and grand-nephew of Alice Baguley, wife of Ambrose Baguley, baptized at All Hallows, May 25, 1561, married in St Saviours, Southwark, Surrey, Elizabeth, daughter of Richard Herrick.

(John Eyrick, ancester of this Richard Herrick, was mayor of Leicester.) Elizabeth's nephew, John Herrick, married Abigail Simpson of Southwark, Surrey, dau of Anthony of Welford, County Northampton, who in his will, 1633 "haberdasher" of London, refers to "son Martin. Martin, "haberdasher of London, in his will, 1693, refers to"Aunt Phillippa Charlton...sister Abigail Herrick..."

The brother of Anthony Simpson, Rev Martin of Hackney, Middlesex, in his will, refers to "sister Mrs Philippa Charlton....nephew Martin Simson money due from John Rose of Southon in New England, planted.... touching transportation of my niece Hester Simson to New England, providing here there." John Rose settled in Southampton, Long Island in 1656.

Philippa Simpson had married Martin Charlton of Southwark, Surrey, and her nephew, Thomas Charlton, had a son, Nicholas, who married Margaret Palmer, the sister of Henry Palmer, of St Mary, Aldermanbury, London, who in his will "marchant", Apr 19, 1739, refers to " my brother Thomas Palmer of Boston in New England." Mr. Thomas Palmer of New England, married Abigail Hutchinson of Boston.

John Marshall mentioned above, was a great benefactor to the Southwark community and a man of considerable wealth.

The tracing of relationships between immigrants of America prior to the emigration has been the pursuit of the

present writer for nearly three decennials.   It   offers   not
only a wide and   interesting   field,   but   is   of   the   utmost
importance, as furnishing us one of the principal   causes   for
the migration to these shores, and the settlement   of   certain
localities.

Removals from these localities, and   marital   connections
between the   settlers   after   the   emigration,   although
interesting, is of slight   importance   in   comparison.   It   is
hardly necessary to say that the difficulties in   ascertaining
these relationships between   the   immigrants   prior   to   their
arrival here are very great, requiring the   investigation   and
copying of   practically   thousands   of   wills,   deeds,   church
records, etc., all over Great Britain.   It   is   the   writer's
opinion that close relationship must be shown,   prior   to   the
emigration, between settlers of any given locality,   and   that
the new immigrants to New England seldom were closely   related
to the settlers of e., g., PA, NJ or NY, or   vice   versa.   It
would be strange, indeed, if an immigrant to any town   in   MA,
for example, in the late part of the seventeenth century,   was
not related by blood to several of the former settlers of   the
same locality and prior to emigration.

It is not difficult to ascribe a cause for this migration
to a given locality, as we find it duplicated, to a very great
extent, even to this day.   Close affiliations existed   between
the new settlers and their relatives and friends on the   other
side, as is evidenced by letters,   wills,   deeds   and   similar
instruments, still in existence.   With   this   digression,   we
will continue the   story   of   the   Marshalls,   with   whom   the
Bagleys were related, and wherever possible similar   excurions
will be made   when   we   reach   the   other   Bagleys   and   their
families.

John Marshall, who had   a   grant   of   arms   from   William
Camden, Clarencieux King   of   Arms,   1631,   made   his   will
"whitebaker, citizen and atllow chandler of Christ Church", of
which he was the founder, May 31, 1619, proved Aug 10,   1625,
in which he refers to his children. He had   20   children.   Of
these, Thomas Marshall, a whitebaker and tallow   chandler,   of
St Sepulcre, extra Newgate, made his will in 1625, in which he
refers to brothers and sisters, sister Pickton, gives right to
fishing in Plymouth in New England.

Edward Marshall, son of John, born in St Dunstan   in   the
West, London, a stone mason, and "master-Mason   of   England,
married Anne Lugg,   and   2ndly,   Margaret   Parker   of   Barnet,
Herts., in St Martin in the Field, 1674.   Edward Marshall took
part in the erection of the   Temple   Bar   in   London   and   the
statue of Charles I, in Charing Cross, London.

Joshua Marshall, son of Edward, master mason   to   Charles
II, twice master of the Masons Company,   in   his   will,   1716,
refers to "son-in-law   Richard   Somers.   These   Somers   were
related to Rev John Wilson, of Boston, MA, the first   minister
there, Robert Taylor of Ipswich,   MA,   Edward   Rawson   of   New
England, etc.

Edward Rawson was Secretary of   MA   colony.   Other
connection have been traced with Robert Wain of Boston, father
of Benjamin Wain of London, who married Sarah Dudley, daughter
of Gov Thomas Dudley of MA, and sister of   Anne   Dudley,   who

married Gov Simon Bradstreet of MA.

William Marshall the son of Edward, emigrated to Barbadoes, was a captain and resided in St Michael's parish, Barbodoes.

Jarvis Marshall, son of Edward, emigrated to Barbodoes, a redemptioner, who received a ticket in the ship James for New York, 1678.

Ambrose Baguley, of Manchester, and Alice Marshall, his wife, had issue as follows:
1.   William, b abt 1480, of whom presently
2.   Charles, who occurs as a "market-worker for white meytte,", i. e.. veal, pork & lamb, of Manchester, in Leet Court Records of Oct 4, 1552, a By-lawman for Whithy Grove, Dec 11, 1552, and selers for lether on Oct 16, 1552. (The word by-lawman is explanatory of his official position, as in ancient records certain personages were described as "yeomen and by-law men for the present year in Easingould" and appear to have been appointed for some purpose of limited authority by the other inhabitants, as the name would suggest, under by-laws of the corporation, in this instance, Manchester).

   i.   George Baguley of Batley and Catherine Clerke, married in Prestbury, Oct 9, 1579, and had:
      a.   Edward, bt July 16, 1580, called "cousin Edward Baggiley and his sisters Elizabeth and Cassandra" in the will of John Smith of London, Dec 7, 1625 (P.C.C. Hele, 116).

In a State Paper, Domestic, Chas. I, CCCCXXVII, Aug 29, 1639 , the Attorney-General writes to Sir Dudley Carleton: "I have this day received of Edward Bagley and Richard Bernet, a patent concerning the searching of leather, dated Apr 13, according to the Council's order."

We find from a State Paper, Dom. Chas. I. CCCCXV, that on Mar 29 the same year there had been a grant to Richard Barrett, Edward Bagley and others for 21 years to enter into all warehouses, shops, cellars, and other suspicious places in a number of counties and cities to search for all leather shipped, etc.

      b.   George Baguley, bt Prestbury, as of Batley, Feb 12, 1583, married as of Allderley, June 22, 1612, Ann Shepeley, and (2), July 6, 1619, in St Martin in the Field, London, as of Manchester, Elizabeth Siggins.
      c.   Elizabeth & Cassandra, b Nov 11, 1585, twins.
   ii.   Nicholas, had children, baptized in Manchester Cathedral:
      a.   Jane, bt, Mar 29, 1574
      b.   Garret, bt, June 1, 1578
      c.   Adame, bt, Sept 16, 1580 of Newton and Taylesworth, had issue"; his wife was buried Jan 29, 1615.
         *John, bt, Oct 8, 1609; d Nov 15, 1629
         *Alice, bt, Oct 14, 1610
         *James, bt, Oct 10, 1613
      d.   John, bt, July 18, 1585
      e.   James, bt, Jan 14, 1587
      f.   Alice, bt, Aug 24, 1590
      g.   Mary, bt, Apr 16, 1592
      h.   Anne, bt, July 24, 1594
      i.   Nicholas, bt, at Newton, Aug 14, 1597; buried

Manchester, Sept 31, 1597
        j. Anne, bt, Dec 17, 1598
    Nicholas Baguley of Newton was buried in Manchester
Cathedral, Mar 31, 1598/9.
        Carrethes Baguley de Newton, lynen weaver, occurs in a
Manchester Quarter Session Roll of May 27, 1620...."in x li."
    In a Subsidy Roll of Salford Hundred, Chester, 1541,
Manchester, we find Nycholas Baguley of Newton taxed for xx li
goods....xs.
    iii. Alexander of Didsbury, who had:
        a. Margaret, bt, Nov 21, 1562
        b. Thomas, bt, Nov 24, 1564, married, of Heaton
Norris, Manchester, July 15, 1599, in Didsbury, Katherine
Jackson and had:
            *Helen, bt, Nov 1, 1601
            *John, Oct 26, 1602
            *Margery (Bigaley), bt Jan 27, 1606; buried Mar
29, 1606
            *Thomas (Bagaley), bt, Jan 4, 1607
            *Jane, bt, Sept 3, 1609
            *Robert, bt, May 27, 1617
            *Anne, bt, July 17, 1618
(Of these, Thomas Bagley, Jr., left issue; he was buried Nov
28, 1644).
        c. Joane, bt, Apr 5, 1566
        d. Elizabeth, bt, Oct 22, 1575
    iv. Robert of Didsbury; buried Feb 17, 1570; had:
        a. Robert, Jr., who married June 1, 1595, Joane
Hoult, and died Feb 28, 1642, leaving:
            *Edward, de Brodston (by Ellen Hall), bt Jan 6,
1597
            *Margaret (Bygeley), bt, Feb 24, 1598; d Dec
25, 1598
            *Thomas (Bagerley), bt, May 5, 1603
He was buried, July 20, 1602, as of Redich.
            *John (Bagley), bt, June 8, 1606
            *Jane (Bugaley), bt, Sept 3, 1609; buried Apr
4, 1611
            *Ann, bt, May 27, 1617
(The variations in spelling are interesting, ascribed, no
doubt, to different entry-clerks of St James, Didsbury, Lanc.
in the ancient parish of Manchester)
3. Richard, who occurs in a will of Thomas Cooke of Eastham,
1520, post festum Assumpcois Bte Mariae Virginia" Dom. Rico.
Baguley deci solidas paia mea ad celebrandu unu trentale" (to
received 10 sol.). He was apparently a preacher in Eastham.

            III. William Baguley
son of Ambrose Baguley and Alice Marshall, his wife, appears
from a Chancery Proceeding of Nov 15, 1503, born about 1480,
occurs in a Final Concord of 3 Edward V., Lancashire, Aug 26,
1549, (m.48) between "William Bagulay, pltf. and James Hulme,
St.def. of a messuage and a garden in Manchester; James
acknowledged the right of the said William and the latter
granted an annuity of 4s from the said tenament." (Fine rolls
of Final Concords, or Pedes Finium, as these records were

called, were actually suits, instituted for the sole purpose of obtaining a proof of ownership of land, which, as in this case, William Baguley intended to purchase of James Hulme for a certain sum of money. No legal and recorded instrument was otherwise kept, while by the suit a copy was furnished to each one of the parties to the transcaction, and another copy was recorded. The annuity of Fines is Greater than the date of the Norman Conquest, and no records have been so well preserved in uninterrupted succession from the reign of Rich. I).

William Baguley of Manchester, was on Sept 30, 1557, appointed a Market Woker for Corne, as appears from a Manchester Court Leet records; on Oct 4, 1557, a "myse gatherer"; on Oct 1, 1561, a "cunstable".

(A Court Leet, "curia letae", was a court of record, held once or twice every year within a hundred, lordship, or manor, before the steward of the leet, for the preservation of peace and the punishment of all trivial misdemeanors. Its original intent was to view the frank pledges, i.e., the freemen of the liberty who anciently were all mutually pledged for the good behavious of each other, hence it was called by the Anglo-Normans, the "view of frank pledge" (visus franci plegiio). It has now fallen into almost total desuetude.)

At a Manchester Court Leet of Apr 6, 1564, the Jury "finde that William Baguley hathe purchased of Thomas Tetloc six Burgage and one close within the town of Manchester, payeth to the Chieff Lorde vy covenante yerelie xii d, and therefore shall prently (presently) be made Burges and do his ffrottri and service to the Lorde of this Manor." (A Burgage was a species of tenure described by old law writers as tenure in socage, where the king or some other person was lord of an ancient borough, in which tenaments were held by a rent certain. Such boroughs had, and still have, certain peculiar customs connected with the tenure, which distinguished it from the ordinary socage tenure. These customs are known by the name of "Borough English", and they alter the law in respect of descent, as well as dower, and the power of devising. By it the youngest son inherits the lands of which his father died seized. A widow, in some boroughs, has dower in respect to all tenaments which were her husband's; in others, she has a moiety of her husband's lands as long as she remains unmarried; and with respect to devises, in some places, such lands only can be devised as were acquired by purchase; in others, estates can only be given away for life. The custom is said by Blackstone to have been derived from the Saxons and to have been so called in distinction from the Norman rule of descent.)

A "close" was an interest in the soil, trees, growing crops, or an inclosed tract of land. The land which William Baguley acquired was, evidently, socage-land, a species of tenure whereby the tenant held his lands of the lord by any certain service in lieu of all other services, so that the service was not a knight's service. The principal feature was that it must be fixed, in this case by a yearly payment of xii d. to the Lord of the manor of Withington in the parish of Manchester, which at that time embraced Manchester, Heston

Norris, Reddich and a large number of villages.

The Jury at the same Court Leet found that the said William Baguley had purchased of Thomas Chaderton, Gt., one close called Sowschill.

William Baguley was a "clothier" of Manchester, and a man of some substance. He made his will, Oct 30, 1572, proved at Chester, Jan 10, 1572/3, in which he "desired to be buried in the parish church of Manchester in or near unto St George Chapel....wife Ellen....son James....daughter Alice to have the house I have lately builded, with the garden belonging thereto in the Dannesgate, with remainder to James Baguley...." The inventory of 3422.17.6, refers to a "pack of cotton."

William Baguley had married Ellen, daughter of William Blesedale of Bowland, who in <u>Ecclesiastical Records of Whalley</u> is styled "grandson of Richard Blesedale, of the Forest of Bowland and aged 43 in the year 1506", which gives us the date of his birth as in the year 1463.

The name Bleasdale occurs as early as 1227, applied to the great forest or moor in the northern part of Lancashire, and part of Yorkshire, formerly in the parish of Whalley, which included the forest of Bowland, Colne, Rochdale, Ribchester, Chipping, and various other localities in Lancashire. The surname was, apparently, taken from the locality, as it does not occur prior to May 25, 1443, when Richard Blesedale is mentioned as a tenant at will of the Forest of Bowland.

At the time of the ecclesiastical court of Whalley, Mar 2, 1514, we find that "Bowland bring no charges and that the jurors were Edmundus and Johannes Parker, Wilhelmus Blesedal and Jac. Bonde, "jurati, nil presente."

In an inquisition post mortem of Apr 16, 1556, there is a deposition of Henry Bleasdale (fil Wilhelmus) and in an inquisition ad quod damnun, Sept 11, 1559, "Henricus Bleasdele et Johannes, fratr. ejus (his brother) had nothing beyond the 2s6d rent with appurtenances in Bleasdell, nor were they wont to be put on assizes or juries nor in any service due therefore to other lords of that fee...."

Johannes Bleasdeale, fil, prim (eldest son of) Wilhelmus Bleasdale, was indicted on Mar 7, 1526, as of Bowland, "pro crimine adulterij cum Johanna Caton, ex qua suscitanit prolem....". Henrici Caton, the husband of Johanna, died in the following year, as she occurs as vidua (widow) de Henricus Caton, de Bowland, in a Lancaster Court roll of 1527, :fined 3d for breach of the peace."

Johannes Bleasdale now married this Johanna, widow of Henry Caton (she appears to have been a daughter of Jacobus Bonde), as is shown by records, in which their son, Henric Bleasdale, refers to "his mother Johanna" alive in 1543, and in fines, where Johannes Bleasale and Johanna, his wife, uxor ejus, are mentioned in 1529.

"At the Court of Halmote, Nov 23, 1529, Johannes Bleasda:le had license to sell flesh and paid the fee, 4d."

"At the Court of Halmote, Jan 21, 1533, Johanna, wife of Johannes Bleasdale was "fined 2d for the escape of 6 pigs."

Johanna, a daughter of Johannes and Johanna Bleasdale,

married John Tomlinson, whose brother was Robert Tomlinson, born in Ulverton, Lanc., where he married 1548, Margaret Lindowe of Fulwood, Preston, Lanc., and had, with other issue a son, Robert, whose grandson, Henry Tomlinson, emigrated to Milford CT, 1652 (Rec Coll Church, All Saints, Derby; St Peter, Derby, Reg.; Har;.M. 2074, Stockport Wills; Vis, of Chester, 1663, Preston rec. and Duchy of Lanc. Decrees, vii.f.202.)

Henry Blesdell, eldest son of Johannes and Johanna Bleasdell, who married in Whalley, Lanc., Jan 30, 1562, a cousin, Johanna Blesdell, was keeper of the Forest of Bowland, Nov 23, 1556, with Reginald Parker.

A pardon was issued July 17, 1570 to Henry Bleasdell of Preston, late of Whalley, for his "outlawry in not appearing to satisfy James Pemberton, citizen and clothier of Manchester, and executor of the will of John Pemberton, father of the said James, touching a debt of 11 pds for the sale of land, worth 8d yearly in rent, in Chipping and Whalley, and 10 acres arable land in Padiham..."

Henry Bleasdell married, 2ndly, June 10, 1572, in Preston, Elizabeth, daughter of Ralph Pemberton, son of John, and sister of the above-mentioned James Pemberton. James Pemberton, by a fine, Dec 24, 1557, had granted to his brother Robert Pemberton of St Albans, Hert., and Catherine, his wife, a messuage, consisting of a toft with appurtenances in Manchester, which the latter sold, by fine, the following day to Henry Bleasdale of Preston.

Robert Pemberton of St Albans and Catherine, his wife, had a son, Roger, who married Elizabeth, daughter of Ralph Moore. Roger made his will, Nov 13, 1626, proved Dec 5, 16217, in which he refers to: "Church of St Mary Bow, London....sons, John, Robert and Ralph....my son-in-law, Robert Wolly....brother-in-law Francis Kempe....daughter Tecle Wolley....daughters-in-law Katherine Pemberton, Susan Pemberton and Frances Pemberton....my cosen and Godsonne Roger William....grandchildren Ellen Wolley and Elizabeth Pemberton."

The grandson of this Robert Wolley, Richard Woolley (Woolery), emigrated to Salem, MA, 1676, and was of Newbury, MA, 1678 (St Albans, Herts. reg; P.C.C. Skynner,117; Ridley, 83; Com. Court of London, 24,50,12, 27).

John Pemberton, son of Roger, was styled "cousin-german" of Roger Williams "beyond the seas" in 1634, who was accompanied by Thomas Angell, a lad of 14, indented as his "servant". John Pemberton had married Catherine, daughter of William Angell, of St Thomas Apostle,m London, who in his will refers to "son Thomas."

Alice Williams, of St Sepulchre, London, in her will, 1634, refers to "sons Sidrach Williams, Roger Williams, now beyond the seas....daughter Katherine, now wife of John Davies, children by her former husband, Ralph Wightman....godson Robert Wolley...."She was the widow of James Williams, merchant tailor and citizen of London, who in his will, 1620, refers to "wife Alice, son Sydrach, daughter Catherine, now wife of Ralph Wightman, merchant taylor of London, my sons Roger and Robert Williams, god-daughters

Elizabeth Pemberton, Ellen Woolery, brother-in-law Robert Pemberton."

Roger Williams, "our famous asserter of religious liberty and freedom", founder of Providence Plantations, had brothers Robert and Sydrach, and was accompanied by Thomas Angell (Ibid).

For the Wightman connections, see further on.

A brother of Ralph and John Pemberton, Robert, had married Susan, daughter of Roger Glover of Beckett, County Berks, and sister of the Rev Jesse Glover of New England. In his will of 1678, he refers to "father-in-law Roger Glover of Bewcott, Co Berks., wife Susan, brother John Pemberton and Katherine, his wife, loving brother Robert Wolley and Tecle, his wife" (P.C.C. Barrington, 69). Rev Jesse Glover was the father of Mrs Sara Winthrop, Mrs Elizabeth Winthrop and Mrs Priscilla Appleton of MA.

Henry Bleasdell of Preston, died prior to Sept 11, 1579, leaving issue: Henry, John, Thomas, Anne, Isabell, Gyles and Elizabeth. Of these Elizabeth, married Thomas Gould of Bovington, Herts., brother of Jeremy Gould of RI, and of John Gould of Watford, wose widow, Judith, in her will, 1650, refers to "son Nathan in New England." Nathan Gould emigrated to Salisbury, MA. (Bovington reg; Archd of Hunt, Mitchin reg. 1,186,111,54; iv, 8,260, 298, 423, v,12.35, Acta 1638; C.C. 145 Pembroke).

Isabell Bleasdale of Chipping, Lanc., and baptized there, Apr 25, 1578, married 1603, Robert Moyse of Holbrooke, Suff., son of Robert Moyse and Alice, his wife, who in his will, 1604, refers to "sons John and Robert Mouse, and his wife Isabell....friends Thomas Aulcock of Paulde, Co. Staff., and John Bleadale of Whalley, Co. Lanc....grandson Joseph Moyse....loving friends John Whiting and Nicholas Stanton...."

Nicholas Stanton of Ipswich, Suff., clerk, in his will, 1648, refers to "mother-in-law Whiteing....Joseph Moyse and his wife living in New England....kinswoman Judith Smith, late wife of Henry Smith, living in New England, and her five children: Judith, John, Elizabeth, Henry and Daniel....wife Mary....Plantation of New England ". Henry Smith came to Dedham, MA. Nicholas Stanton's wife was Mary Whiting, widow of George Cowper. She married afterwards Samuel Slater. Her sister, Anne, married Robert Payne, and "they went to New England", mentioned in the will of his father-in-law, John Whiting, of Hadley, Suff., 1637, "wife Rose, Robert Payne, my son-in-law....son John."

John Whiteing of Hadleigh, Suff., in his will, 1643, refers to "my brother Payne of New England....Brother Henry Whiting." Henry Whiting married Mary, daughter of Robert Crane and Mary, daughter of Samuel Parhawke of Dedham, MA. (P.C.C. 150 Soare;31 Rivers;29 Fairfax; 158 Pembroke; 9 Alchin; 60 May; 70 Foot; 31 Pembroke; 36 Windebank;97 Wingfield; 83 Fenner; 85 Skynner; 143 Essex; 373 Alchin; 30 Brent; 97 Hene; 170 Penn; 64 King; 11 Babington. Harl. MS 6071, 196; Com. Of London, Essex ani Herts> 218. Archd of Essex, Whitehead, L. 103. Do of Colchester, Adam, No 36)

Anne Bleasdale, daughter of Henry, bt in Chipping, Lanc., 1573, married in Caulde, Staff., 1592, John Alcock, son of

Thomas. For the Alcock connection, see further on.

Thomas Bleasdale, son of Henry, bt in Chipping, 1571, administered to his brother John's estate, 1602, and was guardian of his brother, Henry's, minor children. Was related, through his wife, Margaret Barbour, to the grocer, William Barber of London, "who, for his religion, in the reign of Queen Mary, was brought to the stake in Smithfield to be burnt alive, but ere the fire was lighted, news came of that Queen's death, 1558, and the execution was stopped. In memory of such a providential deliverance and in honour of Queen Elizabeth, a valuable jewel was made, in which is a bust of the Queen, his deliverer; and as further proof of the family's gratitude, this jewel was regularly been bequeathed to such sons as named their eldest daughter Elizabeth."

John Bleasdell, bt 1565, son of Henry, married Mabell, daughter of John Parke with whom he was related to Henry Parke of Cambridge, MA, William Forth of New England, Henry Bright of Watertown, MA, 1680, Capt Robert Chapen of Salem, MA, 1630 (Suffolk Willis, 1598, Pleadings Duchy Court of Lanc., etc. C.C.C. 111, Campbell, 332, Berkeley, 24, Dorset, 29, Chor, 90 Lewyn, 13 Hale, etc.)

William Baguley, clothier of Manchester, had only one son, James Baguley, who is mentioned in his father's will, 1572. He had two daughters, Alice and Elizabeth who m John Tapping? in 1558.

IV. James Baguley

In 1572, he "took the place of William Baguley, his father, deceased (Wilhemus Baguley mortuus est) as Birlaman for the Deanesgate in Manchester, as we find from a Manchester Court Leet record of 1572. (A birlieman or birlyman was a petty officer connected with a borough: a birlaw court was used to decide local disputes between neighbors; its was also called "barley-court.")

A Manchester Leet Court Jury, on Mar 26, 1573, "doth present William Baguley to be depted (departed) synce the laste Lete Court, and James Baguley, his sonne to be at lawful age and ought to be entred Burges and to do Suche seruices (Services) as onto suche tennd dothe aperteyne and redit p. ann. iij s." On the same day, James Baguley was admitted tenant and did his fealty, as we find from a Manchester Leet Court record of Mar 26, 1573. (Fealty was that fidelity which every man who holds lands of another owes to him of whom he holds. Under the feodal system, every owner of lands held them of some superior lord, from whom or from whose ancestors the tenant had received them. By this connection the lord became bound to protect the tenant in the enjoyment of the land granted to him; and on the other hand, the tenant was bound to be faithful to his lord, and to defend him against all his enemies. This obligation was called "fidelitas" or fealty. The oath of fealty was one of the essential requisites of the feudal relation, and due alike from freeholders and tenants for years as an incident to their estates, to be paid to the reversioner. It has now fallen into disuse and is no longer exacted.)

On the same day, Mar 26, 1573, the "jurie doth psent

Alice Baguley to haue a gyfte of her father William Baguley a certain Burgage in the Deansgate and she is of the age of 10 years or there abowts."

Alice Baguley was an adopted daughter, as we find from ecclesiastical records of Whalley, relating to the Blesedele family and really a natural daughter of Alice Blesedele, a sister of Ellen, who married William Baguley and who died in childbirth.

On Apr 15, 1574, Jacobi Baguley was on the Leet Jury of Manchester.

James Baguley was old enough (born May 11, 1520) to be a father to his adopted sister, Alice, and he seems to have cared for her all her life with almost paternal affection, until her death, a widow, Apr 3, 1603; she had married John Hutton.

On Mar 1, 1597, James Baguley "has encroached on the river of Irke", we find from a Manchester Court Leet record.

On Oct 5, 1598, Humphrey Houghton of Manchester, clothier, in his will, dated Apr 12, 1598, gave a small bequest to "grandchild James Baguley and William Baguley, his son." (Manchester Court Leet rec, 1598).

Mary Marshall, who had married William Marshall, her cousin, and had a daughter, Alice, who married Ambrose Baguley, had another daughter, Sarah Marshall, who married in 1511, Humphrey Houghton, of Manchester, with whom she had, with other issue mentioned in her will, Nov 2, 1532, a son, Richard Houghton. The latter married Sept 16, 1533, Margaret, daughter of John Alcock of Whalley, Lanc., and had a daughter, Elizabeth Houghton, born in 1536, who married James Baguley of Manchester, Feb 16, 1563.

Among freeholders of Lancashire in 1600, we find Jacobus Baguley de Manchester, Gent., de Salford Hundred. (Subsidy Rolls).

On the jury for an inquest after Edm. Radclyffe, Sept 7, 1604, we find James Baggly of Manchester, Gent. (Lanc. Inq. xix, No 15)

On Oct 1, 1607, at a Manchester Leet Court "the jury doth presente that James Bagley, late of Manchester, Gent, ys departed since the last Court Lete, and that William Baguley is his sonne and next heir and is at full age." On the same day "William Baguley is returned as son and heir of his father, James Bagley of Manchester and of full age."

Humphrey Houghton, whose wife was sister of James Bagley's grandmother, Alice Marshall, and whose granddaughter, Elizabeth, married James Bagley, had a brother, John Houghton of Hocuth, Co. North., whose son, Thomas Houghton of Hocuth, married Mary Green and had a son Nicholas Houghton of London, fishmonger, who married Elinor, daughter of Gregory Newman, as appears from Harl. MS.1476, fo 92. See also Visitation of London, Harl. Soc. xv, p 369.

"Memorandum that Nicholas Houghton, late of the parish of St Margaret, New Fish Street, London, deceased, did on the one and twentieth day of January, 1648, stilo Angliae or thereabout, utter and speak these words: 'I give to my son Robert Houghton the sum of 10 pds, and my ring, to my daughter Mary Norton 40s to buy her a ring, and to my dau. Van Court

none, having never been at the University, nor understanding Latin; but he was my butler, and being put out of my service, got orders, God knows how." In spite hereof Rev Robert Bagley received a call to Norwood and seems to have been satisfactory.
7. John, b Oct 9, 1607; married Nov 3, 1627, Mary Clement and had a son:
     i. John, b Aug 19, 1629 of whom we have no further data unless he is the John Baggeley, ae 14, who emigrated to Virginia, 1634/5 and is supposed to have settled at Saybrook and Watertown, MA, the ages, as given in said shiplists not being very accurate as a rule. On the other hand, this John of Watertown's name is occasionally written Bigelow, which was probably his real name. (Note, the above from "no further data" has been crossed out in the manuscript sent me, as is a marginal note saying he m 1703 Mary Warren)
8. Thomas, b Feb 7, 1611
     John Bagley of Reddich, married, 2ndly, Apr 4, 1610, Alice Alcock of Manchester. She was the daughter of Thomas Aulcock and Dorothy Church, daughter of John Church of Castell Camp, Cambridge, Newborow, Staffordshire and Fingchinfield, Essex.
     Thomas Alcock purchased of Richard Barbour, et al, on the morrow of the Holy Trinity, 14 Jas I, the manor of Braycott in le Clay, connected with the Barber family already mentioned elsewhere.
     John Alcock, eldest son of said Thomas of Faulde, Staffordshire sold land to John Bleadale and Elizabeth, his wife, Oct of St Michael, 1611 "in consideration of one grain of pepper yearly." The Bleadale family has already been referred to.
     Thomas Alcock, Jr., son Thomas, and brother of Alice, who m John Bagley, occurs "on the morrow of the Holy Trinity, 1618, in a final concord, as buyer of land of Thomas Hurst and Anne, his wife, and Henry Read and Dorothy, his wife, of Falde."
     John Bagley had married Thomas Hurst's sister, Elizabeth Hurst, and Thomas Bagley had married his sister, Margaret.
     Thomas Alcock married May 7, 1607, Anne, daughter of Nicholas Read and of Nicholas Clere, one of the aldermen of Colchester, who in his will, 1611, refers to "master Thomas Hazlewood". The latter, merchant, in his will, 1619, refers to "sister Mary Lewis....kinsman Samuel Sherman, kinsman Benjamin Sherman, kinsman John Sherman, kinswoman, Mary Sherman...."
     Mary Lewis had married Robert Lewis and in her will of Colchester, Essex, widow, 1620, she refers to "sister Ann Sherman, Nicholas Read, son of my sister Read, deceased...Ann Anger, daughter of my brother Sherman....my kinswoman Mary Bacon..."
     Anne Cleere, sister of Mary Lewis and daughter of Nicholas Cleere, married Edmund Sherman of Dedham, Essex, clothier, who in his will, 1599, refers to "wife Ann...son Edmund...son Richard...son Samuel...sister Judith Pettfield...brother Henry...kinsman Symon Fenne, clothier of Dedham...."

40s, and for the rest of my goods I give unto Ellinor my wife, and do make her my full executor....in the presence of Artrhur Wind and Susanna Houghton." Administration was granted Mar 2, 1648 to son Robert Houghton (P.C.C. Fiarfax, 33).

(Mary, wife of Fran. Norton of London, is mentioned with her husband, styled "fishmonger" in the Harl. MS. while in the Vis. of London, he is called "haberdasher". Captain Francis Norton emigrated to Charlestown, MA; admitted to the church there, 1642, abd died there 1667).

Robert Houghton, the son, of St Olave, Southworth, co Surrey, brewer, in his will, Dec 25, 1653, proved Jan 7, 1653 (P.C.C. Alchin, 372), refers to "wife Mary 600pds, land in Lawsham which I purchased of Thomas Hill, Gent.., deceased...dau Martha, daus, Sarah & Hannah... dau Mary Planner...Unto my dearly loveinge and pious sister, Mary Norton, wife of ffrancis Norton of Charles towne in New England, 20pds. 500pds due unto my son-in-law John Willcox, who married my daughter Elizabeth...My very loueing brother Mr William Sedgwicke 5 pds to buy a ring. My loueing brother ffrancis Sedgwicke 5 pds."

Robert Houghton had married Mary, dau of Wm Sedwicke of "co Yorke", as it says in the Harl MS 1476. John Sedwick, brother of Mary Houghton, of St Saviour, Southwark, Surrey, brewer, in his will Nov 27, 1638, proved Dec 5, 1638, by Martha, relict, refers to "wife Martha 2000pds...mother Elizabeth Sedwicke of Woburn, co Beds., widow 500pds....my sister Mary Houghton, now wife of Robert Houghton and their daughter Martha. my god-daughter...my brother William, minister of Farnan...my loving brother Robert Sedwicke of Charlestowne in new England 38pds which he oweth me...uncle Stephen Sedwicke. brewer...." (P.C. C. Lee, 181).

Stephen Sedgwicke, brewer, of London, in his will, 1638, refers to "sons Job and Joshua, brother William, brother Norton, cousin Robert Houghton (P.C.C.Fairfax, 192). William Sedwick, Sr., of Lewisham, Kent, in will of 1663, refers to "nephew Zachary Sedwicke, sister Mary Houghton, etc. (P.C.C. Bruce, 22). (This Rev Wm Sedwick was called "Doomsday Sedwick". after his Revelation that Doomsday would be some Day next Week. He was a conceited whimsical Person. sometimes a Presbyterian, at one time called the Apostle of Ely. sometimes an Independent, at other times an Anabaptist, sometimes an Prophet as is said in Newcourt's Reportorium, ii.256).

Robert Sedwick, above named, was a very prominent man in early New England history. He settled in Charlestown, MA, in 1636, was one of the founders of the Artillery Company and chosen Major-General, the highest military office in the colony. Cromwell afterwards appointed him commander of an expedition which captured the French Posts in Acadia, 1654.

Jame Baguley and Elizabeth, his wife had the following children:
1. William, born in 1563, his father's successor; died in 1611 without having married
2. John, of whom presently
3. Nicholas, of Manchester, called "Nich. Baguley in Manchester Court Leet record of Oct 2, 1595, when the jury ordered that the executors of Jas. Radclyffe, deceased, or

Nich. Baguley, if he enjoyes the lease of the house in Fenel
street, to make up the pale before Dec 1st.

   Nicholas Bageley came to London about 1607, and married,
Dec 21, 1609, as Nicholas Bagley, Gent., Agnes Milner in the
St James Clerkenwell church. Mrs Bageley, wife of Mr Nicholas
Bagley was buried Sept 6, 1609, and Nich., Bageley was buried
in the Chauncell, May 30, 1610 (Note: something seems wrong
with her dates)

4.   Alexander, of Manchester, appointed market-looker for fish
and flesh and on the jury, Oct 21, 1621, is mentioned in the
Manchester Constable Accounts, Dec 31, 1621, "unpaid
Allexander Baguley..iiij d."

   In a Court Leet record of Manchester, Apr 13, 1630, we
find the "Jury findet that Alexander Bagley hath purchased of
George Holland certain land in Manchester and is to Come in to
Doe his suits and service." Alex. was sworn to the Lord and
admitted tenant.

   Among officers in the Milnegate for "mastive Doggs &
bitches & great Mungrell Curres that goe abroad in the street
to be kept upp Continually or else Mussled", we find Alex.
Baguley, Oct 14, 1634.

   Administration after Alexander Baguley of Manchester,
buther, was issued at Chester, 1635.

5.   Thomas, of Prestwich, Lanc., married Aug 12, 1609 Margaret
Hurst and had:
   i.   Richard, bt Oct 18, 1610; bur. Mar 19, 1610/11
   ii. Martha, bt Nov 22, 1612
   iii. Amaria, bt Aug 20, 1615
   iv. Elizabeth, bt Apr 19, 1618

   By an inquisition of Apr 16, 1617, after Rowland Mosley,
we find that he had "land in tenure of Thomas Baguley" (Manc.
Inq.xxi, No 68). Thomas Baguley of Heaton Norris, Manchester,
was taxed in gooids, viij s, by the Subsidy of 1622.

   (For the Hurst connection, see further under John Bagley,
brother of Thomas)

6.   Robert
7.   Elizabeth, b 1579, m Richard Jones, b 1567?
8.   Judith, b 1577; d 1635?

                    V.   John Bagley

born Nov 3, 1564, in Manchester, married, first, Sept 11,
1589, Margaret, daughter of John Weld, of London, and 2., Nov
8, 1606, Elizabeth, daughter of Henry Hurst (Hirst), a tanner,
of Leigh, co, Lancaster, and Joane Hatte, his wife, and sister
of Margaret Hurst who married Thomas Baguley, brother of John,
and 3., Apr 4, 1610, Alice Alcock, of Manchester, dau of
Thomas Alcock and Dorothy Church.

   In a Manchester Quarter Session roll of July 24, 1621, we
find: "a precept ad inst. Kath. Cheetam de Reddich, spinster,
vs Johannem Baguley de eadem (same village, i.e., Manchester),
husbandman, p. pare et percipus."

   John Bagley, "tayler", occurs in a tax-list as of
Reddich, Nov 16, 1622.iiijs.

   At a Quarter Session, held at Manchester, Jan 2, 1620/21,
da p'cept at instanc Johis Baguley de Manchester, taylier,
versus Johem Travis de eadem weaver pro pace et percipuciet

compere" was issed ad px session.

In a Sessio pacis tent' apud Manchester decimo octavo die Januarij 1621 cora" Sr G. Booth B.

Will Crompt' debet et Ric Wathous, Jan 20.

Tria Warancit ad instanc et sup sacrum Radi Carler de Failsworth jeom versus Johen Baguley et Robertus fratre ejus (his brother), de Newton, yeom. et Nichol Roades p pace et percipue fac et comp ad px session, Jan 27.

A precept ad instanc Georgij Somister de Reddich gs Ld weaver versus Johem Baguley de ead (of the same place), husbandman, p pace et percipue comp. ad px: gsvd Johes Baguley prd ten in x li. Johes Kemp de Manch., hosier, in v li. Jacobus Baguley de Failsworth, jeom. in v li. p pace et comp ut supra.

All these duits were for debts, evidently of a general business character. They are interesting as showing that John Baguley was engaged in a lucrative business, of some extent, that he was a tailor by occupation and resided in Reddich with a shop in Manchester.

That the Quarter Sessions were used for criminal trials also we find from a Manchester Quarter Session roll of Oct 27, 1618" "Exaiatos of Thomas Bradford of Failsworthe accused for counterfeictinge the hand of John Baguley wch hee hath confessed."

The surname Hurst is derived from "hyrst", a thicket or wood, and occurs, frequently in connection with some other word, e.g., Penhurst, Staplehurst.

Robert de la Hurste occurs as early as 1216, in a Testa de Nevill, sive Liber Feodorum. In Hunts, it is found in 1273 with one Ivo de Hurst in a Hundred Roll, in Writs of Parliament of 1392, as John atte Hurst.

In Lancashire, the name Hurst occurs in 1332, in an Exchequer Lay Subsidy Roll of the wapentake of Derbishire, hundred of West Derbi, with one Hug de Hurst, who then paid a subsidy tax of xi j d.

In Yorkshire the name occurs first in 1264 with one John del Hyrst, "cordwainer", who then became a freeman f York, entitled to continue his trade. A cordwainer was originally a worker in cordwain, or Spanish leather. His son, Willelmus de Hirst, was a "tanner", when he was given his freedom "by patrimony", i.e., as being the son of a free worker.

"Thomas Hirst, skynner, fil, Willemi Hirst, barker" was given his freedom in 1423, The appellation "del" had already been dropped. A "skinner" was a man of greater social standing than a mere "cordwainer", and the family had, evidently, increased in importance. The skinners, in fact, boasted of many royal personages as honorary members, beginning with Edward III, and his queen.

When Johannes Pudsey, a respectable tradesman of York, made his will, July 20, 1552: "Ego, Johannes Pudsey, civis et textor Ebor....sep. in cimiterio ecclesiae meae parochilais Beatae Mariae in Castelgate, &c", he gave to "Thomas Hirst, skynner, arcum meum cum le grene batt et vij sagittas parockfederde."

He is also mentioned in the will of Johannes Pudsey's widow, Emma, of June 1st, 1445: "To Thomas Hirste a little maser adorned with silver and gold..."

Thomas Hirst's brother, Johannes, a steyner, had a son, Nicholas de Hyrst, who held a small part of the manor of Hurst, or Hyrst, in Lancashire in the parish of Ashton under Lyne, originall a village for the manufacture of pottery.

Johannes Hirst, son of Thomas, was a carpenter and became a freeman in 1454. He had four sons: John, Richard, William and Robert. Richard was Prior of Nostell Abbey, in the West Riding of Yorkshire; William occurs in several Lancashire pleadings in the Duchy Court as of Leigh, Lanc.; Robert resided at Leeds, Yorkshire, where he made his will Mar 13, 1498/9, as "Robert Hirste, of Ledes, to be buried in the parish church of Ledes, under the litill bell..." gave bequests to the church of Ledes "to pray for my soule, and the soules of my fader, modir, childre, brod and susters and all my frendes, and of all them that I have injured or wronged...to every man, woman and childe ther like wisse being that er poore and will receive it, to pray for my sould, j d...for every torche burning abowt my body frome my house to the church....To my broder and lord the prior of Saint Oswoldes, Richard Hirst, an old noble weing a riall, which my brodir, Mr John Hirste owned... to dompne William Hirste, my son, my Portus and a silver spone...Thomas Hirste my newowe and his heires.... daughters (mentioned by name), wife &c... (York reg 1499, Reg Text. iii. 336A)

Johannes Hirst, the eldest son was a "wright", as appears from an instrument of 1485, when Oliverus Bowkra, "nupr.appr.Johannis Hirst, wright" became a freeman of York, as an apprentice of said Hirst. Of his children, Jacob Hurst was one of the clergy of Prestbury, Cheshire; William was of Great Marsden, Lancashire, and occurs in halmote rolls of Colne, 1541, etc., of which he was a "Greave" in 1545; Robert was a constable of Marsden as appears from a Court roll, 1549, preserved at Clithero castle. A Greave was the chief officer or steward of a Saxon manor.

Thomas Hirst, the eldest son of Johannes, styled nephew in his uncle, Robert Hirt's will, married 1529, Margery, a daughter of Oliver Ward of Marston, Prestbury, Cheshire, where his children were buried. The family settled about then miles northeast of Marston, at Poynton in Prestbury parish.

Of Thomas Hirst's children, Henry, born in 1530 , a tanner, resided for some time at Durham, and appears in ecclesiatical proceedings relating to "laying violent hands upon a clerk when he deposeth: "Henry Hirst, yeoman, aged 30 years, saith, that being at his shop workinge he heard a sturr in the streit, and therewith lap furth and saw William Taylye have William Lee by the coller; then imminst put them sonder. Examined what words he hard bitwixt them, he saith that thei childd and brawled lyk wyves (wives) but whatt words they wer he cannot depose upon..."

In a deposition in regard to the Rebellion of 1569, of June 13, 1570, Richard Hutcheson of Elvett, in the suburb of Durham, brasire, ae 60, saithe...they mett at the examinate's house, where was also Henry Hurst.

Henry Hurst shortly afterwards moved to Leigh, Lancashire, where he married, Dec 8, 1574, Joane Hatte, as appears from the registers and where he was buried June 23, 1521 (must be an error). He had two daughters, Margaret, who married Thomas Baguley, and Elizabeth, who married John Bagley.

John Hurst, brother of Henry, settled in Ecclesfield, where he married and had issue. Oliver Hurst, another brother, came to Prestbury, Cheshire, where he married and had issue.

Richard Hurst, brother of Henry, Oliver and John, came to Prestbury, Chester, in the part called Poynton and married Ellen Cottrell, daughter of Thomas, closely related to the Cottrells of Lincolnshire and Middlesex, of which family were Sir Clement Cotterell, Groom Porter to King James I., Sir James Cotterell, Master of Ceremonies, ambassador to Brussell and grandfather of Bishop Wm Cotterell of Leighin and Fenns.

John Hurst, youngest son of Richard Hurst and Ellen Cottrell, married 1624, Dorothy, daughter of John Robinson of Little Marsden, Lancashire and removed thither. In a deposition, Lanc. Royalist Composition Papers, in a petition of Ann Blundell, wife of Robert, of Ince Blundell, on behalf of herself and children, Feb 2, 1651 (i.ser.cviii No 3, 253).

"John Hurst, of Little Marsden, husbandman, aged 60 years, sworn, saith that he had been occupant of an estate lying in Marsden, by lease from John Robinson, Gent., for 16 years then lasp part..."

Of their children, Richard Hurst and Andrew Hurst, were "transported to Maryland, 1662, 1673 and in 1675. William Hurst had a grant of land from William Hooke of Great Marsden, late in the occupation of Andrew and Richard Hurst, "who did longe since departe out of thys country." George Hurst, a brother of Richard and Andrew, married Elizabeth, daughter of Samuel Feild and had two sons, Samuel and John. The latter had two sons Abraham and Joseph, and emigrated in 1629 to Ann Arundel Co, MD. Joseph settled afterwards in Dorchester Co, MD, and Abraham was of Baltimore county.

John Bagley had with his first wife, Margaret Weld, eight children:
1. William, b Dec 3, 1590, of whom presently
2. Peter, b oct 11, 1591, who occurs in a Manchester Constables Account of 1627/8, "Paid to Peter Baguleye, souldyer, which had a passe paid him towards his reliefe, Jan 22d....6d." Peter married, June 19, 1632, Ellinor, daughter of Robert Barber pf Kensworth, Co Hants.. and Susan, daughter of William Bull of Wells, Co. Som., as a second wife and had a son
   i. George, who married in St James, London, June 17, 1668, Anne Lister, by banns, daughter of "Rich. Lister of Marias, ux ejus". Richard Lister was sheriff of Shropshire and brother of Thomas Lister of Alberbury, whose son, Edward Lister, emigrated in 1620 in the Mayflower, as "servant" to Stephen Hopkins, "a youth."

Thomas and Richard Lister were sons of Richard Lister of Rowton, Shropshire, Alberbury parish, and Jane, daughter of Thomas Jennings of Wattlesboro, whose daughter, Christian, married (1) Thomas Wells, and (2) John Doughtie, a recusant, "six months in the common gaol, a very noyson place, replenished with misery." (State Papers).

Ellinor Barber was sister of Richard Barber, who emigrated to Dedham, MA, prior to Nov 23, 1638; William Barber who was "transported to St Christopher in the barque Mathew of London, with warrant from ye Earle of Carlisle, May 21, 1635, ae 22. He settled at Dorchester, MA, and removed to Salem, finally buying land in Watertown, MA; Susan Barber, who married 1632, Edward Bassett of St Albans, Herts. (son of Edward Bassett of Uley, Co Gloucester, whose daughter, Jane, married John Deighton of St Nicholas, Gloucester, and sister of Thomas Bassett who emigrated in "Christian", Mar 16, 1634, to Windsor, CT and removed to Fairfield.)

"Here lies the bodies of John Deighton of this city, 6t, and Jane, his wife, daughter of Edw. Bassett, of Uley....He spent all his time in the study of surgery and attained a great knowledge therein" (St Nicholas, Glouceter cemetery)

John Deighton's daughter, Katherine, bapt in St Nicholas, 1614, married Samuel Hagburne and emigrated to Roxbury, MA. After his death, she married Gov Thomas Dudley and after his death, Rev John Allin of Dedham, MA. Frances, sister of Katherine, married 1632, Richard Williams (son of William of Wotton under Edge, Glouc.), who emigrated to Taunton, MA, with his sister, Elizabeth Williams and are mentioned in the will of his sister, Jane Williams of Whegenhurst, Glouc. 1650 "my bro. Rich. Williams and my sister Elizabeth Williams that are now in New England...." (P.C.C. Aylett 292; Lort 208; Cons Ct Glouc.)

Anne Barber, sister of Ellinor (p 96), married 1633, Richard Church (son of Rich. and Alice Church of St Martin Orgar, London, and brother of Arnold Church, who married Margaret Ward, sister of Nathaniel Ward, who was of Hartford, CT and removed to Hadley, 1656.)

Robert Barber, brother of Ellinor (p 96), ae 28 in 1634, when the Visitation was taken, had letters of adm to his father, Robert Barber's estate, and married 1643, Rebecca, daughter of James Styles of Langley, Bucks. She married, (2) 1646, George Burroughs of Lewisham, Co Kent.

Thomas Barber, brother of Ellinor (p 96), became a member of the Stiles party sent out by Sir Richard Saltonstall in the barque "Christian" of London, 1634.

Sir Richard was the first of the 18 assistants named by the MA Bay Charter and came over with Gov Winthrop in 1630, casting in his lot with the Watertown people. He returned to England in 1631. From there he wrote to the ministers of Boston: "It doth not a little grieve my spirit to hear what sadd things are reported daily of your tyranny and persecutions in New England, as that yoy fyne, whip, and imprison men for their consciences. These rigid ways have laid you very low in the hearts of the saynts. We pray for you and wish you prosperite euery way and not to practice these course in the wilderness which you went so far to preuent. The Lord give you meeke and humble spirits."

Thomas Barber was invited in 1661 by the town of Northampton, MA, to settle there.

Robert Barber, father of Ellinor Bagley (p 94), was son

of Robert Barber and Anne, daughter of Thomas Dunscombe of Birckhill. He married, 2dly, Anne, daughter of John Dunscombe of Barley End, Co Bucks, and was son of William Barber of Kensworth, Herts., as we find from the Visitation of Oxford 1634. The grandson of this John Dunscombe, also named John, was in 1635 "transported to Virginia in the Assurance." Robert Barber married 3dly, 1571, Sarah, daughter of John Seaman of Yeldham and Chelmsford, Co Essex, and his wife Mary Chaplin.

For the Seaman-Chaplin connections with the Bagleys, see further on.

Thomas Barber, son of Robert, Sr., and brother of Robert, whose daughter Ellinor married Peter Bagley, had sons: Giles and Jeremy, who both married daughters of Thomas Mulliner of Ipswich, Suffolk. Thomas Mulliner of Ipswich, "joiner" who made his will 1625, refers to "son Thomas and his daughter Elizabeth....dau Elizabeth, wife of Gyles Barber....bro Jeremy Barber..." Thomas Mulliner emigrated ot New Haven in 1639, and was called a "chronic litigant." Among other things he made up his mind that his pigs were bewitched, so "he did cut of the tayle and ears of one and threw into the fire." (New Haven Col Rec).

Francis Barber, son of Robert, Sr., married Margaret, daughter of Richard Aluey of Corber, derby, whose daughter, Mary, married John Bate. ("John Bate and my dau, Mary, his wife....Francis Barber and Margaret my daughter, his wife....Will of Richard Aluey). James Bate (brother of John), had son James, who emigrated in "Elizabeth" 1635, to Dorchester, having married Alice Perret, widow of William Parker. She married, 3rdly, James Woodward, and his brother, John Woodward, married Alice Morden, widow of Walter Washington, brother of Lawrence Washington, who emigrated to Virginia, the great grandfather of Pres. George Washington (P.C.C. Cobham, 31; Fines 112; Fenner 42; Barrington 69; Twisse 160; Parker 1; Swann 99; Pile 123; Pembroke 68).

George Barber, son of Robert, Sr., married 1611, Sarah, daughter of Francis Whightman of St Albans, Herts., and had George Barber, "transported in the Transport to Virginia, 1635, settled in Dedham, MA, and Francis Barber who emigrated to Virginia in "Plaine", 1635.

For the Whitman connections with the Bagley family, see further on. Sources for the above connections: Vis of Somerset; Harl MS 1141; Dorset Adm., 1613, fo 98; Som. & Dors. N. & Q.ii.73; Collinson, H. of Som. iii; P.C.C. 22 Campbell; 135 Hene; 67 Cottle; 405 Berkeley; 40 Harte; 15 Meade; 193 May; 151 Laud; 108 Laud; 95 Wootton ; 68 Duke; 124 Duke; 139 Hare; 8, 137 North; 292 Hylett; 208 Lort; 159 Ent; 152 Huber; 27 Isham; 69 Barrington; 83 Ridley; 49 Lee; 117 Skynner; Mis Gen & Her i 171; Landsown MS No 857; Vis Harw; Reg of parishes mentioned; Harl MS 2119; Essex, MA deeds, vii; Cons. Court of Glouc; Com Court of London, 24, 50, 12, 27; Som Wills, 17 Stokton 133; 33 Medfelds, etc. Note: P.C.C. always stand for Prerogative Court of Canterbury; vols. not numbered but named from first will, e.g., camp, the figure mentioned is the page.

3. Alexander, b Sept 18, 1592 of Bolton, Lancashire, and

married, as Alexander Baggeley de Manchester, Feb 1, 1642/3, Katherine Banister; having children:

     i.   Richard, bt Dec 10, 1643
     ii. Jane, bt, Oct 28, 1644
     iii. William, bt, July 13, 1646
     iv. Alexander, bt Jan 15-23, 1647
     v.   Henery, bt, June 6-24, 1649

Alexander was buried in Bolton, Lancashire, Feb 28, 1657/8.
4. Edward, b Feb 10, 1593 of London, called "kinsman Edward Bagley, citizen of London, "in the will of Elizabeth Barnard, wife of Sir John Barnard of Abington, Co Northampton, Kt. Jan 29, 1669, in which she also refers to "cousin Edward Nash, Kinsman Thomas Hathaway, late of Stratford on Avon, Warw. Dame Barnard was the widow of Thomas Nash, daughter of John and Susanna Hall, and granddaughter of William Shakespeare. (P.C.C. Penn 35; Pile 115; Fines 127). Edward Bagley had married Sarah, daughter of John Hall of Manchester, Nov 3, 1639, who, evidently, was related to this Dr John Hall of Stratford On Avon, Warw, father of Dame Barnard.
5. Mary, b Sept 7, 1594; m 1626 in Killarry Co Lanc.. Humphrey Barrett ?
6. Richard, b Apr 17, 1595, who on Feb 9, 1637/8 occurs in a State Paper Dom. Chas I. ccclxxxi, in a "Petition of Richard Bagley to the King: Sir Richard Harrison being lord of the manor of Hurst in Berks. and petitioner having a copyhold of inheritance in the said manor worth 10pds per annum, (John Bagley, his father had died in 1635, leaving this property, acquired by his first wife Elizabeth Hurst, to son Richard, by a grant of Oct 4, 1616, i.e. at the majority of said Richard) Sir Richard through vexatious suits about four years since enforced petitioned for peace sake to surrender his copyhold for no consideration at all, but only with promise to surrender it again, if he did not help petitioner's son to his marriage portion of 2500pds, which as yet he cannot get. Petitioner who is a poor man and hard pressed of Sir Richard is utterly undone, having spent all his estate, which was worth 2000pds, and is much indebted, prays for relief.
     "Order to let Sir Richard see the petition and send his answer in writing."
     Richard Bagley again petitioned "to see Windebanck, being referred by Lord Cottington to him, after waiting three weeks in town for the answer of Sir Richard", Apr, 1638. ccclxxxviii.
     Richard Bagley was married, May 1, 1616 to Elizabeth Seaman, and their son,
     i. Richard, Jr., b Feb 21, 1617, had married, Jan 7, 1638, Sarah, daughter of John Clement of Manchester, "butcher ", who left a large estate. Sir Richard Harrison was related to this John Clement, and claimed part of his estate. For the Clement and Seam connections, see further on.
6. Robert, b Dec 11, 1599, is mentioned in State Paper of Oct 25, 1638, Dom. Chas I. cccc, as of Iver, in a letter from Sir John Lawrence to Sir John Lambe "Being requested by the inhabitants of Norwood to testify my knowledge concerning Robert Bagley of Iver, where I live — he can read very well under a preaching minister, but preacher and scholar he is

Richard Sherman emigrated to New England in 1637. Samuel Sherman married Esther Burges, who in her will, 1644, refers to "sister Bacon in New England."

Edmond Sherman's brother, Henry, was father of Mary, who married Philip Bacon, and emigrated to New England, 1634. Henry's son Samuel Sherman married Esther Bacon and emigrated to Boston. Henry's son Richard emigrated to New England. Henry's son Ezekiel, who married Priscilla Burges. Priscilla married (2) Thomas Fownes, styled "nephew of Thomas Winthrop". Henry's daughter Anne Sherman married Anthony Whiting and John Angier.

John and Ann Angier had a daughter, Mary, who married Nathaniel Sparhawk, who emigrated to New England.

Thomas Alcock married, (2) Margaret Harris of Bucks., daughter of John of Aylesbury, Bucks, 1622, and was "accidentally killed by a blow on the head with a fire-pan by one John Boyd", as appears from inquest.

Margaret Alcock then married, 1632. Christopher Chalfont of Aylesbury, Bucks, son of Thomas Chalfont and Margaret, widow of Francis Cornwallis, already referred to previous page. Margaret Chalfont of St Sepulchre, London, in her will, 1678, refers to "daughter Sarah, widow of Timothy Norris...daughter Mary, wife of Stephen More....gd child Samuel Hardie...sister Susanna Harris of New England".

Margaret (Harris, Alcock) Chalfont's daughter, Mary, had married (1) Robert Hardie, who in his will, heberdasher of London, 1661, refers to "wife, Mary, son Samuel, mother Margaret Chalfint, widow". Samuel Hardy emigrated and became town clerk of Beverley, MA.

Mary Hardie now married Stephen More, clothworker of London, and in her will, 1670, refers to herself as "Mary More, wife of Stephen More, clothworker of London...my son Samuel Hardie in New England...children of my deceased brother of New England...mother Margaret Chalfont...Aunt Norris..."

Thomas Alcock and Anne, his wife, had sons Francis and Thomas and a daughter, Elizabeth, who was one of the maidens "pressed", i. e., kidnapped, on the Assurance, July 24, 1635, to obtain wives for the settlers of Virginia.

Francis Alcock emigrated in Bemis for New England, 1638; Thomas Alcock married Abigail, daughter of David Hoare and Abigail Porter and emigrated to Newtown, now Cambridge, MA, in 1632/3. His name was written Olcott in the records of the First Church of Hartford, Alcott in the list of early settlers, and Alcock on the map. In his will, 1653, he refers to "dear and tender mother, Mrs Margaret Charfount...sister Mrs Mary Hardy...mother Horar."

For sources, see the following: Vis of London, 1633; Lincoln Ped. Harl.MS.1052; Lansdowne MS 207, 273; Lin. Mar Lic.; Lin. Dioc. Bishop Repington reg. fo. 169, 47; Bishp Longland's reg. fo 180; Bishop Gray's reg 151. Final Concord Staff. Jas I.; Lichfield Episc reg. fo 772; Vis of Cheshire, 1613; Harl.MS. 1070, fo 87; 1535; State Papers Dom; Letters and papers for. & dom. Chancery series; Court of Wards and Liveries,46, No 79; 25;105;38;8;;61;159;72;39;74;21;88;63;91;8 6;236. Chancery Proceedings 1621-5, Ser.ii. No 64, bundle 368, 388; 1626-9, bdl 419. Cal of Patent Rolls, P.C.C. Hale

28; Reeve 112;108; Laud 155; Soame 6.8.9.32.55.63; Dorset 60;
Rowe 39; Butts 20; Seager 100; Scott 20; Meade 15; Woodhall
47; Harvey 151; Laud 67; Aylett 292; Barrington 14; Montague
56; Lawe 110; Capell 89; Hare 139; Lee 79; Brent 394.

    Thomas Bagley, ae 24, emigrated in the Amitie, George
Downes, Master, bound to St Christopher, Oct 13, 1635
(believed to be the Thomas of Virginia and NC; see Notes on
Bagley Lines)

9. Adam, b Dec 23, 1612, of Manchester, signed on Oct 22,
1643, a petition by the inhabitants of Manchester, to the
Sequestration Committee, praying for allowance to the
ministers of the chapels of the Collegiate Church, according
to the order of the deputy lieftenants made at Preston, Oct
22, 1643.
10. Humphrey, b Oct 17, 1614, of London, married Mary Harris,
Feb 15, 1636. They had a son
    i. John, bt Feb 1, 1638 in St James
11. Philip, b Jan 3, 1617, emigrated on Paule, Leonard Bette,
Mr., to Virginia, July 6, 1635, ae 19.
12. Jane, b Mar 2, 1617, married William Pierce of Nuthhurst

VI. William Bagley

b Dec 3, 1690, son of John Baguley and Elizabeth Hurst, his
wife, of Manchester and Reddich, married (1) by license, Sept
17, 1616, Elizabeth Hurst of Wilmslow.
    In a Manchester Court Leet record of Apr 17, 1620: "the
jury orders William Bagley to remove his Dunghill from the
wall of William Radscliffe."
    In 1622, in a Subsidy Roll of Salford Hundred,
Manchester: William Baguley was taxed iiij s, for j li.lans."
    "An Extracte and Certificate Indented and made xviij daie
of April In the yeare of the Raigne of or most gratious
Sovaigne Lord James by the grace of god of England, France and
Ireland Kinge Defendor of the ffaith &c in the Nineteenth and
of Scotland the ffowre and ffiftith Comprysing the names and
surnames of all and every of such pson & psons within the
Hundred of Salford in the Countie of Lancaster as are
chargable for Lands and goods to the payment of the first
Subsidy graunted to our said Souaigne Lord the Kings Maitie in
Parlamt Houlden att Westminster in the Eighteenth years of his
Haignes Raigns and Presented and Taxed att Manchester in the
said Countie the daie and years aboue written; Before John
Radclyffe Cecil Trafforde and Thomas Barton kingts and Edward
Holland Leonard Asshawe John Greenhelghe & Oswald Mosley esq.
Commyssoners by vertue of his mats Comyssion to them and
others in that behalfe directed appointed and lymitted..."
(Chetham Libr.MS. 8015).
    William Bagley was on the jury at the Inquisition after
Robert Meall of Butterworth, Apr 26, 1683 (Lan.Inq.p.m.xxiii,
No 22).
    William Baguley, widower, had a license to marry
Katherine Potterof Manchester, widow, Aug 18, 1624.
    In a Manchester Constable's Account of Oct 13, 1629, we
find "In arrears: William Baguley...2s" and on the following

days: "Received of Mr Baguley to Redeem a Siulver spoons was Destrayned p.12 Condite laie...2s".

William Bagley, widower, had a license to marry Ann Dodd of Chester, May 30, 1631.

By a Manchester Leet Court of Oct 19, 1647, William Bagley was ordered "to make up his hedge which is fallne downe betwixt his landes and the landes of Marshall Dickonson." On the same day he was ordered to "cause a ditch in the acres belonging to him to be cleaned."

By a Manchester Court Leet record of Oct 10, 1648, it appears that: "the Jury found that William Bagley is deceased & Alexander Bagley is his son & heirs of lands in Manchester & is to Come in to doe his suit and service."

It is interesting to note that both John Bagley and his son, William Bagley, married women by the name of Elizabeth Hurst. William Bagley's mother, Elizabeth Hurst, was daughter of Henry and niece of Oliver Hurst. The latter settled at Pynton, Prestbury, and married Jan 27, 1563, Ellen Hurst, with whom he had a son Oliver, who married Apr 15, 1590, Olivia Martin and had a daughter Elizabeth, born Nov 11, 1593, who married her cousin, William Bagley of Manchester (Mar. Licenses Chester). (The Hurst family history had already been given).

William Bagley had with his first wife, Elizabeth Hurst, a son

1. Alexander, b July 11, 1617, heir after his father. William, in 1648. On Oct 10, 1648, Alexander Bagley was fined 6s8d for not findinge a passage for the Accers ditches, by a Manchester Court Leet. On Apr 24, 1650, Alexander Bagley was fined 4s for not coming in to doe his suite & service. On Oct 9, 1650, Alexander Bagley was fined 1s for not paveinge the Street over against his howse in the Deanesgate. The last data is interesting as showing that the family still owned and occupied the house and land at Deanesgate, in Manchester, which had been in their possession for a long time. He had mortgaged the house to one Samuel Sandford, mercer of London, and in 1657, the latter had to sue to recover, as we find from an Exchequer depositon by Commission, Lanc. 1657. East No 21: "Sam. Sandford, mercer of London, vs Alexander Baguley, mortgage of houses, etc, in Manchester."

William Bagley's second wife was Katherine Potter of Manchester, a widow, whose maiden name is unknown as not given in the marriage license.

William Bagley's third wife was Ann Dodd of Chester, whom he married by License, May 30, 1631. With her he had issue:

2. Anne, b Dec 11, 1632, married, June 14, 1651, Thomas Burrell of St Albans. Herts.... son of George Burrell, a brewer, and his wife Grace Davis.

William Burrell of Berwick, Northumberland, and Frances, daughter of Rowland Howard, had issue: (1) Richard whose daughter, Elizabeth, married John Chalfont and had a son Richatd Chalfont who died in Rotterdam in 1648; (2) Thomas who married 1589, Eleanor Robinson and had the above mentioned George; (3) Daniel Burrell, a citizen and grocer of London, who married 1590, (1) Hannah, daughter of Samuel Wheeler, and (2) Lydia, daughter of William Acton, portman of Ipswich Co, Suff (Will, 1616, P.C.C. 20 Meade). She married (2) Rev John Ward, rector of Dinnington, Suff., and St Clemens, Ipswhich (Add.MS. 15520, fo 15; Chandler Ped Harl;. MS. 6071, fo 483; Tanner MS, 180, 109, 257. Rev John Ward was the son of Rev John Ward of Haverhill, whose will was proved 1598 (p.C.C. 85, Lewyrn), and whose wife, Susan, married (2) Richard Rogers of Wetherfield, CT.

Rev John Ward of Haverhill was connected through marriage with the famous Samuel Gorton of Warwick, RI, Clement Chaplin of New England, and John Ward of Haverhill, MA. (Arch Sudbury, Coleman, fo 686; P.C.C. Fines, 69; Pembroke 68; 332 Berkly; 47 Coventry).

Daniel Burrell's son, George, emigrated to Lynn, MA with son Francis.

John Burrell, brother of Daniel, married, 1576, Margaret, daughter of Tobias Winter (Berwick reg.), and had 14 children. of these, John, bt in Berwick, North., 1597, married, in Minsden chapel, Hitchin parish, Herts., 1628, Hester Winchester, and had 8 children, and emigrated with son John, son Zachariah and wife to Wetherfield, CT, afterward to Milford and his son, John Burrell, settled in Weymouth, MA, 1643 (Minsden reg.; Milford reg; Hartf. Prob. Rec.iv 14: Co. Rec.; iii.155; Weymouth rec).
3. Elizabeth, b Oct 9, 1633, married, Sept 7, in Stockport, James Porter, brother of John Porter, who emigrated to Weymouth, MA, with wife Deliverance.
4. Samuel, b Aug 12, 1634, of whom presently:
5. Phebe, b July 2, 1635, married Oct 11, 1654, John Taylor and was "across the seas" in 1656, when her sister-in-law, Sarah Martin, wife of Samuel Martin of Manchester, "leather-seller", claimed the estate of their father, John Taylor, Sr. There was a John Taylor of Weymouth, MA, who had a wife Phebe, and he was probably son of John Taylor and Rebecca, who in his will, 1668, refers "to wife Rebecca, son John" (Nor. prob rec).

Anne Dodd, the third wife of William Bagley, was daughter of Rev John Dodd of Stockport and his wife, Elizabeth Hay, of Manchester, as appears from Court Leet records. George Dodd, the brother of Anne, was a mariner and came to Boston in 1647, purchasing land in Cambridge. He returned to England, and his widow, then in Suffolk Co, MA, on June 23, 1663 "petitioned the court....that her husband, George Dod some years past departed this life in England, leving with me fouer smale Children to take care of...desires an allowance out of said estate, in Virginia and some in New England." The Court on July 31, 1663, "allow her the best bed bolster, one pillow, one pr of blankets, Rugg, bedstead & Coard, & 5. in money."

Lidia Dodd, sister of Anne, married, July 14, 1629, Richard Sylvester of Manchester, who emigrated to Weymouth, MA where they had children baptized in 1633.

Abigail Dodd, another sister of Anne Dodd, born May 17, 1597, married Sept 4, 1636, John Whitman, who emigrated with his brothers, Robert and Zacharaiah Whitman, prior to Aug 13, 1639 to Dorchester, and had children born and baptized in

Weymouth, MA, 1641. He died in Weymouth, MA, 1692.

Peter Whitman , father of John, Robert and Zachariah, had married Alice Eaton, aunt of Margaret Eaton, daughter of Mathew Eaton, who married Edmond Lane, and in her will, of London, "widow", Jan 16, 1661, refers to "my late husband Edmond Lane....sister Martha, wife of William Eaton, now, I think, in New England and her five children, cousin Sarah Barrett, daughter of my late brother (in-law) Daniel Jenkin and now wife of John Barett..."

William Eaton of Staple, with wife Martha and three children, emigrated in 1637 to Watertown, MA.

Ellen Axtell of Bovington, Herts., in her will, Mar 15, 1602, refers to "late husband, Thomas Saunders, son Mathew Eaton, Thomas Hayes, son of Thomas Hayes, Nathaniel Hayes, another son, and Abiezer Hayes, another son of Thomas Hayes. Thomas Goulde, the son of Thomas Goulde, my sister Isobel Hayes, wife of Thomas Hayes..."

Ellyn or Elnere Axtell, daughter of William Golde of Bovington, Herts., who in his will, 1568, refers to sons and daughters. His sister, Joan Goulde, married, (1) Henry Axtell, and (2) James Wells. Henry Axtell's sister, Alicia, married Henry Whitman, grandfather of Peter Whitman.

Joan Gold Axtell Well's daughter, Joane, who married Thomas Heart, had a son, James Hart, who had a son Edmund Hart. (One Edmund Hart emigrated to Weymouth, MA).

Ralph Whightman, in his will, refers to sister Eaton, i.e., the wife of Mathew Eaton, brother of Alice Eaton, wife of Peter Whitman.

Elizabeth Brooke, in her will, refers to "William Whetman and his sister, Elizabeth Whetman , children of my brother Peter Whitman

James Whitman of Albury, Herts., merchant, George Whitman of London, chemist, William Whitman of Albury, Herts., and Elizabeth Alcock, sons and daughters of the deceased Peter Whitman of Albury, Herts., were bound to administer the estate of their brother, Ralph Whitman of London, Aug 15, 1640. James Whitman and Margaret Alcock, his wife, out of natural love and affection convey to their son Zachariah Whitman of London, a tenement with appurtances in Old Jewry, London, late in the possession of Zachariah Alcock, Oct 3, 1647.

Elizabeth Whitman, daughter of Peter, and sister of John of Weymouth, MA, married Sept 7, 1618, Henry Alcock, Jr., son of Henry, Sr., and Sarah Church, sister of George Church of Aylesbury, Bucks.

The Alcock family history had already been given, above.

Zachariah Whitman, brother of Elizabeth, emigrated in Truelove, with wife Sara (Biscoe, daughter of Richard, and married at Chesham, Bucks, 1630), and son Zachariah Whitman, to Milford, CT.

Ralph Whitman, brother of Stephen, is mentioned above. He had married (1) Judith, daughter of James Bate of St Albans, and sister of Edward Bate, who emigrated to Weymouth, MA, children of Thomas Bate of Lydd, Kent. Ralph married (2), Catherine, daughter of James Williams, merchant taylor of London and his wife Alice. (See above)

Stephen Whitman, brother of Peter and Ralph, is mentioned

in the will of William Dyre of Sussex Co., PA, proved in
London, 1690, in whihc he refers to "eldest son William Dyre,
now in Boston on New England, to wife, land in Narragansett
Co., in New Englnad, estate of my late father William Dyre
upon Rhode Island...400 acres land at Beaverwick, formerly in
partnership with Stephen Whittman....". William Dyre's mother
was hanged in Boston during the persecution of the Quakers.

Elizabeth Whitman, sister of Peter, married John Brooke
of London and in her will, 1599, widow, refers to "late
husband John Brooke....dau. Joane Foote....Wm Whitman my
brother's son, and his sister Elizabeth Whetman....son-in-law
Robert Foote..."

Robert Foote of Shalford, Essex, in his will, 1608,
refers to "wife Joan....land in Royston, son Joshua, dau Mary,
wife of John Hewes".

Joshua Foote, ironmonger of London, emigrated to Roxbury
and Providence, and when he died administration was granted,
in 1655, to Joshua Hewes of Roxbury, son of his sister, Mary
Hewes of Royston."

John Foote, grocer, of London, in his will, 1616, refers
to "daughters Priscilla, wife of Robert Clement and Elizabeth,
wife of John Hays, wife Harriet."

Widow Margaret Foote, of St Benet, in her will, 1634,
refers to "daughter Priscilla Garford, sons-in-law John Hayes,
Richard Garford and Charles Harris, his sister Meryall
Harris..."

Walter Harris, brother of Charles, emigrated to Weymouth,
MA, after 1636, and had land adjoining John Whitman, Samuel
Bagley, etc. Thomas Dyre also had land in Weymouth, MA.

To Weymouth, MA had emigrated a number of relatives of
Samuel Bagley, son of William Bagley of Manchester who had as
his third wife Anne Dodd, whose brother-in-law, John Whitman,
settled in Weymouth, MA.

VII. Samuel Bagley

born in Manchester, Aug 12, 1634, in the house at the
Deanesgate, which had been in the possession of his family for
many years. (For this complete line, see Notes on Bagley Lines
by Norton R. Bagley). He died Feb, 1710/11 "old" as it says in
Weymouth records. Mary, his wife, d Dec 29, 1713 (Braintree
town records).

Weymouth, MA was then in the county of Suffolk,
adjoining the town of Braintree or Brantrey. In the
Weymouth vital records, we find that

1. Samuel, son of Samuel Bagley and Mary, his wife, was
baptized there Sept 7, 1658. He married Elizabeth Nash, was
of Braintree, and is apparently the Samuel Bagley, mason, who
on May 1, 1710, sold to Samuel Copeland, blacksmith, for 10pds
land in Braintree, as we find from Suffolk Deeds, 35, p 62.

On Dec 1, 1714, Joseph Green of Weymouth, Co Suffolk, and
Anne, his wife, sold to Samuel Bagley of Brantrey, Co Suffolk,
for 5pds, one fifth part of third allotment of land called
Boston Common in Braintree (ib 28:198).

Samuel Bagley of Braintree and Elizabeth, his wife, sold
to John Clark, et al, as commissioners for 25pds, 50 acrss of
land on Cochato river, adjoining land of James Bagley, Feb 13,

1716 (ib.31:145).

On May 23, 1723, Samuel Bagley, "out of love and affection unto my said son, James Bagley, tract of land in Braintree acknowledged his grant thereof, June 20, 1715 (37:37).

Ebenezer Thayer and Ruth, his wife, on Apr 6, 1724, sold to Samuel Bagley land in Nraintree called the Middle Division (37:207).

2. James, son of Samuel Bagley and Mary, his wife, bapt Feb 21, 1663, made his will, Aug 2, 1690, as "James Bagley of Boston, glazier....upon the present expedition to Canada against the Common Enemy....friend Richard Cheever of Boston, cordwainer..." (Suff. wills, 8, p 16).

i. James, son of James Bagley and Jane was bt in Braintree, Mar 1, 1714.

ii. John, bt Aug 18, 1725

James Bagley presented to the town of Braintree what is now called Randolph cemetery.

3. John, bt Dec 12, 1668, son of Samuel Bagley and Mary, his wife, had in 1699 of the town of Braintree, as of Roxbury, 4pds "to keep Abigail Neal (Braintree rec).

4. Joseph, bt Dec 18, 1672, son of Samuel Bagley and Mary, his wife.

5. .....died in 1697, a child of Samuel Bagley.

The family afterwards settled in New Hampshire, and here we find them in 1790 in Grafton County of Orangetown and Thornton, Samuel and Winthrop Bagley; in Hillsborough, County, Campton. (This paragraph is incorrect; the New Hampshire Bagleys were descendants of Orlando Bagley of Amesbury, MA, not of Samuel of Weymouth and Braintree)

The New England tradition is that Samuel Bagley of Braintree, Orlando Bagley of Amesbury and Boston, and Thomas Bagley of Rhode Island, were brothers. There has been no proof found of this tradition and the above Bagley data do not bear the tradition out unless there are sons of William Bagley, father of Samuel, of which no record had yet been found.

SOURCES FOR BRITISH BAGLEYS OTHER THAN THOSE LISTED IN THE TEXT

Brestbury, Lanc. Registers
Wills, Chester, 1635, 1646, 1590, 1594
Lancashire Inquisitions Post Morten, xix No 15
Exchequer deposition by Commission, Lanc., 1657, No 21
Plundered Ministers Account 1644
Manchester Quarter Sessions Rolls, 1618, 1620, 1621
Marriage Licenses Chester, 1667, 1672, 1662, 1640, 1641
Finald Concord, 3 Edw V. m 48
Winwick Church inscriptions
Manchester Cathedral registers
Manchester Constable Accounts, 1621, 1625, 1627, 1629
Manchester Court Leet Records
St James Diasbury Reg, Rochdale, Lanc Reg
Bolton, Lanc. Reg; Prestwich, Lanc Reg
Visitation of Cheshire, 1580, 147. 148-49, 150
Harl MS 1424, fo 62

Manchester School Registers
Wills and Administrations of Chester
Lanc. Inq. xxi. No 68, xxiii, No 32
Wilmslow. Nortcliffe reg
Church Lawton Manor reg
Bishop of Manchester Vis. of Manchester, 1592
Close Rolls, 19, Ed II. m. 21; 20 Ed II.m 9; 16 Ed II. m 24; 5
Ed II.m 30
Patent Rolls, 12 Ed II.i.m.17' 7 Ed II.i 12; 3 Ed II. 19;
19 Ed II. i. 3; 19 Edw III.i.m4; 4 Edw III. iv.i.m 4
State Papers, Domestic, Chas I. dxxxix; ccccxxvii; cccc;
ccccxv; ccclxxl; ccclxxxviii
Lanc. Pea Rolls, 1471.30m.2d
Northamptonshire wills, V. 1578-89
Fenland Notes & Queries, iii. 76
Hist of Cheshire, Ormerod
St James, London, reg
St Martin in the Field, London, reg
Chester Prergoative Court, adm 1677, 1679
Subsidy of Clergy of Dio of Chester, 1624
Do Salford Hundred, 1541. 1622
Freeholders of Lancashire, 1600
Chamberlain Accounts, Cheshire
Freemen of Chester, 1476, 1663, 14-15 C.11

MISC. BAGLEY NOTES

These are notes from various records and persons sent through
the years; some are taken from Census records. They are
presented here in this form in the hope that more can be put
into the lines we now have, or make it easier to formulate
other Bagley lines.

Aaron C.. Census of 1850 for Ohio; first two letters refer to
Co; last to town, number, page of Census HM W2 162

Aaron, ae 49, b NY; living Erie Co, No East PA; Census of 1880
Lydia A., wife ae 46, b NY
John, son, ae 32, b NY
Carrie, dau, ae 19, b NY
George, son, ae 4, b PA

Aaron, b June 7, 1791, son Aaron & Elizabeth, Hollis, NH

Abbie Dennett Bagley m John Gale, 1892, at Kensington, NH

Abby Ann, dau Zebedee Bagely & Elizabeth lived Seneca, MI

Abigail Ellis, bDec 18, 1870, Southport, ME; d Portlaand, ME,
May 17, 1935, wife of George Bagley, and dau Alex Tibbetts, b
PEI

Abigail, dau John of Watertown, MA , b Feb 4, 1663/4; m Dec
10, 1684, Benjamin Harrington. Mentioned in father's will

Abigail; m Robert Anderson, May 24, 1722, Braintree, MA

Abigail, b Deerfield, 62, d Mar 1876, widow, nurse, father, b
Northfield; mother, b Deerfield, dau Joseph Robinson & Abigail
Brown. Sold land in Candia, Jan 1, 1863; Rockingham Co NH
Probate R (widow Jonathan?)

Abigail, m Mark, son of Moses Sawyer, June 26, 1823, Topsham,
VT

Abigail, m William M. Quimby, Nov 3, 1839, Salis MA R

Abigail, m Eliphalet Spofford, Jan 5, 1769, at Springfield, VT

Abigail, m George Langdon of Boston, May 15, 1836, Cambridge,
MA R

Abigail, dau of John Couch & Polly Gordon, m Bagley Colby, she
b about 1775; he settled Salisbury, NH

Abner, b & d Dover, MA., Feb 23, 1855

Abner m Abigail Green, Jan 30, 1831, Portland, ME
Mary Jane, b Portland, Feb 1, 1831
Sarah, b Portland, ME, Aug 18, 1835
Abner, b Portland, ME, Sept 28, 1842; d Sept 12, 1843.

Portland
Hannah, b Portland, ME, Jan 22, 1833
Addison Holey of Kennebunk, ME was appt adm, Abner given as of
Newbury, MA

Abner's wife Caroline, dau of James Decker, d 1855

Widow Abner's child, Abner Bagley, b July 24, 1819, Topsham,
VT, might be Bailey

Abner & Sarah Whittier had a dau Mary J. of Pittsfield, NH,
who m Charles Green of Pittsfield, NH, Dec 10, 1892, NH R

Abraham F., m Mar 3, 1813, Rachel R. b Barnard, VT, Nov 15,
1792, dau Eleazer Myrick & Rachel Richmond, History of Barnard
VT & VT R

Ada H. Baglee, given as ae 24 on Census of 1880, Orano, ME

Ada , m John W. Fisk, both of Randolph, VT, Mar 30, 1877, VT R

Adaline D, d Nov 9, 1889, ae 3, b & d Norwood, dau George F. &
Lydia, both b Boston, MA R

Adam, had dau Mary, d Oct 10, 1857, ae 26, b Milford MA. His
wife, Mary, d Oct 10, 1857, ae 26 , b Hopkinton; d Milford
(don't know what story is on this one)

Addie V., of Richmond, ME; m Charles A. Price of Richmond,
June 6, 1891, Augusta ME R

Addis Alfred, son Francis Marion & Ellen Thompson, b July 8,
1876, given as married

Adelbert , ae 30, b Susquehanna Co PA
Lizzie, wife ae 26, b PA
Maud, dau ae 6, b PA (might be son E. P. Brooklyn, PA line)

A. G. & Ann had dau Elizabeth, d Sept 1, 1855, ae 4 mos,
Pitttsfield, MA

Agnes, b Malden, had son Frederick who d Jan 30, 1901, at
Boston, ae 3 mos MA

Agnes, d June 15, 1960, ae 79, b Eng, d Bedford, MA; dau Mark
W. & Ann M. Smith, both b Eng.

A. J., d Nov 2, 1879, ae 29, Middletown, Conn

Alanson Horr, b Dec 28, 1827, at Hartland, VT, son Benjamin &
Hannah, VT R

Alanson, his child, d Apr 12, 1839, Clinton CT R

Alda E. Adams, d Sept 23, 1934, ae 31, b NJ, d Attleboro, MA
her husband was Bernard J. Bagley, and she was dau George

Adams & Mary A. Grant, b NJ

Alena Maud, m Henry, Leanell, Dec 19, 1914, son Henry William
& Edna Newton. She m (2) Alton Aldrich, Sept 13, 1927, VT R
at Montpelier.

Alexander Dudley had wife Edith Alden Brooks, dau Charles &
Mary Stanwood, who d May 4, 1937, ae 61, b Boston, d Townsend,
MA, he d Apr 1, 1932, ae 63, b Birmingham, Eng., d Townsend,
MA. (I stopped once in Townsend and talked with one of these
Bagleys. They appear to be a distinct family in this
country.)

Alexander, Albany NY, sold land in Albany, Mar 28, 1889

Alexander, b MA, m Annie McClinton, b TN, had a son Lawrence
Brooks, b Aug 5, 1950, Nashua, NH
Alexander T., b Eng, (1838), son Richard & Elizabeth, b b Eng,
d Boston, Apr 13, 1884, ae 42; his wife, Mary, b Eng, d
Boston, Sept 4, 1912, ae 70, dau John Evans & Mary, both b
Wales (she b 1842)
1. Richard P., d Jan 15, 1874, at Boston ae 11 dys
2. Florence W., b & d Boston, Feb 23, 1881, ae 3
3. Edward Cartwright, d Aug 8, 1937, ae 62, b Boston, d
Winthrop, MA, wife was Bessie Louise Colley, MA R

Alfred, ae 14, son Edward & Amarilla of NY, Census of 1860,
see Edward

Alfred Howard of Rosette Park, Union Co NJ, d Apr 8, 1947.
His wife was Marie Annette; dau was Margaret Annette. He was
son of William Lloyd Bagley.

Alfred N., d June 9, 1942, wife was Mabel Bagley (in notes
containing will of Valentine Nye Bagley of Catskill, NY, but
Valentine son's were Arthur & George)

Alford, given as ae 6, Census of 1880 for Howland, ME in
family of Alford & Julia Buzzell

Alfred, b Seabrook, NH & Mamie Kelley b Ireland, had son
Alfred J. b & d Apr 11, 1912, at Newburyport, MA

Alfred had son Walker, d Apr 24, 1892, ae 39, b Washington DC;
d Boston MA

Alice S., d Dec 7, 1887, ae 7, b & d Newburyport, MA, dau John
F. & Maria, both b Newburyport, MA

Alice E., b Aug 1859, d July 15, 1920, m a Mitchell, Cemetery
Lee, Hill, NH

Alice, ae 11, b Ohio, dau William & Sarah, Census of 1850,
Sciot, Portage, OH

Alice, b Mar 9, 1849; d Sept 1, 1921, New Britain CT

Alice had son Joseph, who d Apr 4, 1905, ae 3 mos, b Salem, d
Boston, MA

Alice H. of Merrimac, MA, m William Gray, and their dau Annie
M. Gray, m Charles Webster, 1898, East Kingston, NH

Alice of Lowell, MA had dau Estelle, d Nov 14, 1911, ae 4 mos,
b Nashua, NH, d Boston, MA

Alice , b Lowell, MA ae 22, had Mary, an illegitimate child at
Manchester, NH, b July 1, 1909

Alick, m Theresa Miller; their son, Paul, d July 13, 1958, ae
57, Sioux Falls, SD, his wife was Helen who d July 13, 1958;
no children listed.

Almary, b ME & H. T. Drew of Enfield, NH, had son Jacob, who
m a Drew at Enfield NH 1897

Almeda, ae 7, possibly dau John of Green, PA, 1880 name may
have been Almina

Almon & Maria (Stone), had son Almon, b Dec 21, 1835,
Marlboro, NH (See Almon, son Oliver & Polly)

Alonzo J, ae 21, b Oct 2, 1838; d Islesboro, ME, May 4, 1893,
single ME R

Alta, b Mar 4, 1879, dau John of Logan, OH (Civil War Vet)

Alvin, ae 48, physician, b NY
Jane, ae 50, b NY
C. A. Van Valkenburg, 19, b NY
H. R. Van Valkenburg, ae 13, b NY
Census of 1850 OH, Ashtabulam Co, Conneault

Amanda, b July 4, 1817, dau Henry & Bethiel of Campton, NH

Amasa, m Nancy Brown Dec 1, 1803, at Wrentham, MA and had dau
Belinda, d Oct 18, 1809, ae 2

Amelia Janet, b Feb 13, 1938, at Milford, NH , dau Edward F. ,
b Lowell, MA & Emma Leachout

Amos, b Mar 9, 1756, son Jonathan & Martha Clark, Salem NH

Amee, ae 3 dys, dau James b Eng, Census of 1869 for Essex VT

Andisa, dau of Daniel, Census 1850, Jackson, Union Co, OH

Andrew & Nancy Ann, his wife, sold land to William Kirpatrick,
in County of Meigs, Ohio (Greene Co NY Deeds)

Andrew of Peterboro NH, corporal in MA Regt in Revolution

Andrus Bagley, Census of OH, 1850 AB CO, p 327

Angie C. m July 28, 1900, William H. Shaw, b Nov 24, 1868,
Sgt 1 Co D, Texas Inf. one child Shaw Record

Ann, dau Edward, b 1810 & Elizabeth Bennett of Bradford, PA
m ______Town

Ann, m Robert Dickerson, Aug 21, 1853, NY Marriages

Ann , m Croyden Bush, Mar 3, 1833, NY Marriages

Ann Kasper 1881-1929, Bridgeport, CT Cemetery

Ann T. & Clarence Clemence of Southbridge, intentions of m,
July 13, 1834, Salis MA R

Ann & John Dutenbogert, m Jan 17, 1758, NY marriages: their
son Johannes John christened Sept 13, 1762, m Nov 16, 1788,
Ann Smith, dau William and Sarah (Montange), christened Oct
20, 1763. Children were Maria, b June 8, 1789; and Ann, b Aug
28, 1792

Ann, b 1784, d Dec 8, 1863, ae 79 at Monson, MA

Ann of Montville, ME m Thomas Peavey, son John C., b & d
Montville, Sept 22, 1928, ae 65

Anna E., m Edward B. Hartshorn, Aug 23, 1862, Bedford, NH

Anna, m Ned Keely or Kelly, Feb 27, 1827, Topsham, Vt, he of
Bradford, VT

Anna, b 1800, W Newbury, MA, d June 13, 1845; m Orlando Howard
Sargent, b Amesbury, MA, Aug 22, 1809, d July 13, 1884, both
of Merrimac, m Nov 27, 1834. He was a carriage manuf.
Children: Arthur, b June 7, 1845, d Nov 9, 1847; Edmund
Howard, b July 29, 1849; William Bernard, b Nov 15, 1851;
Augustus H., b Feb 9, 1856, d Mar 11, 1891, unm The Sargent
Record

Anna, now of Windsor town of Hartford, VT ordered to leave
town, Nov 15, 1806, see Daniel

Anna of Waterbury, CT 1900-1918

Anna, widow of Merrimac, MA, m Perry Sargent, Dec 6, 1890

Anna, ae 13, b 1857, dau Nelson on Census of 1870 for New
Baltimore, NY

Anna A of Goffs Falls, NH , dau C. J. & Mary of Dover, NH , m
H. R. Jones of Goffs Falls, June 17, 1868, NH R

Annah Elizabeth, dau John, son of John & Dolly, b at Ferry,
Aug 30, 1847, Amesbury, MA

Anne Marie, ae 3, Census of 1870, <u>New Baltimore</u>, NY, dau Horatio

Anne, b Aug 6, 1768, dau Joseph & Deborah of <u>Pelham, NH</u>

Anne, b Mar 4, 1774, dau Joshua & Anna, <u>Hopkinton, NH</u> R

Anne E., dau Frederick & Almira, ae 20, Census of 1860 for St <u>Johnsbury, VT</u>, b 1840

Anne Hawkins, b Apr 28, 1869, d Apr 26, 1945, dau Philanda Warboys & Edward Hawkins, <u>VT</u>

Annette, d Nov 28, 1954, ae 91, b Eng, d <u>Everett, MA</u>, dau Noel & Ann Jennings, both b Eng

Annie, d Jan 4, 1944, ae 93 (b 1851), b <u>Houlton, ME</u>, d <u>Lowell, MA</u>, husband was John Bagley, dau Albert Johnson

Annie A., ae 20, Census of Bangor, ME, 1880; on same card as Ellen, ae 43

Annie C., b <u>MA</u>, single, d <u>Norway, ME</u>, July 30, 1932, ae 84

Annie S., ae 1, dau James A., b <u>Carroll, PA</u>, 1880

Anthony, son Rev David, b 1761, <u>NJ</u>, wife b NJ, d <u>IL</u>, wife b 1763, NJ; d IL
1. Aaron, b 1784, St Clair, IL
2. Icabod, b 1785, St Clair, IL
3. David, b 1787, St Clair, IL
4. Rachel, b 1788, St Clair, IL
5. Job, b 1789, St Clair, IL
6. Mary, b 1790, St Clair, IL
7. Abram, b 1791, St Clair, IL
8. Elizabeth, b 1793, St Clair, IL

Anthony, ae 25, d Dec 7, 1857, b 1834, in <u>Wenham, MA</u>

Araminda Minerva, dau James of <u>PA</u>, b <u>VA</u>, ae 8, 1880

Archie G., <u>Springfield, ME</u>, ae 21, b Winn, ME, father unknown; mother, Hattie, b Lee & Mary Hanscom of Lee, ae 17, b Lee, ME, dau Preston Hanscom & Martha Roberts, m July 2, 1923, at <u>Lee, ME</u>

Armour W., son Edward, b 1810, m Elizabeth Bennett in <u>Bradford, PA</u>; family dispersed through <u>OH</u> & IA (See Stephen)

Arthur, ae 12, son Edward & Amarilla of <u>NY</u> Census of 1860

Arthur, d Aug 31, 1961, ae 62, b 1899, <u>Topsham, VT</u>, d Dennis, <u>MA</u>, wife Lucy Canfield; a mechanic

Arthur C., b 1827, son Josiah & Elizabeth, Census of 1850 for

<u>OH</u>, originally from <u>VA</u>

Arthur, m Helen MacDonald, who d July 10, 1941, ae 30, at Boston, parent was Ronald, b <u>PEI</u>. Child: William D., d July 3, 1934, at <u>Boston</u>, ae 1 yr

Arthur S., b <u>ME</u> & Stella Elliott, b ME. A male child, b about 1910, 3rd ch

Arthur, b St John's, New Bruns, m Rosetta, b <u>Canton, MS</u>, had child George Francis, d June 1871, stillborn

Asa & Abigail of <u>Haverhill, MA</u> had son Asa, b Oct 16, 1775

Asa, b May 5, 1815, <u>Pittsfield, MA</u>, son of David & Ann Hannah

Asa & Ann had son Daniel H., d Jan 5, 1858, ae 6 mos b & d <u>Oakham, MA</u>

Asa, b May 12, 1845, son Edward & Elizabeth, <u>Salem, NH</u>

Asa, m Marintha Sanders, June 28, 1835, <u>NY marriages</u>

Asenath Dolly, m Volney Tanner, Apr 12, 1812, <u>NY marriages</u>

Ashman, LKPA, p 189, Census of 1850, <u>Ohio</u>

Augustan, ae 18, son Edward & Amarilla of <u>NY</u> Census of 1860

Augusta, wife A. S., d <u>Bangor, ME</u>, Dec 24, 1917, b <u>Granby, VT</u>, July 6, 1861, dau Stephen Austin, b Lunenburg, VT & Phoebe Cleveland, b Stratford, VT

Augustus, b Oct 2, 1796, son Enos & Patience Sullivan, <u>NH R</u>

Rev A. W. of <u>Jefferson, OH</u>, m Oct 13, 1897, Edith Field, dau Dexter & Eliza Assity; she was b May 26, 1872. He was son Ferric Field Bagley, b Jan 28, 1899 (Field Genealogy)

Azor, b July 20, 1757, enlis 1778, at Fishkill, NY, Dutchess Co; lived in <u>OH</u>, widow Martha received pension 1837.

Mr Bagley, m Abigail Sargent, b Jan 22, 1753, dau Orlando & Sarah Belch Sargent (The Sargent Record); probably <u>Amesbury</u>

Miss Bagley, d Jan 11, 1825, <u>Amesbury, MA</u>

Child of Mr. Bagley, d Jan 7, 1787

Barger (?), son Schyler, Census of 1870 for <u>New Baltimore, NY</u>, ae 1

Barnard, b Wednesday, Eng, m Mary J. Smith, b Cambridge, MA, had a male child, b Jan 13, 1932, stillborn, at <u>Foxboro, MA</u>

Benjamin, son Prudence, late of <u>Greenville, Greene Co.NY</u>,

<u>117</u>

nephew Seth Bixby co-executor. Benjamin given as of Coxsachie, Jan 30, 1832. She d Dec, 1831

Benjamin of Millerburg, Scholarie Co, NY, sealed Jan 23, 1832, son Prudence

Benjamin on tax list of Falmouth, ME, 766, 3 polls, see John

Benjamin m Maria Rosen, Apr 17, 1961, ae 77, b & d Boston

Benjamin M of Cedar Point (IA?), son Edward, b 1810, and Elizabeth Bennett of Bradford, PA

Benjamin, b Ireland, m Elmira Millet, b Ireland; Son Charles, b Ogdensburg, NY, 2nd m wid ae 25 of Skowhegan, ME., m Agnes L. Booth of Skowhegan, ae 21, dau William Booth & Anna O'Neal, m Nov 15, 1905, at Skowhegan. She d there Oct 14, 1918, ae 32

Benjamin & Hannah Harding, m Sept 6, 1850, both born ME, probably Troy, had at least two children:
Loisa E., d Oct 18, 1877, ae 16, b ME, d Lowell, MA
Frank, d Aug 30, 1887, ae 30, b Dixmont, ME; d Somerville, MA

Benjamin J., farmer, Dixmont, ME, ae 32
Hannah J., ae 33
Hannah, ae 6
John Frank, ae 4, 1860 Census Penobscot Co, ME

Benjamin m Julia Twitchell. She d Jackson, ME, Oct 15, 1866, b Jackson, Oct 1841, dau Joshua & Elizabeth (Jones)
Dau Medora, m Jackson, May 22, 1866, 1st ch, m Ezra Abbott Carpenter, b Nov 20, 1861 at Thorndike, ME. Their children: Chloe, b Mar 31, 1866; d Mar 1, 1893; Elizabeth, b July 18, 1887; and Medora Lena, b May 28, 1890 (George Abbott Descendants)

Benjamin had wife Lena S., d Apr 20, 1910, ae 62, b Marshfield, ME. Father Jonas Berry.

Benjamin m Juliet Woodruff. She b Nov 15, 1806, dau Sylvestre & Polly Peck of Bristol, CT

Benjamin, b 1799, in Chatham, CT
May fit into David of Chatham line

Benjamin F. of Newbury, VT m Emmeline Smith of Chelsea, Jan 5, 1929, Chelsea, VT

Benjamin & Hannah had son Alanson Horr, b Dec 28, 1827, Hartland, VT

Benjamin & Rebecca had son John F., d 1851, ae 3 mos, at Boston

Benjamin, b Boston & Evaline, b South Reading, MA, had dau Evaline, d June 4, 1860, b & d Boston

Benjamin of Concord NH, b Abigail Boynton of Warren, NH, Feb 18, 1807

Benjamin of Topsham, VT, Census of 1830, 1 M under 5, 1 M under 10, 2M 10 under 15, 1 M 20 under 30, 1M 40 under 50, 1F under 5, 1F under 10, 1F 30 under 40.

Benjamin MOST, p 243, Census 1850, Ohio

Benjamin m Ann Clifford and had dau Serence C., b Plum Island, d Lynn, MA, Dec 31, 1890, ae 80

Bernard, d June 29, 1947, ae 46, b Heleb, ME, d Seeconk, MA, wife Elizabeth Tiprot, son William Bury of Canada & Margaret Rose Green

Bernard Ethran, b Sept 14, 1935 at White Wright, TX, son Beryl & Mildred Mickeroy.

Bernard, son John & Prudence, Saratoga Co and Greeneville, Greene Co. NY, m Phoebe Stoddard, see card for John & Prudence Ellen Wesley

Bertha E. Vaughan Bagley, d May 13, 1925, ae 49, b Lynn, d Danvers, MA, dau Sam C, b Moore's Forks, NY & Hannah Ramsdell b Lynn (probably old 2064)

Beryl E., b abt 1908, Nacodoches TX, father Harvey, mother Mable Connley, m abt 1934, Mildred Mickeroy, b July 13, 1911, Nachodoches TX, dau David McKleroy, mother Mary L. Halton.
1. Bernard Ethran, b Sept 14, 1935 White Wright, TX
2. Tommy Earl, b June 24, 1937, Jefferson, TX

Bessie W., m William Royce, Aug 29, 1882, Moretown, VT

Bessie Colley, d Aug 17, 1953, ae 75, d Worcester, MA, b Marblehead, MA, husband Edmund C., dau Herbert, b Portland, ME & helen Snow, b Marblehead, MA

Betsey m Joseph Davice, Jr., Jan 10, 1807, AMES MA, children on Ames or Salis MA R. A Joseph Davice "hung himself in his garrit", Sept 8, 1810 Ames MA

Betsey Chase, b Sandown, Aug 27, 1788, father Joseph, mother Marey NH R

Betsey m Matthew Perkins Sanborn, son Ensign John Dearborn Sanborn, b Hampton, Sept 14, 1765. His mother was Lydia Perkins, Matthew, b July 26, 1796, lived Laconia, NH. She d May 20, 1853. He d Sept 26, 1843. Sanborn Genealogy

Betsey, married, d Aug 11, 1847 in Pembroke, NY (near Darien), ae 68. Pembroke Historian

Bettie, dau Henry of Bedford, PA, ae 6, b PA, 1880

Betty Bagley & Valmore Page, had son Ernest Page, d Apr 5, 1923, ae 3 mos, b Amesbury, MA. He b Upton, MA, she Milford, MA

Betty published to Stephen Morse of Newton, Jan 1, 1789, Ames MA

Blanche, ae 3, on Census of 1880 for Newburgh, ME. See R. C. Bagley in same household

Bridget McLaughlin, d Aug 23, 1863, ae 21, b Ireland; d Medford, MA
Bridget & Peter Bagley of Medford, had son John, who died Aug 3, 1863, ae 12 dys, b & d Medford, MA
They had son Thomas, who d Dec 24, 1863, ae 3 mos (might be twins, looks as though mother died in childbirth)

Bridget 1853-1916, West Haven, CT

Calvin, son John of Windham, NY, Census of 1860, ae 2/12

Calvin A., m Dorothy F. Kilborn, dau John D. & Sarah Carroll. She b Ipswich, MA; d Danvers, MA, Apr 3, 1957, ae 50; John, b Newburyport, MA; Sarah, b RI

Candalace Bagley, d Mar 17, 1852, ae 25, Waterbury, CT

Carl Gardiner, 1898-1918, both WWI (other is Charles Gardiner) on large cemetery stone in East Machias, ME, marked Bagley
A Mrs Margaret Bagley, b Sept 8, 1897, in E Machias, ME, dau Adelbert & Lara (Gardner) Ackley, d Sept 26, 1988, Machias. 2 daus, Ruth Sullivan of Dennysville, ME, & Hazel Davis of Marshfield, ME; a special step-dau Kathleen Faloon of E Machias; 3 sons, Perley H. F. Gardner, Myles Gardner and Clayton Gardner of E Machias. Predeceased by 2 sons, David in 1988 & Clarence in 1939. A grandson, Clarence Gardner, d Aug 28, 1987, ae 38, son David Rand and Dorothy (Berry) Gardner

Carle Francis, son Henry Stone, b Peabody, MA & Lillian Cornwall, m Thelma Foster Nichols, Aug 25, 1932, at Center Conway, NH, 25-30, 2nd, divorced, dau Carleton W. Raymond & Edith Hersey

Carleton W. (See Charles Frederick), m Oct 4, 1936, at Augusta, ME, Althea Drew of Bucksport, ME, b about 1912, dau Clyde & Lillian Walker

Caroline Draper , dau George E. b Dedham & Cordelia Draper, b MA, d Dedham, b there, June 5, 1870, ae 19

Caroline, dau John & Susan, ae 6, Census 1880 for PA

Caroline, dau Ralph of Shaler, PA, ae 14

Caroline, ae 17, b NY, dau William & Sarah, Census of 1850,

Sciot, Portage, OH

Caroline, wife John T. Clement, 1874, Amesbury, MA tombstone

Caroline, ae 19, b 1851, Census of 1870 for New Baltimore, NY,
dau Nelson

Caroline, m Ahillus Sanford, Dec 26, 1822, VT R

Caroline W., of Springfield, MA, m William H. Bubage, July 7,
1844, at Enfield, CT

Caroline, ae 1, dau James B., b Eng. Census of 1860 for Essex,
VT

Carrie Sexton, d Jan 16, 1955, ae 86, d Newton, MA, b
Lawrence, MA, dau Jonn K., b Sparta, GA & Elizabeth A. Fields,
b Malden, MA

Carrie, ae 6, dau William A., b Conn., PA Census 1880

Carrie, dau Aaron, ae 19, 1880, Erie Co, PA

Carrie Evelyn, b Sept 13, 1862, Fowler, IL, dau George Rodney
& Ellen Chase, m Alvin A. Dewey

Carrie L., m Dec 7, 1872, at Laconia, NH, Robert Seeley, NH R

Carrie, dau George, m William Edson, Oct 22, 1873, Pomfret,
VT, ae 18, b Brandon, VT

Carrie Jane, m July 2, 1890, Herman Summer Rollins, b Sept 27,
1862; living 1934 on Hampton Rd, Exeter, NH, son Gilbert &
Abigail (Hayes); no children, Descendants of John Hayes of
Dover, NH

Catherine Bagley, ae 69, b VA
N, ae 16, laborer, b VA
Zephr, ae 11, b Ohio   Census of 1850, Salem, Muskingum Co, OH

Catherine & Charles Stewart, m Oct 26, 1781, NY marriages

Catherine A. Holland, d Oct 14, 1918, Waterbury, CT

Mrs Catherine H., d Deering, ME, Oct 24, 1891, ae 50

Catherine, dau Calvin Sawyer & Clausia Sumber or Summer, b Apr
29, 1846; d Dec 16, 1924, VT

Catherine, Orvidence Twp, Bedford Co, PA, 1F 50-60

Catherine, b Islesboro, ME, d Dec 23, 1899, ae 88-7-12, wid,
dau Robert Combs & Lucy Thomas

Catherine, dau Catherine, d Sept 7, 1890, ae 4 mos, at Boston

Catherine, d Jan 31, 1889, ae 45, b Ireland, d Newton, MA, dau
Thomas & Catherine Launeau (record is not clear if this was
her maiden name and if she m Bagley or not)

Catherine A. (Graham), b Nov 215, 1894, ae 51, b Newburyport,
MA; d Haverhill, MA, dau William & Mary (Whelna), b b Ireland

Catherine (Golden), b Ireland, d Boston, wife John, d Mar 5,
1879, ae 25, dau James & Ann, b b Ireland

Catherine (Doherty), d Mar 2, 1890, b Ireland, d Boston, dau
John & Bridget, both b Ireland

Charles Frederick, b About 1878, Census of 1880, gives ae 2, m
Apr 3, 1898, Waterville, ME, Jennie Roberts of Bangor, dau
Henry & Mahaley Mahoney; m (2) Bessie R. Wing, dau William &
Annette (Choate), Sept 20, 1922, Augusta, ME. Given as
widower, ae 44. She ae 29.
1.   Female, b June 19, 1898, Bangor, ME
2.   Evelyn, b Aug 17, 1900, Bangor, 2nd ch
3.   Frederick Charles, Jr., b ug 7, 1903, Millinocket, ME
4.   Laurence Roberts, b Dec 27, 1907, Millinocket
5.   Carleton W., 5th ch, b May 26, 1911, Millinocket
6.   Anne V., b June 5, 1926, Augusta, ME, first ch by 2nd m, d
June 7, 1926

Charles, b 1746, son John from Eng, Montgomery Co. NY

Charles, b Ogdensburg, NY, 2nd m, Wid, ae 25, m at Skowhegan,
ME, Agnes L. Booth of Skowhegan, Nov 15, 1905. She d there Oct
18, 1918, ae 32

Charles Wildes, d Salem, MA, ae 78, husband of Helen
(Chandonnet), former resident of Manchester, NH. Survived by
widow and son:
David Bagley of West Newbury, MA (no date, but in 1980's)

Charles, given as of Peacham, VT, m Hannah Kincaid of W
Topsham, VT, Nov 28, 1835

Charles E., Bangor, ME, m Ella Rines, Bangor, May 13, 1876, by
Rev W. S. Brown at Bangor.
Census of 1880 for Ward 4, Bangor, ME, gives Charles, ae 25,
Ellen, ae 26, and Charles F., ae 2

Charles & Catherine, had dau Melissa, b Oct 16, 1836

Charles H., ae 22, b Hallville, CT, son William H. & Lura
Dyer, b RI, m Anna Trafton of East Rochester, NH., Nov 28,
1906, dau Frank & Carrie (Grant) at N Chelmsford, MA.
1.   Lila Margaret, b Jan 6, 1909, East Rochester
2.   Martha Ann, b Apr 23, 1918, East Rochester

Charles, b Nov 20, 1768, son Charles & Abigail, Haverhill, MA
(could be NH)

Catherine Coan, b Bennington, VT
1. Leeward Clayton, d Apr 10, 1930, ae 3 mos, Holbrook, MA

Clifford Howard, ae 32, in 1943, b Amesbury, MA., m Mary
Doody, ae 36, b Boston
1. William Francis, b Portland, ME, Jan 3, 1943

Colin, m Fern M. Perkins, d Mar 13, 1960, ae 43, b Brockton; d
Foxboro, MA, dau Leon, b Brockton & Hilda McLean, b Salem, MA

Connelly, son Schlyer, Census of 1870 for New Baltimore NY, ae
19, b NY

Cora Estelle (Wilcox), d Sept 4, 1899, ae 29, wife Walter, b
Hyde Park, VT, d Milford, MA, dau Cyrus, b Cambridge, VT &
Augusta Bullam, b Hyde Park, VT

Cora, b Cobbleskill, NY, 1867, m Frank Lethbridge Holcomb, b
Apr 13, 1854, d June 18, 1917, at Anadarko, OK. Frank was son
of Lysander Lethbridge Holcomb, Albion ? NY, Concordia, Kansas
and Davenport, IA; m at Hinesburgh, VT, June 25, 1845, Jane
Pelton, b 1828, d Mar 29, 1902, a Mayflower descendant. They
had five children, b Concordia, KS. One of the five, Nettie
Helen, b May 28, 1866, m Grover Chandler, who d 1908, at
Andarko, OK. The Holcombs, Nation Builders by McPerson

Cordelia m Charles Reed. Their dau Elizabeth Adams, b San
Francisco, July 21, 1857, d Seattle, Wash, Mar 15, 1928. She
was b Hilldale, MI, May 5, 1831, dau Edward & Elizabeth Adams
(Barnard) Bagley, m (apparently second husband) James E.
Hubbart of Seattle, brother was Walter Reed Bagley (NE Gen
Register) (probably David of Chatham, CT branch)

Cordelia d Dec 10, 1871, ae 35, East Lyme, CT

Cornelius & Joanna, both b Ireland
1. John, d May 11, 1868, ae 65, b Ireland, d Boston

Cornelius & Ellen (Calleghan), both b Ireland
1. John, d Jan 13, 1890, ae 50, b Ireland, d Salem, MA

Cornelius F., b Peabody & Catherine C. Woods, b Ireland
1. Female, d Feb 22, 1911, stillborn

Cornelius & Mary Austin, both b Peabody
1. Male, b Feb 18, 1902, b & d Peabody, MA

Cornelius & Catherine, both b Ireland
1. Marget, d July 9, 1878, ae 2, b & d Boston
2. Female

Cornelius & Mary, both b Ireland,. She d Feb 7, 1902, ae 48,
b Ireland, d Peabody, dau Dennis Kelly, b Ireland.
1. John, d Mar 10, 1879, ae 9 mos, Peabody, MA
2. Julia, d Feb 17, 1881, ae 1 yr, Peabody, MA
3. Margaret, d Mar 26, 1883, ae 1 yr, b & d Peabody, MA

Charles & Abigail, <u>Haverhill, MA or NH</u>, had son Charles, b Nov 20, 1768 NHR

Charles Frank, son Thomas & Ellen Colville, b Nov 27, 1884, Lincoln Co, TN.; Wash. & Lee University ; banker <u>Fayetteville, TN</u>, m Sept 25, 1918, at Nashville, Jemima H. Higgins, dau Mary Hill & Joseph Higgins, b Nov 30, 1893, grad Belmont Col.
1. Charles F., Jr., b Sept 21, 1919, <u>Nashville, TN</u>
2. Jose Higgins, b Jan 28, 1923, (Ebenezer Hill of Mason, NH)

Charles of <u>Manchester, NH</u>, m Adeline P. Noyes Putney. They had son Frank Edson who m at Manchester, NH. Ella Rogers, b July 9, 1858 at Manchester. She d Aug 31, 1908. M Sept 20, 1882

Charles, ae 39, bridge builder, b <u>Rutland, VT,</u> d Jan 25, 1894

Charles R. , 1785, <u>Southington, CT</u>

Charles A., ae 24, Manchester, m Alice M. Pattee, ae 23, at <u>Manchester, NH</u>
Female child, b Jan 2, 1911, <u>Salem, NH</u>

Charles F. & Rose M., of <u>Enfield, NH</u>, sold land Apr 28, 1914, Grafton Co, NH R. Charles L. was sole heir of Rose M., deceased, May 21, 1918

Charles m Elizabeth Stephens. May 27, 1882, <u>Burlington, NJ</u> Court R

Charles F., Jr., b Sept 21, 1919, <u>Nashville, TN</u>, son Charles Frank & Jemima M. Higgins

Charles, son William, Census of 1870, <u>Coxsackie, NY</u>, ae 17, b NY

Charles, ae 21, b NY, son William & Sarah. Census 1850, Sciot, <u>Portage, OH</u>

Charles H. of North Dakota, son Edward, b 1810 & Elizabeth Bennett of <u>Bradford, PA</u>

Charles of <u>Berlin, NH,</u> b Ireland

Charles & Christina (Thomas), both b Ireland
1. Christina T. d Dec 21, 1881, ae 75, b <u>Boston, d Higham, MA</u>

Charles, ae 19, son Edward & Amarilla of <u>NY,</u> Census of 1860

Charles of <u>Cohansey, Salem Co, NY</u> and his wife, Elizabeth:
Jean under age
Sarah under age
Charles under age
Elizabeth   card reads 1699 which must be mistake
Jean
Mary

Charles E., b Bangor, Feb 5, 1854, father Edward, b Herman, ME, and mother Margaret; husband Ellen Ryan, m May 13, 1876, Bangor, ME, Census of 1880 gives
1. Charles E., ae 25
Ellen, ae 26
Charles Fred, ae 2. He d Augusta, ME, Dec 19, 1933

Charles L. m Emma, b Newburyport, MA
1. Charles A., d Jan 7, 1870, ae 2 mos, b & d Newbury, MA

Charles B., Northampton, MA, & Jacqueline Pelletier, b Southbridge had son Joseph, who d Sept 31, 1944, at Worcester, MA

Charles, b 1832, son Josiah & Elizabeth. Census of 1850, OH family from VA

Charles A., son William, b Plattsburg, NY, & Mary Goodsill, b Ireland, d Jane 22, 1936, ae 48, b Springfield, MA, d Agwam, MA; wife was Laura E. Kimache

Charles Edward, son Dennis & Mary E. Lane, b & d Southboro, MA,; m Ida Louise Mourse. He d June 30, 1937, ae 51. She died Aug 20, 1949, ae 64, b & d Southboro. dau Warren C., b Medway, MA, and Carrie Stone, b Shrewsbury, MA

Charles Elmer, ae ,10, b PA, son of James, b VA Census of 1880, PA

Charles N., ae 3, son William A, b Conn, Census of 1880, PA

Charles F., b Berkeley, RI, d Plainville, MA; m Caroline E. Barter. He d Apr 24, 1955, ae 77, son Henry W., Valley Falls, RI, & Sarah D. Potter, b Scituate, RI
1. Henry Reingold, d Mar 4, 1905, ae 3 mos, No Attleboro, MA
2. Bernice Elsie, d Mar 8, 1909, N Attleboro, MA

Charles F., b Dorcester & Nellie A. McCarthy, b Boston
1. Charles, d Boston, Mar 16. 1894, ae 1 dy

Charles of Lowell, MA
1. Charles W., d Aug 23, 1860, ae 10 mos b & d Lowell, MA

Charles N., b Richmond, RI & Emma J. Stodard, b Preston, Conn
1. Lydia W., d Apr 7, 1892, ae 5 MA R

Charles m Helen Crowe, who d Mar 13, 1908, ae 48, b Malden, d Cambridge, MA, parents b Canada & Ireland

Charles D., m Mary Etta McCleary, who d Oct 17, 1926, ae 65, b Red River, Canada, d Haverhill, MA, dau Ans Johnson, b Scotland

Charles, given as ae 24, Census of Bradford, ME, 1880

Charles S or S of Hartland, VT, occupation, golddigger, CA, ae 32, m Helen Dunbar of Hartland, ae 26, Apr 13, 1857

Charles R. & Florence K, of Hanover, NH, sold land Sept 12, 1953, Grafton Co Deeds

Charles, b ME & Mary Baker, b Gloucester, MA, lived St Johnsbury, VT, m at Portland, ME, July 1, 1885, given as b Vinal Haven, ME.
1. Olivia L., b Mar 19, 1891, St Johnsbury, b Richmond, ME; d Mar 20, 1891, ME R
2. Pearl Olive, b Apr 18, 1893, St Johnsbury, VT
3. Edward S., ae 22, b Richmond, ME, m at Dover, NH,. both residing Portland, ME, Louise Houghton, ae 19, dau Fred Houghton & Alice J., of Portland
    a. Female, b Nov 15, 1907, Portland, ME
    b. Alice Houghton, b Feb 22, 1909, Portland, 2nd ch
Charles D., given as b Richmond, ME, living Portland, ME, ae 45, d May 1, 1907 (VT R)

Charles H., b Seabrook, NH, d Salisbury, MA, Apr 15, 1900, ae 37, son Valentine & Elizabeth (Fowler)

Charles L., d Jan 7, 1926, ae 45, b 1881, b ME; d Cambridge, MA, wife Bessie

Charles W. & Elsie Hayward or Maynard of Topsham, VT. She m (2) Sept 9, 1908, at Topsham, ae 30, dau John Hayward & Elvira (Avery), Dau by first m, Eva Bernice , b Apr 4, 1900; d Topsham, VT, Mar 22, 1911. Charles & Elsie were m Aug 26, 1898.

Charles H., b Boston & Mary A., b Stockton, ME
1. Gracie A., d Aug 14, 1874, ae 4 mos, b & d Somerville, MA
2. Marion F., d Boston, July 23, 1882, ae 5 mos

Charles E., b Lebanon, NH & Achasa L. Allen, b Hyde Park, VT. Achasa A. Allen, d Oct 18, 1927, ae 55, b Hyde Park, VT, d Cambridge, MA, dau Leonard & Cynthia (Bassett) b VT
1. Reginald S., d Sept 13, 1913, ae 14, b Greenwood, SC; d Worcester, MA

Charles L. Gardiner, 1895-1917, on large stone in cemetery in East Machias, MA, marked Bagley

Charles H., m Mary C., who d Dec 15, 1909, ae 60, b Searsport, ME; d Boston

Charles, b Searsmont, ME, m Ellen Campbell, b Exeter, NH
1. George C., d Livermore Falls, ME, Feb 12, 1907, ae 27, b Corinth, ME

Charles H., b Boston & Mary C., had Marion F., d July 23, 1882, ae 5 mos, b & d Boston

Charles m Mary, who d July 12, 1906, ae 95, b Eng; d

<u>Cambridge, MA</u>

Capt Charles, Census of 1850, <u>Belfast, ME</u>, ae 50, master mariner

Charles, d Nov 1, 1861, ae 60, ME R

Charles, b Montague & Carrie Wambeck, b N B
1. Female, d May 5, 1931, stillborn, b & d <u>Worcester, MA</u>

Charles, ae 30, millman, b ME, Census 1860, <u>Oldtown, ME</u>

Charlotte m John Edmunds, both of <u>Montville, ME</u>. He d <u>Searsmont, ME</u>, Mar 27, 1841 when she was adm of his estate. He left heirs over 21 yrs old

Charlotte m Charles H. Trott, <u>Providence RI</u>, Dec 19, 1866

Charlotte of Pawtucket, RI, m Joseph W. Miller, Apr 30, 1820, <u>Providence, RI</u>

Christopher m Jan 6, 1820, <u>Topsham, VT</u> (could be born on that date)

Christopher, b NYC, Census of 1790 for <u>Hillsdale, NY</u>

Christopher, 1 - 3, <u>NYC East Ward</u>, Census of 1790

C. J. of <u>Dover, NH</u>, m Mary had
Anna A. of <u>Goffs Falls</u>, who m H. R. Jones of Goffs Falls, NH, June 17, 1868

Clara, dau Michael of <u>Philadelphia, PA</u>, ae 5/12, Census 1880

Clara, dau George & Clara of Lowell, MA, ae 20, m Phineas Whiting, widower of Lowell, ae 28, son Phineas & Sarah, June 26, 1848, <u>Lowell, MA</u>

Claire, dau Francis P. & Ruth of <u>Dorchester, MA</u>., m -----Amidon and lived <u>Stone Mountain, GA</u> in early 1970's when her mother died

Clarence, son Schyler, Census of 1870, <u>New Baltimore, NY</u>, ae 7

Clarissa G. B., m Glendon Washburn, Nov 26, 1936, VT, she dau Edward John Bourdon & Delia E. Ross (must have been Bagley widow)

Clarence, son George Ward & Elizabeth, b May 18, 1860; d Aug, 1860, ae 3 mos, <u>Providence, RI</u>

Clarice H. (Yates); d Oct 3, 1961, ae 78, b Eng, d <u>New Bedford, MA</u>., dau Alfred & Ellen Ashton, both b Eng

Clayton m Mary Madeline Ahern, who d Mar 5, 1934, ae 34, b Rockland, ME; d <u>Holbrook, MA</u>, dau James F., b Ireland &

4.   Julia, d Feb 10, 1884, ae 24, d Peabody, MA

Cornelius & Annie, both b Ireland. He d Sept 5, 1883, ae 55,
b Ireland, d Boston. son Matthew & Mary, both b Ireland
1.   John, d July 2, 1873, ae 1 yr, b & d Cambridge, MA

Daisy, late wife of Torrill A. Nute or Nutt, b 1876

Daniel & Margaret (Sheehan), both b Ireland
1.   Mary, d Aug 9, 1896, ae 45, single, b Ireland, d Boston

Daniel & Mary of Newton, MA, He b Ireland, d Newton, MA, Aug
10, 1858, ae 65
1.   Thomas, b Ireland, d Newton, July 20, 1861, ae 32
2.   Catherine M., d Nov 23, 1870, ae 5 mos, b & d Boston

Daniel J., m Anne Kelley, who d Apr 10, 1951, ae 78, b
Roxbury, d Boston, dau Michael J. & Mary Ryan, both b Roxbury

Daniel & Catherine McDonald, both b Chelsea had son John, b
Chelsea, MA, d Boston, Sept 12, 1956, ae 33.   Catherine, d
Apr 28, 1921, ae 30, b Oct 5, 1890, b & d Chelsea, MA, dau
Alexander & Catherine McMarish, b & d Nova Scotia

Daniel W. Bagley m Mary T. Dodge, both of Bangor, ME, Jan 7,
1859, by George W. Snow. Bangor, ME R

Daniel, son David & Christina Decker, christened Prattsville,
NY Oct 9, 1798 (Daniel of Broom & New Baltimore?)

Daniel E. b Holyoke, MA & Harriet E. Waters, b Westfield MA
1.   Male stillborn, Nov 17, 1910, at Westfield, MA
2.   Edward M., d Mar 22, 1909, ae 14, at Westfield ; gives
father's name as Dennis, but mother's correctly.   Harriet
Waters, d May 13, 1946, ae 72, b & d Westfield, MA, dau
Martin, b Ireland & Ellen Brad, b Hamilton, Ont.

Daniel Bagley, Census of 1850, OH, Ashtabula Co, Conneaut
Clarissa M. ae 9, b PA
James P., ae 6, b PA
Daniel, ae 76, b NY
Elizabeth, ae 76, b NY
Anndy Law, ae 19, farmer, b PA
Andrus, ae 53, b NY
Letta, ae 50, b NY
Sarah Ann, ae 22, b PA
Nancy J., ae 16, b PA all in same household

Daniel witnessed land deed of William Harcum and wife Polly
made by Elisha Harcum, Apr 3, 1790, Northumberland Co, VA

Daniel, son of David & Christine Decker, b Oct 9, 1798, NY

Daniel of Bangor ME, 2nd Regt Inf Civil War

Daniel, b Nov 23, 1837, son Jacob & Sarah M. , b Bangor, ME

Daniel F. m Ellen M. (Goddard), b Spencer, MA, d Worcester, dau Joseph Goddard, b Canada & Mary Powers, b Ireland

Daniel & Nancy Howard, both of Burlington, VT, m Jan 23

Daniel, residing in Hartland, VT, depart this town no return according to law given under hand at Hampton, Sept 29, 1807 (see Ann)

Daniel, son David, b Sept 4, 1818, IL

Daniel, ae 39, Census of Jackson, Union Co, Ohio, 1850
Mary, ae 33
John, ae 10, twin
William, ae 10, twin
Andisa, ae 8
Martha, ae 6
Nancy A., ae 5
Thomas C., ae 2

Daniel, land grant in Montgomery, NY, Nov 19, 1737

Daniel in Schenectady, NY, July 28, 1737

Daniel of Haverhill, m Judith Emerson of Chester, NH, Oct 3, 1816

Daniel m Unes Rider, Nov 2, 1783, 1st Baptist Church at Bangall, Dutchess Co, NY

Daniel William, m Mary Wear Smith, int May 13, 1834, nothing more on Newburyport, MA R, given as Bayley under intentions but Bagley under marriges

Daniel O'Bagley lived ME, dropped the O and went west. Grandson was Gerald A. Bagley, 6745 Sutter Ave, Carmichael, CA

Daniel, b 1741, son of John from Enmg, in Montgomery Co, NY

Daniel m Ethelynn Ruth, May 14, 1939, VT R

Daniel m Katherine McDonald, VT R (son of David?)

Daniel, son of David & Ann Hannah, b Mar 17, 1813, Pittsfield, MA

Daniel, son of John of Watertown, MA, b Dec 1, 1650; mentioned in father's will in 1703

David, d Mar 17, 1897, ae 84, b & d Amesbury, son William and Dorothy, both b Amesbury

David Bagley, private Capt Henry Tiebout's Co, Col Goose Van Scharck's 1st NY Regt; muster roll of Jan-Mar, 1781, dated West Point; reported discharged Mar 18, 1781, in exchange for

William Reede

David, tax payer, First Parish, Falmouth, ME, 1760; see James, Joseph, Joseph, Jr. & William

David, Census of 1790, Hillsdale, NY

David, a seaman from Conn, 1776, Dec

David C., m Thura Baker at St Albans, VT, July 4, 1868, he ae 22, resided Ellensburgh, NY, dates right for David of James, Maine line

David of Hartland, VT and wife, M. E., son of George, b Sept 29, 1868

David, b Ireland, m May Murphy, b Ireland, had son Daniel, b Nov 20, 1861, d May 25, 1938, VT R

David of Plattsburg, NY, served 3 days in Sept, 1814, in company f Capt James George of Topsham, VT, Ref Book, A80, p 67 & 70

David m Ann Hannah
1. Daniel L., b Mar 17, 1813, Pittsfield, MA
2. Asa, b May 5, 1815, Pittsfield, MA
3. John, b Oct 1821, Pittsfield, MA

David, 1 3 1, Woodstock Town, Ulster Co, NY, Census of 1790
David, third son David & Fanny, b Providence, RI, Dec 1, 1861

David, on Census of Ulster Co, NY, 1790, with 4 males under 16

David on Census of 1810 for Scipio, Cayuga Co, NY

David & Polly Cotton, intentions Great Pond Settlement, July 3, 1798, at Alna, ME

David had cider & vinegar works in Niagara Co, 1835, NY

David, son John A. & Prudence, ae 16, Spring twp, Crawford Co, PA Census 1850

David & Lydia Ann both of Pawtucket, RI, m Nov 17, 1821

David m Cornelia Baumhau, Dutch Reformed Church, Claverack, Columbia Co, NY, Sept 27, 1795

David & Christina Decker (see Abner of NY and his wife) had a son Daniel, christened Oct 9, 1798, Prattsville, NY. In same records, Sally Bagley a member

David ae 25, stone cutter, b VA (Census of 1850, Muskingum Co, OH, Salem)
Gilman, ae 20, stone cutter, b VA

Davis of Putnam Co. GA, b 1807, son William & Mary (Runnels),
dau G. Dudley Runnels & Fannie Habert of Caswell Co. NC; Davis
m Martha Pearce. dau of Thomas & his first wife, Betsy
Roberts. Davis moved to Chambers Co, AL, before 1845 as his
son Josephus was b there 1845. From Rufus Beuregard Bagley,
3520 Gilman AVE, Montgomery, AL, 36105, July 31, 1986

David & Dorothy had dau Rhoda W. of Lowell, MA, who m Isaac B.
Chaplin of Dracut, MA, ae 27, a carpenter, son Samuel & Eliza,
May 31, 1846, Lowell, MA

Delia, d Portsmouth, NH, Sept 24, 1894, ae 30, single

Della Elizabeth Quinn, d Jan 16, 1919, ae 63, b Springfield,
IL; d N Attleboro, MA

Della G., m Solomon L. White, she b Mar 12, 1856; he b Sept
Sept 21, 1861, d Sept 21, 1907, Bradford, NH Cemetery

Demetrius H. of Whitefield, NH, whose father Demetrius was b
NC, ae 29, m Leola Nolin, ae 34, b Jefferson, NH, m Aug 21,
1945

Dennis, b Southboro, MA, m Mary E. Lane of Boston
1. William J., d July 7, 1942, ae 55, b & d Southboro
2. Charles Edward, d June 30, 1937, ae 57, b & d Southboro
His wife was Ida Louise Mourse
3. Leo F., d Sept 26, 1918, ae 30, b & d Southboro, a soldier
Ida L. Mourse, d Aug 20, 1949, ae 64, b & d Southboro, dau
Warren C. & Carrie Stone, he b Medway, MA; she Shrewsbury, MA

Dennis & Margaret, both b Ireland
1. Margaret, d Boston, Sept 11, 1881, ae 5

Dennis m Margaret (Garran), who d ae 58, May 11, 1893, at
Boston, b Ireland, dau Michael & Jane O'Malley, both b Ireland

Dennis, b Peabody & Catherine Roach, b Salem
1. Mary F., d Mar 5, 1902, at Peabody, ae 1 yr

Derwood of Lamoni, IA came from Mich, Other relatives, Mrs.
Mary Wright, 214 West 12 Ave, Einfield, IA, and Pearl
Robinson, 2318, So Mead Ave, Wichita, KA

Dolly m Moses Nichols, Mar 9, 1815, Amesbury, MA. She d June
20, 1823, Ames MA R; no children on Ames or Salis MA R

Dolly Bagley m John Colby, Mar 8, 1812, Salisbury, MA.
Children on Salis MA R:
1. Annah Edwards, b Jan 2, 1831
2. Charles Abraham, b Nov 9, 1820
3. Edwin John, b July 31, 1812
4. Elbridge Berry, b May 10, 1815
5. Elizabeth Ann, b Aug 15, 1817
6. John Bagley, b July 28, d Feb 23, 1830
7. Lorentz Spitzenfield, b July 31, 1812

8.   Patrick Henry, b Jan 27, 1826
9.   Sarah Bagley, b June 3, 1823

Dolly Bagley m Moses Nichols Barzin.   Their   dau   Betsey   J.
Barzin, d May 3, 1892, ae 72, at Danvers, MA

Donald B, Sr. of Pine Hill Road, Warren, NH
1.   Daniel Burt
2.   David
3.   Donald, Jr.
Donald Sr's mother was Ruth Bagley of Franklin, and wife's
parents were Mae & Elmer Heath of Warren (I have written twice
to this Donald but received no answer)

Dora, dau Henry of Windham, NY, Census of 1860, ae 1

Dorcas, b Mar 7, 1754; m Richard Gooding, b Feb 14,   1754,
Falmouth, ME, June 30, 1776. Dorcas died Jan 29, 1820; he d
July 30, 1834.
1. Lemuel, who d Sept 28, 1864, Portland, ME; m Sarah
Mitchell, who d Sept 30, 1861, Portland, ME; m Jan 18, 1800.
Lemuel, b Oct 14, 1779, Falmouth; Sarah, dau Solomon Mitchell,
b Aug 2, 1782, North Yarmouth, ME (Desc of Edward Small)

Doris Loise, d Jan 22, 1908, ae 7 mos, b Ames, MA; d Merrimac,
MA

Dorothy m Amos Webster of Rumney, Oct 30, 1847, son Amos of
Plymouth.   She was his third wife, Stearn's History of
Plymouth, NH

Dorothy, d Sept 18, 1778, ae 2, Portland, Conn

Earl H., son Hope & Laura, b Nov 9, 1896, Providence, RI

Edgard, son Elisha, b PA, ae 4, 1880

Edith m William H. Drury, Sept 28, 1929, Montpelier, VT
1.   Their son Bert Stevens, m Emma Royce, VT

Edmund & Esther M. Hazard, m Providence, RI, Aug 15, 1815

Edson Pierce, son James W., b MA & Anna Pierce, m Dorothy
Grammon of Littleton, NH, June 17, 1957, at Littleton.She ae
19, dau Floyd Grammon & Thelma Pierce, she ae 21 NH R

Edward Cartwright, son Alexander T, b Eng & Mary Evans, d Aug
8, 1937, ae 62, b Boston; d Winthrop, MA, wife was Bessie
Louise Colley

Edward S. m Martha Vigren, July 19, 1891, lived Bloomfield,
NE; had large lumber yard; lost everything in Crash of 1929;
living after 1930; Martha d 1916, and he m (2) Marie----, and
they had two daus Alta Marie & ----.   Mrs Marie lived
Lincoln, NE, 1942 and kept boarding house at Univ of NE with
younger dau; older dau Alta Marie away teaching.

Dau of Edward & Martha, Helen Martha Bagley, b Mar 9, 1898, graduate Woods College, Fulton, MO. Teacher in Idaho. Became nurse in 1921, and m J. Harry Mattson, Feb 14, 1922, at San Francisco. They went to Hawaii in 1923 and stayed there. Helen taught school and d Mar, 1938, ae 39. Mattson m again & d July 31, 1968. A dau is Ms Kaiulani Mattson, 1200 14th Ave, San Francisco CA, 94122. Has photos taken in Whitewater, WI & Sandhorn, IA. (Suggests the Samuel line but can't find Edward)

Edward, d Sept 29, 1900, ae 43, b & d Boston, son John & Rosanna, both b Ireland.

Edward James, son William & Mary Goodsill, d Nov 14, 1937, ae 62, b & d Springfield, MA. Wife was Mary Conlin

Edward, b 1810, m Elizabeth Bennett in Bradford, PA.
1. Stephen m Mary Allen; see Stephen for children

Edward M, d Dec 25, 1948, ae 67, b & d Boston, wife Catherine Nugent, son William H, b ME & Mary Lannin, b Ireland

Edward, d Oct 12, 1962, ae 32, b Revere, MA, d Danvers, MA; wife Barbara Dunne, father was Forrest, b ME and mother Elsie Stonewall, b Boston. Edward d Oct 12, 1962, ae 32.

Edward J., d Mar 28, 1901, ae 21, b & d Malden, MA, son Thomas, b Montreal & Annie Campbell, b Providence, RI

Edward F. & Hazel Boyle, both b Lowell, MA
1. Male, Apr 28, 1954, stillborn at Brockton, MA

Edward H. & Mary Jones of Gardiner, ME, m Oct 12, 1827

Edward LKPA, p 179, Census of 1850, OH

Edward J., m Angela Kennedy, both b Foxboro, MA
1. Female, d Feb 26, 1954, ae 2 hrs, Attleboro, MA

Edward J., d Apr 19, 1947, ae 46, b Dedham, d Boston, son William Vincent, b Dedham & Mary Ann Taylor, b Ireland

Edward Francis, ae 43, 2nd m, m Hazel LeCourt, ae 34, 2nd m, dau William Boyle & Cecilla Van Court, Apr 14. Son Patrick & Margaret Cassidy of Lowell, MA

Edward, Census of 1790, Hillsdale, NY, gives 1-1-4

Edward, ae 45, hotel keeper, Hamden, NY, all children b Delaware Co, NY, Census of 1860
Amarilla, ae 44
Mary, ae 23
Charles, ae 19
Augustan, ae 18
Imogene, ae 16
Alfred, ae 14

Arthur, ae 12

Edward of <u>Charlestown, MA</u>, son John, d Jan 19, 1851

Edward & Della Ashley of <u>Concord, NH</u>
Pauline, d Manchester, Aug 19, 1897, ae 3 mos

Edward, b <u>NH</u>
William C., d July 4, 1926, ae 46, b <u>Haverhill, d North
Hampton</u>, wife Pearl Hyde (doesn't say whether, NH or MA)

Edward R., b <u>St Johnsbury, VT</u>, son Frank or Franklin & Melissa
Rowell, ae 25, m July 1, 1893, Lizzie Goring, 18, dau Turser
Young of Franklin, m Elvira Ashley of <u>Concord, NH</u>

Edward of <u>Manchester NH & Lowell, MA</u>; m Emelia, who d Lowell,
MA, Mar 12, 1912, ae 50

Edward F., b Lowell, 25 & Emma D. Leachout, b Ludington, Mich
1.   Edward F., Jr., b Jan 31, 1936, <u>Nashua, NH</u>
2.   Amelia Janet, b Feb 13, 1938, <u>Milford, NH</u>

Edward & Mary
1. Maria, b <u>Providence RI</u>, Oct 4, 1855

Edward, son Peter, d <u>Providence RI</u>, Jan 7, 1866, ae 2 and 3
mos
Edward, son of Peter, d Providence, RI, Nov 21, 1869, ae 5 mos

Edward N., d May 24, 1934, ae 53, <u>MA</u>

Edward & Elizabeth
1. Asa, b May 13, 1745, <u>Salem, NH</u>

Edwin, b Boston, m Mary Russell, b NFL
1. Male, d <u>Boston</u>, Jan 19, 1897, ae 10 dys

Edwin S., b Medway, ME & Charlotte Aldrich, m May 18, 1883, ae
30, she b New Bruns.. He given as son John & Mary (Ashley) m
<u>Derby, VT</u>

Effie of <u>Seabrook, NH</u>, m Charles Fowler, son Wilbur 1893, at
Seabrook, suggests Morris Bagley's wife Effie Fowler

Effie Laurette, dau James of <u>PA, b VA</u>, ae 6, 1880

Effie, dau Mary of <u>Carbondale , Lack. Co PA</u>, ae 7, 1880 (try
Orlando of Brooklyn line)

Effue ? Bill, ae 12, possibly son John of <u>Green, PA, 1880</u>

Elaine, dau Francis Murphy & Henrietta Jones, b <u>Cohoes, NY</u>, ae
34, m (2) Manchester, Vt, Feb 20, 1942, Warren Fonda

Eleanor N. of <u>Haverhill, MA</u>, Will, dated Feb 15, 1896 with
codicil dated Apr 29, 1896. Niece Ellen E. Allen of Hudson

MA, Essex Co MA Probate R

Eli m Eunice Goodrich, b May 20, 1793, <u>Hamden, Delaware Co.
NY.</u> Ae 67 1860 Census
1. Church, b 1818, d Dec 30, 1835, ae 17 (See Edward of
Hamden; he may be son of Eli)

Elias, 1867, William C. Potter, Adm

Elijah, d Feb 19, 1801, <u>Craftsbury, VT</u>   (Have him in as a
posible in main line)

Elisha, ae 26, b <u>Tioga, Tioga Co, NY</u> (Census of 1880 for <u>PA</u>)
Sarah J., ae 25, b PA
Edgard, son, ae 4
May, dau, ae 3

Elisha & Louise Daniel
James, b 1841 at <u>Pittsfield, ILL,</u> d about 1862, at Pittsfield.
Family probably came from <u>VA</u>, supplied by Thomas Jones cousin
in 1877

Elisha & Sarah
1. Jennie, b May 1881, m Charles Deming (apparently <u>NY</u>)

Eliza (Farell), d Mar 13, 1898, ae 66, b <u>Quebec, d Boston, dau</u>
Michael, b Ireland

Eliza (Dunn) & Matthew she d Feb 18, 1879, ae 72, b <u>Ireland, d
Boston,</u> dau James & Eliza, both b Ireland

Eliza E., b 1835, dau Josiah & Elizabeth, Census of 1850 <u>OH,</u>
family came from VA

Eliza of Newton, MA, m John Sargent of <u>Newton,</u> Oct, 1812,
Newton (This should probably by NH as on NH R)

Eliza M. m Charles Worthen of <u>Salisbury, MA,</u> Feb 22, 1868, at
<u>Exeter, NH</u>

Eliza of <u>Braintree</u> m Capt Stephen Salisbury, intentions, Aug
13, 1831, Weymouth MA R (probably Samuel line)

Eliza, Aug 5, 1877, <u>Hamden, Conn</u> (probably death)

Eliza, m Stephen Milborn, b Oct 11, 1796, son Ambrose & Sarah
(Whitman), Sept 1, 1831. Desc John Whitman of <u>Weymouth, MA)</u>

Elizabeth A., d Mar 8, 1959, ae 89, d <u>Boston, b San Francisco,</u>
dau Daniel & Sarah Smith

Elizabeth, dau John of <u>Watertown,</u> b June 18, 1657, m John
Stearns, Jr. Mentioned in father's will in 1703

Elizabeth, m John Burtine, Feb 25, 1774, <u>NY marriages</u>
1. Sarah, b Augm 1775 NYC

Elizabeth J, dau William, b Conn, Census of 1880 PA

Elizabeth Gregg, dau Henry of Green, PA, ae 20, 1880

Elizabeth, dau Joseph & Mary of Portsmouth, m Frank Varney of Portsmouth, Jan 17, 1867; another record says Jan 20, 1866

Elizabeth M, d Sept 1, 1897, ae 2 mos, b & d Lynn, MA, dau John F, b Peabody & Agnes Crowley, b New Bruns

Elizabeth of Raymond, m Samuel V. Osgood about 1852, at Raymond, NH

Elizabeth, dau John & Caroline, b Sept 9, 1826, m Jan 1, 1855, Hiram, son Calvin & Caroline (Richer) Tuttle, b Mar 30, 1833. Farmer at Smith Mills, Chautauqua, NY
1. Frank Deward, b Dec 29, 1858

Elizabeth m David Cole of Clinton, ME, intentions, Sept 29, 1838, Clinton, ME

Elizabeth, ae 20, m Thomas Enright, ae 25, of Lowell, MA, June 2, 1848

Elizabeth (Bayler), intentions, & Gideon Lowell, m Nov 20, 1777, Ames MA, Second Church. No children on Ames or Salis MA R, Another record gives Nov 20, 1776

Elizabeth & Nicholas Saragent, m Feb 16, 1819, Ames MA.   A Nicholas, d Oct 17, 1842, ae 59. No children Ames or Salis MA R

Elizabeth of Amesbury, MA, Anne T. Plaisted petitions herself to be adm of estate as only next of kin of Deceased, Nov 5, 1900, Essex Co MA Probate R

Elizabeth Badgerley, ae 20, b OH Census of 1850 OH, Brown Co, Eagle Springs
Adaline Badgerly, ae 8, b OH
David Badgerly, ae 4, b OH
All in household of William Obertaker, ae 35, b KY and Sarah Obertaker, ae 45, b VA

Elizabeth, at Chittenton, VT, b Canada, d July 20, 1874

Ella (Saunders), m Frank E. She d Nov 6, 1952, ae 85, d Williamsburg, MA, b Westville, NY, dau John M. & Maria E. Bronson

Ella May, b Jonesboro, m Samuel E. Lord, b Whiting, ME
1. Lawson Edwin, b Apr 22, 1915, Jonesboro, 1st Ch, d Jonesboro, ME, Aug 15, 1915

Ella, d NY Greene Co, Sept 23, 1892, sister of Mary J. Bourke

Ella, dau Henry of Bedford PA, ae 4, 1880

Ellen, widow of Haverhill. Hard Bagley apt adm of her estate,
May 13, 1924, Essex Co MA Probate R

Ellen, wife Patrick had guardian appt. Guardian was William
Bagley, June 1, 1915; husband living, Essex Co MA Probate R

Ellen, m Horace H. Hie (Hite?) St Johnsbury, VT, Oct 20, 1859

Ellen M., widow Joseph, b Ireland, d Brunswick, ME, Mar 30,
1902, ae 78

Ellen (Donahue), d Apr 2, 1885, ae ?5, b Ireland, d Monson, MA

Ellen (Dailey), d Brockton, MA, Oct 14, 1882, ae 52

Ellen H., dau Frederick & Almira, St Johnsbury, VT, Census of
1860, gives ae 11, b 1849

Ellen given as ae 43 on Bangor, ME Census 1880. In same
household is Annie A. Bagley, ae 20

Elmeda, ae 7, female, b Freen, Ind Co, PA, enumerated with
John Bagley

Elmer J., m Mae Tilton, she d Oct 17, 1957, ae 80, b Groveton,
MA; d Haverhill, dau Newton & Harriet (Carleton)

Elsie, dau Henry of Bedford, PA, ae 11/12, b PA, 1880

Elvira of Salisbury, MA, widow, granted to Albert Follensbee
of Woburn, MA, May 19, 1884, Essex Co MA R

Elvira of Barre, VT, m David Bradbury, Oct 14, 1867, at
Montpelier, VT

Elvira T., m Lt Levi Pillsbury, at New Ipswich, NH, Sept 15,
1842, NHR (Try Nathaniel of New Ipswich)

Elycum & Judith, 1st to arrive after the Mayflower. Elycum
went to Boston. Jonathan & Samuel stayed in Boston,
Worcestershire, Eng

Emaline m Thomas Peckham, Dec 28, 1837, NY marriages

Emelia, d Lowell, MA, Mar 12, 1912, ae 50, prev res
Manchester, NH, wife Edward Bagley, NHR

Emeline Bagley, m George Rowe

Emily Sawtelle, d Jan 1, 1881, ae 50, b Turner, ME, d
Stoughton, MA, dau John & Lucinda, both b Turner, ME. Second
death certificate gives parents as Joseph, b Bridgewater, NH &
Ellen M., b Cambridge, MA

Emily of <u>Greeneville, Green Co, NY</u> sold land in Catskill, Feb 3, 1897 and Apr 1, 1881

Emma, dau William N. & Catherine, b Taunton, MA, d Nov 9, 1853, ae 13 mos, <u>Providence, RI</u>

Emma & Gertrude, minors, <u>Chelsea, VT,</u> Jan 21, 1936

Emma, ae 18, b 1852, dau Nathan of <u>New Baltimore, NY,</u> Census of 1870

Emma, dau John & Susan, ae 4, Census of 1880 for <u>PA</u>

Emma C, m Fred A. Smith, Dec 25, 1904, at <u>Randolph, VT</u>

Emma Jane Ramsdell, d Mar 15, 1928, ae 76, d <u>Norfolk, MA,</u> b <u>Charlestown, MA,</u> dau Ramsdell, b NH & Eunice Roby, b Danbury, NH

Emmanuel, son John & Jane, both b <u>Eng, d Fall River,</u> MA, Apr 28, 1898, ae 42, b Eng. His wife was Clara A., b Eng.
1. Annie, d Dec 14, 1881, at Fall River, as 8 mos

Emory R. of <u>Maxfield, ME</u> & Mrs Frances Emerson of Howland, ME, m Mar 13, 1862, at <u>Atkinson, ME</u>

Enoch, <u>Amesbury, MA,</u> 1810 Census; 1M-10; 1M 15-20; 2M 20-30; 1M 30-40; 1F 10-15; 2F 15-20; 1F 20-30

Enos & Patience
1. Augustus, b Oct 2, 1796, <u>Sullivan, NH</u>

Ephraim, b Oct 1, 1837, <u>Hampstead, NH</u>

Eric m Nettie L. Wright, who d Oct 9, 1931, ae 78, b <u>Troy, ME,</u> <u>d Boston;</u> dau Isaac, b Gigton, ME & Abigail, b Troy

Ernest Page, d Apr 5, 1923, ae 3 mos, b <u>Amesbury, MA,</u> son Valmore Page & Betsey Bagley, she b <u>Milford,</u> he b Upton, MA

Ernest, b Springfield, MA & Catherine, b Agwam, MA
1. Ernest J., d July 2, 1912, ae 3 mos, b & d <u>Springfield, MA</u>

Estelle, d Nov 4, 1911, ae 4 mos, b <u>Nashua, NH, d Boston,</u> dau Alice Bagley, b <u>Lowell, MA</u>

Esther m Edwin Lannon of <u>Middlebury, VT,</u> Feb 18, 1821

Esther, dau Isaac & Lizzie, <u>Bedford, PA,</u> ae 7, 1880

Ethel M, dau George R. & Mary Lowell, m George Hanna at <u>Cabot,</u> <u>VT,</u> Feb 12, 1927, ae 49, 1st m

Ethel C., dau Frank of <u>Gloucester, MA,</u> m Alfred Ireland

Etta M., m Alfred M. Morrill of <u>Amesbury, MA.</u> Tombstone in

Amesbury, MA, gives his dates as 1875-1921; hers as 1875-1931

Eunice of Plainfield, NH, m George Gould of Hillsboro, NH, dau
Harriet H. Frink, m Joseph Marshall of Lempster, her second m

Eunice Gibbs & Thomas L., She d Oct 16, 1962, ae 66, b
Plattsburg, NY, d Chelsea, MA, dau Peter, b Canada

Eva H. Hodgdon, d Feb 8, 1950, ae 75, b Lawrence, MA, d
Haverhill, NH, husband Frederick E., dau Charles G., b
Meredith, NH & Helen Wentworth, b S Berwick, ME

Eva M. of Springfield, VT, d ae 31, Oct 16, 1918, b Chelsea,
MA, father Joseph Keyzer, mother Ida M. Whynot

Evaline, d June 4, 1860, b & d Boston, dau Benjamin, b Boston
& Evaline, b S Reading, MA

F. James, given as ae 7, Census of 1880 for Howland, ME,
living in family of Marseilles & Nellie Plummer

F. Harry divorced from Florence, May , 1929, Bangor, ME

Faye of Newbury, VT, m Mary Eddy, Dec 12, 1811, Chelsea, VT

Fenton, attorney, Zanesville, OH, Newton, Twp, Muskegum Co,
Oct 10, 1838, enl in 78th OH Vol. In Nov, 1861, discharged
Aug 1862, commissioned 1st Lt, May 1864

Ferdinand, d Nov 10, 1955, ae 50, b Southboro, MA, d
Marleboro, MA, son Thomas H. of Carleton 7 Mary A. Carriagn, b
Westboro, MA

Fernald, son James F. , Argyle, ME, & Winifred Stimbles m
Orano, ME, Feb 10, 1934, son Edward Howard & Bertie Sherrer

Fernald S., ae 23, in 1934, b Newton, MA, m Gladys M. Howard,
ae 22, b Ruegelsville, PA
1. Alberta Winifred, b Southeast Harbor, ME, Sept 24, 1934,
1st ch

Feric Field, b Jan 28, 1899, son Rev A. W. of Jefferson, OH,
who m Oct 13, 1897, Edith Field, dau Dexter & Eliza Assity,
she b May 26, 1872

Florence Bagley, Will, 1934, Braintree, VT

Flora E., m Lafayette Jerome, b Warren, VT, m Nov 25, 1895, ae
34

Forrest, b ME & Elsie Stonewall, b Boston
1. Edward, d Oct 12, 1962, ae 32, b Revere, MA, d Danvers,
MA; wife Barbara Dunne

Forrest G. m Tida Peer, who d Aug 31, 1943, ae 55, b Dover,
NJ, d Boston, dau George & Nellie of Dixon, NJ

Frances J. m Joseph E. Rice, Apr 1850, Randolph, VT

Frances Jackson, d Feb 2, 1949, ae 47, b Salem, MA, d Lynn, husband, William W., dau John, b Salem & Mary Dupree

Francis P. of 53 Hamilton St, Dorchester, MA, m Ruth, who died at Chester, NH, early 1970. She was 58. She given as native of Boston and had lived in Dorchester & Chester. Family is given as three daus: Mrs. Claire Amidon of Stone Mountain, GA; Mrs Joan Davis of Derry; Miss Ruth Bagley of Chester. Sons: James J. Bagley of Chester & Robert J. Bagley of Dover, NH. Sister Mrs Henrietta Duffey of CA

Rev Francis H. m Isabella Lee Van Rennsselaer, dau Stephen & Amanda Strong, Mar 7, 1826

Francis G. m Cook Co, ILL. History of Cook Co, says he married at bride's father's place

Francis M., b May 15, 1841, East Liverpool, OH, d Sept 4, 1901, father William in Civil War

Francis E., ae 2, Census of 1850, Belfast, ME, household of John P.

Frank G. & Catherine Gary, who d at Boston, b Boston, Aug 26, 1898, ae 29, dau Jeremiah & Johanna Minnehan, both b Ireland, given as Carney
1. Mary, d Feb 6, 1897, ae 1 dy Boston

Frank m Joanne Tillymans, both b Foxboro, MA
1. Male, d May 26, 1959, ae 1 dy at Attleboro, MA

Frank & Mary his wife, Josephine H. Lusk & Adaline Hallock, all of Greeneville, Greene Co, NY, sold land in that town. Harry Bagley was notary public. Those signing deed: Stanley Vincent, Catskill, NY; J. Everett Vincent & Ann, his wife, Islip, NY; Ansel M. Elliott, Ludlow, Kenton Co, KY; Augusta M. Elliott, Ludlow, Kenton Co, KY; and Adaleine H. Elliott, Ludlow, Kenton Co, KY

Frank & Julia Leary, both b Boston
1. Francis, d May 12, 1907, ae 3 mos, Boston

Frank J. m Nellie V. Leary, who d Oct 13, 1951, ae 80, b Bridgewater, d Boston

Frank G., ae 1, son George & Emma, b Bedford, PA, ae 1 in 1880

Frank B. Bagley's land in Durham, NY mentioned in estate of Peter Snyder of Greenesville, NY, Mar 31, 1899

Frank B., Amesbury, MA m Sarah E. Cook, b Brunswick
1. Sydney Gilbert, d Sept 10, 1898, ae 1 yr, b & d Amesbury, MA

Frank Edson, son Charles of <u>Manchester, NH</u> & Adeline P. Noyes
Putney m at Manchester, Sept 20, 1882, Ella Rogers, b July 9,
1858, at Manchester, who d Aug 31, 1908

Frank Vaughan, son George F. of <u>Woonsocket, RI</u>, and Margaret,
ae 22, student, m June Cook, dau Leslie Cook & Ingeborg John,
Apr 17, 1953, a Greenville, NH

Frank, 50, b Bangor, ME, and Melissa Rowell, m <u>Bradford, VT,</u>
Oct 7, 1855. Estate of J. Franklin Bagley of <u>Newbury, VT</u> was
probated 1922, He d Andover, NH, lived there 10 yrs, previous
residence Bradford, VT, d Sept 15, 1912, ae 82, b Wheelock,
VT, Nov 15, 1830, widower, son George, b Bow, NH, hotel keeper
and Miss Mills, b Bow, NH, NH R
1. Edward R. ae 25, b <u>St Johnsbury, VT,</u> m July 1, 1893,
Lizzie A. Goring, ae 18, dau Turner Young of Franklin & Elvira

Frank M., Co G. 9th Regt VT Vol Inf, b <u>Haverhill, NH,</u> farmer,
enl. June 3, 1862, at <u>Bradford, VT,</u> apt 3rd sgt, July 1, 1862,
2nd sgt, Mar 26, 1863,prisoner of war, mustered out June 13,
1865; promoted 1st sgt, Mar 1, 1865, detached service.
Child's Gazateer says he was from <u>Topsham, VT</u>

Frank N. of <u>Lynn, MA,</u> d July 9, 1883. Charles Burdette of
Boston, adm of estate, Essex Co MA R

Frank B., ae 39, farmer, b KY
Nancy J., ae 26, b Ind
Robert Thomas, ae 31, b KY same house
Edward Cavanaugh, ae 26, b Ind, same house
Census of 1870 for town 11 Range, 5 postoffice, <u>Siuard, IL</u>

Frank F., b Dec 29, 1860, d Jan 18, 1901, buried <u>Detroit
Lakes, MI</u>
Lena , b Jan 13, 1868, d Jan 31, 1939, she bt lot
Annette, b Feb 8, 1870, d Nov 13, 1913
Eay F., b Oct 20, 1871; d Nov 13, 1918

Frank E. widower of <u>Gloucester, MA,</u> d Oct 30, 1927; grandson
Harold F. Blake of Gloucester; daus Nettie M. Andrews, widow
of Chester Andrews and Ethel C. Ireland, widow of Alfred
Ireland, of Salem, MA

Frank, b <u>Barre, VT,</u> m Mary Wilson
1. Joseph, d July 16, 1955, ae 42, b & d <u>Boston,</u> wife
Catherine Mallou

Frank, b <u>Amesbury</u> & Mary, b Newburyport
1. Mary A., d Dec 1, 1877, ae 5, b <u>Lawrence,</u> d <u>Haverhill, MA</u>

Frank, b Whiting, ME m Mattie McLaughlin
1. Female, 1st ch, b May 11, 1895, <u>Whiting, ME</u>

Frank, son Benjamin & Hannah Harding, d Aug 30, 1887, ae 30, b
<u>Dixmont, ME,</u> d <u>Somerville, MA;</u> Hannah b Troy, ME

Fred E., d 1921, son Jonathan & Helen of Merrimac, MA

Fred Eastman, b Concord, NH., Jan 21, 1885, d Nashua, NH, Aug 14, 1945, son Jonathan of Haverhill, MA & Addie or Abigail Eastman. Will, Nov 12, 1941, mentions wife. Adm was Eva Augusta Bagley, Oct 3, 1945

Fred Bagley of Concord, m Charlotte Wright, live-long res of Concord. She d there Aug 21, 1933, ae 50, b Concord, 1883, dau William Wright, b Ireland & Jane Campbell, b Ireland

Frederic Charles (See Charles Frederick), m Ruth Robinson of Augusta, ME, ae 31, dau George & Gertrude Staples (Cole), June 20, 1927. She divorced previous husband named Stearns.
1. Eleanor Bertrude, b Augusta, ME, Oct 1, 1929

Frederick, d Oct 4, 1915, ae 29, b Waukegan, IL, d Norwood, MA, son Frederick P., b Detorit and Grace Hodges, b Champaign, ILL
Frederick P., d Oct 29, 1933, ae 73, b Detroit, MI, d Boston, MA, wife Grace Hodges, an ink manuf, son George Bagley & Caroline Philips, b b Detroit. Grace d Aug 22, 1944, ae 84, b Campaign, IL, d Boston, dau Leonard, b Richmond, VT & Almeia Murphy, b Mt Vernon, OH

Frederick G. was referee in court action about land mortgage in Greene Co, NY, Apr 3, 1893

Frederick, d Andover, NH, Potter Place, res 38 yrs, prev res Claremont, d 1936, July 29, ae 70, b Bradford, VT, Mar 21, 1866, RR section; son Franklin P. Bagley, b Wheelock, VT & Melissa Rowell, b Bradford, VT

Frederick E. m Eva A. Hodgdon who d Feb 8, 1950, ae 75, b Lawrence, d Haverhill, MA., dau Charles G., b Meredith, NH & Helen Wentworth, b S Berwick, ME

Frederick, ae 48, Census of 1860 for St Johnsbury, Caledonia Co, VT
Almira, ae 47
Anne E., ae 20
Mary, ae 15
Ellen H., ae 11
Jane, ae 7

Frederick & Kate
1. Stillborn infant, Mar 4, 1879, Plymouth, VT

Frederick & Bridget
1. Thomas, b Portland, ME, Nov 18, 1863
2. Catherine, b Portland, ME, Feb 12, 1866

Frederick of Westwood, MA, m Catherine Bodell
1. Frederick Hunter, Jr., ae 28, m Anne Barry Hawes of Westwood, MA, ae 24,, dau Frederick Barry & Rachel Grinnell, m

Frederick, b Eng & Eliza Phinney, b Canada
1. Female stillborn at <u>Salem, MA</u>, Feb 6, 1894

Freelove & Luther Stockwell, m May 5, 1805, at <u>Shaftsbury, VT</u>

Freeman, d Sept 1, 1801, ae 18, at <u>Boston</u>. Record of deaths
in Boston & Vicinity

Gaultia of <u>St Johnsbury</u>, m Aaron Smith of <u>Danville</u>, VT, July
27, 1882, dau Thomas Hill of Colebrook, NH

Bena L., b Jan 16, 1899, dau William Scott & Ellen Stone, De
<u>Kalb Co, NY</u>

Genevieve, dau Thomas F. & Mary of <u>Providence, RI</u>, b Aug 17,
1899

George of <u>Blackstone, RI</u> m Elizabeth Nichols of Boston. She d
Feb 21, 1921, ae 20, b Boston, d Blackstone, dau William &
Bridgett, both b MA
1. John E., d Nov 28, 1942, ae 23, b Blackstone, d Boston.
Wife, Olive W.

George A., <u>Charleston, ME</u>, Civil War, Co D, 2nd ME Cavalry, d
Aug 24, 1864; buried veterans cem in FLA.   Susbstituted for
Leland F. Brigham

George D., d Apr 28, 1942, ae 70, b <u>Braintree, d Weymouth, MA</u>,
son Timothy & Rosa, both b ME.   His wife Mary Elizabeth
Wilson, d Feb 1, 1958, ae 69, b Kenswick, Eng, dau William &
Margaret Tyson, both b Eng

George E., m Margaret Woodward, who d Mar 27, 1943, ae 63, b
<u>ME, d Boston</u>, dau Arthur, b Mason & Jennie Monroe, b Nova
Scotia

George F., b Cranston, RI m Alma Johnson, b E Greenwich, RI
1. Charles F., d Dec 4, 1909, at <u>Taunton, MA</u> ae 1 dy

George m Claudia. He d Aug 20, 1947, ae 64, b <u>Providence, RI,
d Boston</u>, son Thomas & Eleanor Harveley, both b Eng

George, d July 1, 1887, ae 24, mariner, b & d <u>Boston</u>, son John
& Mary, both b Ireland

George F., d Aug 20, 1863, ae 24, b & d <u>Boston</u>, son George D.,
b Nova Scotia

George V., b 1843; on same record with Jane, dau William H.
and Jane E. and Nelson, son of Moses & Abigail, but may have
no relationship

George D., d Apr 28, 1942, ae 70, <u>Braintree, d Weymouth, MA</u>, m
Mary E. Wilson. He was son of Timothy & Rosa M, b ME

143

George, d Feb 27, 1917, ae 23, d Milford, MA, soldier, son Hattie & John, both b Worcester, MA

George & Lucy Dow
1. Maggie Dow Bagley who m Leon Sawyer at Bradford, VT, July 21, 1900, ae 21

George, d Jan 12, 1902, at Leominster, MA, son Thomas P. & Mary A. (Kennedy)

George H. ae 9, b PA, son of Samuel of Bedford PA, 1880

George, son William of Green, PA, 1880, ae 6

George W., b Eng, m Jessie Williams, b Wales. He was 40, she 31
1. William, 1st ch, b Claremont, NH, Oct 7, 1922

George & Clara
1. Clara of Lowell, MA, ae 20, m Phineas Whiting, widower of Lowell, MA, ae 28, son Phineas & Sarah, June 26, 1848, Lowell, MA

George A. & Mary Perkins
1. Sarah Louise, b Aug 22, 1861 in VT

George H., lived Rindge, NH, 2 yrs prev res Lowell, MA. Buried Lowell, d May 13, 1908, ae 47, single

George R., b VT, m Mary Lowell, b VT
1. Ethel M. m George Hanna at Cabot, VT, Feb 12, 1927, ae 49, first m

George H., 1863-1924, Meredin, CT

George W., b Chelsea, VT, b 1843, see Alexander T, of Jane dau William H. & Jane E.

George Bagley of VT, will probate June 5, 1882

George W., son John A. & Prudence, ae 7, b PA, Spring Twnsp, Crawford Co, PA

George Washington, m Sarah Musey, m Providence, RI, Mar 4, 1849

George Ward & wife Elizabeth
1. Clarence, b Providence, RI, May 18, 1860

George, ae 32, b Bedford (Baydstown, Bedford Co PA)
Emma C, ae 31, b PA
James B., ae 10, b PA
Hattie J., ae 8, b PA
Frank 0., ae 1, b PA

George F., Woonsocket, RI, b MA, m Margaret Vaughan of
Blackstone, MA.
1. Frank Vaughan, m June Cook, dau Leslie Cook & Ingeborg
Johnson, Apr 17, 1953, at Greenville, NH; a student

George Rodney, b abt 1836, Fowler, IL; d Jan 27, 1906, Purdin,
MO, m Oct, 1861, Ellen Jean Chase, b Apr 23, 1844, Paloma, IL,
d Apr 12, 1865, at Fowler, father David W. Chase, mother Lydia
Tomlinson
1. Carrie Evelyn, b Sept 13, 1862, Fowler, IL; m Alvin A.
Dewey
2. Lydia Ellen, b Sept 13, 1863, Fowler, IL, m William Kramer
(supplied by James Tomlinson, uncle in law)

George (third husband), m Eleanor Folsom, dau Jeremiah & Polly
Rand, b 1822, d 1854
1. Major (Folsom Genealogy) probably Exeter, NH

George W., Skaneatiles, NY, m Rebecca Sherman of Sennett, NY,
Oct 12, 1849

George
1. Carrie, who m William Edson, Oct 22, 1873, Pomfret, VT, ae
18, b Grafton, VT

George
1. Aaron, Erie Co, PA, ae 4, 1880

George, ae 29, b Philadelphia, PA, Census 1880
Emma, wife, ae 26, b PA
Sarah, ae 7, b PA
Mary, ae 4, b PA
Laura, ae 2, b PA
George, Jr., ae 2/12, b PA

George H., m Margaret, 5th ch of Jane Hamilton & James
Latimer. James L. & Jane H., m June 6, 1803 and moved to TX
in 1833. Jane Hamilton was 2nd ch of James Hamilton & Jane
Gwinn who were m Gilford County, NC. He d Carroll County, TN,
having had 12 children.
(Calhoun, Hamilton & Related Families)

George W., ae 19, d July 8, 1844, at St Albans, VT

George A., & Mary R.
1. Mary C., m John Knowlton, Dec 12, 1867, Springfield, VT

George, son Daniel of Scholarie Co, NY, 1855

George, Rev soldier from Salisbury, NH (History of Salisbury
by Dearborn) I think these must be Bayleys

George H., m Mary Jennie Stratton, ded by 1893, She later m
Paul Kelly of Northumberland, NH, May 15, 1880, dau Horace
Stratton of Northumberland, NH.

1. Edna, b Strafford, m George Stoddard of Columbia, Sept 30,
1886, went to Canada
2. George Ezra, b about 1871, Strafford, NH (probably the
George E. Strafford, b June 23, 1871, d Concord, NH, July 29,
1947; m (1) Abbie Tibbetts of Bath, ME, ae 21, b Southport,
ME, dau Alexander & Sarah (Hawley), Aug 6, 1893; m (2) Nea
Edmonds ?, b Guiildhall, VT, Sept 16, 1860, d Portland, ME,
Aug 26, 1947, dau John Hopkins & Margaret Lyford).
a. Ruby B., b Oct 2, 1896, Southport, ME, 1st ch
b. Harriet G., b Apr 14, 1899, Bath, ME, d Sept 6, 1899, 2nd
ch
c. Myrtle, b Aug 1, 1900, Bath, ME, 3rd ch, drowned in 1931
at Portland, ME, called herself Gladys & m a Parker
d. Georgie Gertrude, b Jan 26, 1910, Portland, ME, m 1933, Dr
Westbury Thomas, d 1948; m (2) George Barstow. They were
divorced and remarried, Dec 24, 1912

George, Jr., son George of Philadelphia, ae 2/12, 1880

George, ae 9, b 1861, son Nelson of New Baltimore, NY, Census
of 1870

George MGVK, p 82, Census of 1850, OH

George E., 1852-1920 & Ardella M., wife, 1848-1923, buried
Rockport, ME., does not appear to go with H. Augustus line.
On same lot is Sarah Corthell, dau William & Susan, and Abby
Benjamin F.

Georgianna, d Littleton, NH, Nov 15, 1959, ae 49, prev res
Laconia, b Apr 1, 1909, m , dau Clavin Hancel, b Canada,
farmer, & Hattie Seymore, b Westfield, VT, body removed to
Meredith, NH

Georgie E. Bagley Ayers, 1864-1933, Newburyport, MA Cem

Gertrude & Emma, minors, Chelsea, VT, Jan 21, 1936

Gideon, who lived Albany, VT
1. Marie May, b Apr 28, 1881; d Sept 26, 1889 (May be 885,
Vol 1

Glen Arthur, d Aug 31, 1942, ae 3 mos, b Norwood, d
Tewksbury, MA, son Louis C., b Norwood & Dorothy Sutpher, b
Newark, NJ

Grace M., of Littleton, sold land, May 25, 1931, Grafton Co NH
deeds

Grace had child, b Gerrish NH county farm, b & d same day,
June 8, 1936, 2nd ch, father unknown. Grace was b Littleton,
NH, ae 31; d Boscawen, NH, prev res Concord, June 8, 1936, ae
31, county farm

Grange L., b c 1816, Lunenburg Co, VA, m there May 11, 1841,
Cornelia Edwards, b c 1820

Grant A., d Aug 14, 1874, ae 4 mos, b & d <u>Somerville, MA</u>, son Charles H., b Boston & Mary A., b Stockton, ME (not sure of first name)

Gretche Susanne, b May 14, 1934, at Berne, IN, dau Harmon & Josephine (Reusser) at <u>Berne, IN</u> (may be d)

H. J. of <u>Dixmont, ME</u>, m Julia A. Jewell of Jackson, ME, May 10, 1866, at Jackson.

HBC, b <u>ME</u> & Elvith Greene b ME,
1. Julia Joseph, d June 10, 1871, ae 28, b Boston, d <u>Cambridge, MA</u>

Hannah m Holdridge Hiel, July 4, 1845, <u>St Albans, VT</u>

Hannah m Zebulon Winslow at <u>Loudon</u>, Mar 31, 1766, NH

Hannah Nichols Bagley, b Feb 1, 1831, dau Will & Hannah Nichols Bagley. m James Francis, son James Bradley Lovejoy & Nancy Augusta Shattuck, b <u>Pepperell, MA</u>, Oct 19, 1833, d there Dec 28, 1877, m Lawrence, MA, Nov 7, 1859
1. Nora Grace, b Lawrence, Sept 19, 1872

Hannah m Samuel Stevens, int June 17, 1791, Salis MA R.   A Hannah Stevens d June 7, 1839, ae 77, <u>Salis MA R</u>.   A Samuel Stevens d Dec 31. 1833, ae 66, Salis, MA
Children on Salis MA R
1. Betty, b July 22, 1791
2. James, b Sept 2, 1794; d Aug 20, 1795 (given as son Samuel)
3. John, b Sept 9, 1801
4. Mehitable, b Feb 5, 1797
5. Sally, b Aug 9, 1806

Hannah & Noses Nichols, m Mar 3, 1825, <u>Ames MA</u> No children on Ames or Salis MA R

Hannah, <u>Danville, NH</u>, 1810 Census

Hannah M., m Peter Shirlon, July 5, 1867, Craftsbury, VT. She ae 50; he b Troy, NY, farmer, ae 53, <u>Irasburg, VT</u>

Hannah, Apr 16, 1836, <u>Stonington, CT</u>

Hannah Fifield, dau Benjamin & Hannah (Peterson), b Dec 21, 1752, m a Bagley. No trace of this family in <u>Salis NH cem</u>. Might be Bagley Colby

Hannah Jane m George W. Patterson, at <u>Belfast, ME</u>, Mar 10, 1839, Certificate Mar 24. Goes with James, son Thomas

Hannah, b NH, m Charles Boyles, b MA or NH
1. Charles Bagley Boyles, b 1815; d 1901, in MN, b MA, a baker, lived Weeks Mills and <u>China, ME</u>, during 1840 and

1860's; went to MN about 1869. He m Rachel Peva, b 1821,
Windsor, ME, d 1907, MN. Their dau Roselia Boyles. b 1852,
China, ME, d 1915, St Paul, MN. m Alphonso Bonney, b 1847,
China, ME, d 1915, St Paul, MN. Their son Frederick Bonney,
1884-1964, St Paul, m Marion Mulliken, 1885-1974, St Paul, MN.
Their son, Richard Bonney, b 1911, m Frances Bradbury, b 1911,
who wrote inquiring about this family

Hard S. appt adm of estate of Ellen F. of Haverhill, MA,
widow,. May 13, 1924, Essex Co MA R

Harietta H., d Dec 19, 1902, North Haven, CT

Harmon, b June 30, 1907, Berne, IN, m Josephine Naomi Reusser,
b Aug 8, 1908, at Bern, IN, dau Dr Amos Reusse, & Clara H.
Bixler
1. Sally Elaine, b Mar 2, 1930, Detroit, MI
2. Gretcher Suzanne, b May 14, 1934, Berne, IN

Harold W., d July 29, 1904, ae 1, Lynn, MA

Harold William, b Sept 22, 1900, son William Scott & Ellen
Stone, De Kalb Co, NY

Harriet W., m John Gordon, both Old Town, ME, Oct 8, 1940,
Bangor, ME R

Harriet, PEMD, p 371, Census of 1850, OH

Harriet Sargent Bagley, d Oct 25, 1878, ae 24, b & d
Shrewsbury, MA, dau William R. of Oxford & Arenath M.
Laughlin, b Shirley, MA

Harry L, m Lillian R. Cornwall, who d June 7, 1928, ae 43, b
Marseilles, Ind, d Melrose, MA, dau William N, b Milford, CT,
& Laura Gates, b New Haven, CT

Harry & Elmer Snyder, executors of last will of Peter Snyder,
late of Greeneville, Mar 31, 1899

Harry William, b Holyoke, MA, ae 32, m Josephine Holland, ae
31, at Prov RI
1. William Atherton, 2nd ch, b Lewiston, MA, Apr 4, 1942

Harry Albert, Jr., of St Louis, Mo, ae 25, b St Louis, son
Harry A. & Edna Simmonds, b July 17, 1943, at Brunswick, ME,
Dorothea Clayton of St Louis, ae 22, dau Robert & Lucille
(Lemmon)

Harry A., son Edward, b 1810, m Elizabeth Bennett in Bradford,
PA

Harry, son Henry of Green, PA, ae 11, 1880

Harry C., d Newbury, VT, Aug 9, 1879; m Sarah Amelia. dau Dr
Calvin & Sally Parker Jewett of St Johnsbury, b Sept 30, 1815,

m Sept 23, 1850. She d July 11, 1903, Jewett Genealogy

Harry Watts, b Paterson, NJ. m Kathryn Eavers, b Rutherford, NJ
1. Harry Watts, Jr. m Lois Ella Bashaw at Burlington, VT, Nov 6, 1941, he ae 26, b Highland Mills, NJ
a. Kent Watts, b June 29, 1942, Burlington, VT

Harvey C., divorced Inez B., Sept 1947
Flora divorced Harvey C., Jan, 1953, Bangor, ME

Harvey & Mable Conley
1. Beryl, son, b abt 1908, Nacodoches, TX

Hattie J., dau George, ae 8, Bedford, PA

Hattie E., wife George E., d Belfast, ME, July 12, 1913, ae 59-10-6 b Columbia Falls, dau Richard Dorr, b Columbia & Margaret Leighton, b Indian River, ME

Hearne, son Schyler, Census of 1870, NY, New Baltimore, ae 11

Hearyy ? Calven, son James of PA, & VA, ae 1, 1880

Helen, dau T. K. & Carrie Aiken, b Bedford, NH, Feb 27, 1892

Helen M., dau Michael & Bridget, Providence, RI, b Nov 14, 1893

Helen Miller, d July 8, 1963, ae 102, b Concord, MA, d Stoneham, MA, hus Jonathan, dau Edwin A. of Concord, MA & Emmaline Varney, b Alton, NH

Helen Louise, May 3, 1926, 1st ch of William Vincent of Dedham, MA, 29, and Hilda Kennedy, 27, b Nova Scotia

Helen C., m (2nd wife) Joseph M. Taylor, b Effingham, NH, 1832, d Lynn, MA, Feb 8, 194-, n June 15, 1899 (Anthony Taylor of Hampton & His Desc)

Helen m Joseph Bachelder, Dec 30, 1873, Albany, VT

Henry W., b Valley Falls, RI & Sarah D. Potter, b Scituate, RI
1. Charles F., b Berkeley, RI, d Plainville, MA, wife Caroline E. Baxter, d Apr 24, 1955, ae 77 (could be Barter)

Henry E., m Esther B. Smith, who d Apr 8, 1940, New Bedford, MA, d Boston, nurse, dau Joseph Smith & Barbara Gould, b Germany

Henry A., b PA & Emily Nichols, b NY
1. Hazette Chaffen, d Aug 9, 1913, ae 20, b Fla, d Easton, MA (Try Michael Hodge line, Newburyport, MA)

Henery or Hennessey & Sally Benoit of Middlebury, VT, m Bridgeport, VT, July 10, 1797

Henry of <u>Bridgeport, CT</u> & Polly Byington, at Bridgeport, Feb
24, 1805

Henry A. had wife Sarah J. Cloon, who d Mar 23, 1926, ae 76,
at <u>Peabody</u>, b Marblehead, MA, dau Thomas & Mary (Glass), both
b Marblehead

Henry, Ae 37, b Bedford, <u>Bedford Co, PA. Census of 1850</u>
Sarah J., ae 37, b PA (NR)
Myrtie, ae 14, b PA (NR)
Ida, ae 12, b PA (NR)
Sallie, ae 10, dau b PA
Charles, ae 8, son, b PA
Bettie, ae 6, dau, b PA
Ella, ae 4, dau, b PA
Elsie, ae 11/12, dau, b PA

Henry, ae 41, b <u>Green, Ind Co, PA</u>, Census of 1880
Catherine, wife, 38, b PA
Samantha, dau ae 18, b PA
Harry, son, ae 11, b PA
James, son, ae 9, b PA
May, dau, ae 6, b PA
Ida, dau, ae 3, b PA
Elizabeth Gregg, dau ae 20, b PA
Maude Baker, granddaughter, ae 5, b PA

Henry & Bethiel
1. Benjamin, b Plymouth, July 18, 1820 NH
2. Amanda, b July 4, 1817, <u>Campton, NH</u>

Henry, ae 66, b Eng
Mary Anne, ae 29, b Ireland Census of 1850, <u>Summit Co,
Detroit No 1400 Stowe Twnps, OH</u>

Henry, 1748, in Rev War, son of John from Eng, <u>Montgomery Co,
NY</u>

Henry Stone, b <u>Peabody, MA</u>, 46, m Lillian Cornwall, b
Marseille, IL, had son Carle Francis. He m Thelma Foster
Nichols, Aug 25, 1932, at Center Conway, NH, 25-30, 1st, 2nd m
divorced, dau Carleton W. Raymond & Edith Hersey

Henry M, b ME, m Marion McKinley, b <u>ME</u>
1. Robert William m Marjorie Twitchell of <u>Milford, NH</u>, he ae
34, 2nd m, and she 33, dau Ralph Twitchell & Millie MacDonald
of Milford, July 3, 1957 (may be Willian whose wife d 1954)

Henry Census of 1840 for <u>Liberty, ME</u> 1M 5, 1M 10-15, 1M 30-40,
2F 5-10, 1F, 15--20, 1F 30-40

Henry L. Census of 1850 for Waldo Co, ME, ae 33, b VT
Lucinda, ae 23
Roxanna, ae 11
James, ae 8
Creander, ae 4
Emaline, ae 3
Elizabeth, ae 1
There was a Henry L. supposedly son of Jefferson & Fidelia
Gallup of Hartland, VT, m Mary Thurber and went to Waldo Co,
town of Montville and in Census of 1880 had 5 children

Henry of <u>Davistown ME</u> & Betsey Baker of Balltown, ME,
intentions, Sept 9, 1799

Herbert J. m Dec 26, 1898, Lulu May, b Oct 11, 1878, dau E.
Lee Rowley & Mary Amanda Bell, <u>Scholarie, NY</u> records

Herbert R., d Jan 6, 1950, ae 37, b <u>Blackstone, VA, d Boston,</u>
negro

Hope & Laura Bagley of <u>Providence, RI</u> had dau b Aug 21, 1898
They had son Earl, b Nov 9, 1896

Horatio, Census of 1860, New Baltimore, not on Census of 1860,
may be Badeley
Horatio N., 44, farmer, b NY 1816
Elizabeth, 38, b 1822
Stephen, 15, farmer, b NY 1845
James K. P. 12., b 1848
Rachel Ann, 6, b 1854
Anne Marie, ae 3, b 1857

Howard G m Mattie Emma Pease, d Dec 25, 1960, ae 71, b
Merrimac d Amesbury, dau John, b Merrimac & Mattie Perry, b
Sherman Mills, ME

Hugh & Sarah, both b Ireland, He d Jan 8, 1876, ae 65, b
Ireland, d Boston,, son James & Catherine, both b Ireland.
Sarah d Sept 28, 1895, ae 58, b Ireland, d Boston, dau Joseph
Storey & Mary Colgaan, both b Ireland
1. Margaret, d July 25, 1864, ae 3mos, d Roxbury, MA
2. Mary, d June 29, 1864, ae 1-6, b Buffalo, d Roxbury

Hugh & Mary, both b Ireland, He d Aug 28, 1889, ae 52, d
Boston

Hugh b Providence, RI & Frances, b Boston
1. Mary F., d Jan 6, 1883, ae 6, Southbridge, MA

Hugh & Margaret, Somerset township, Bedford Co, PA

Ida, dau Henry of Green Co, PA, ae 3, b PA, Census of 1880

Idella M. wife pf George F. d Rockport, ME, Mar 1, 1923, b
Rockport, Oct 7, 1847, dau William Corthell. He d NY,
previous residence Rockport, 1928, ae 76-2-29

Imogene, ae 16, dau Edward & Amarilla of NY, Census of 1860

Irene G., dau Jonathan & Helen F. of Merrimac, MA

Isaac m Sabra Warren, Feb 27, 1827, Alfred, ME R

Isaac m Ruth of Newbury, VT
1. Harvey W. m Julia Dutton of Newbury, VT at Hartford, VT,
Jan 26, 1865, ae 25, 1st m

Isaac, (may be Bayley) m Betsey, dau Thomas & Elizabeth
(Lowell) Johnson, b Feb 28, 1880 (Wells History of Newbury,
VT)

Isaac, ae 27, Bedford St Bedford, Bedford Co, PA, Census of
1880
Lizzie, wife ae 22, b PA
Esther, ae 7, dau, b PA

Isaac, b Dutchess Co, NY, 1807, see David of Dutchess, Co

Isaac, ae 8, son John & Susan, Census of 1880, PA

Jacob & Charles, both Troy, ME, a quitclaim deed recorded July 27, 1830, on Sept 3, 1829, they bought land owned by Thomas Bagley of Troy, ME

Jacob of Bangor, ME, 12 Regt Civil War

Jacob of Davistown m Lydia Green of Green, ME, Oct 31, 1810

Jacob Bagley, 51, farmer, b ME, Town 11 Range 3, post office in 1860, Zanesville, in 1870, Giuard, IL

1860 Census	1870 Census
Jacob, ae 41, b ME	68
Agnes, 38, b Scotland	42
Joseph, 27, carpenter, b ME, not on 1870	
Thomas, 13, b ME	26, b ME
Van Amburg, 12, b VA	22, b VA
Robert Hinston, 10, b Scotland	not on 1870
Andrew, 1 yr, b IL	20, b VA
Hannah, 3, b IL not on 1870	
G. W. 7/12, b IL given as George	11, b IL
	John ae 5, b IL
	Anna, ae 9, b ME

See Ella Susan, old 1493

Jacob, ae 82, d Oct 28, 1852, at Barton, VT, b about 1770

Jacob, of Bangor, ME, m Sarah M. Dodge, Nov 6, 1834.   A   Jacob of Bangor, d Feb 9, 1874, at Bangor, ae 62-7

Jacob Bronson, b Nov 5, 1839, son David of IL

Jacob, ae 27, or 77, at Weare, NH, & Betsey Woodman
1. Damuel, b Aug 28, 1792, at West Newbury, MA

Jacob, possibly son of John of Green, PA, 1880

Jacob, son Almary, b ME & H. T. Drew of Enfield, NH, m
_____ Drew of Enfield, NH., 1897

James, tax-payer First Church Parish, Falmouth, ME, 1760, see David, Joseph, Joseph, Jr., and William

James B., son George , ae 10, 1880, PA

James J., son Francis P. & Ruth of Dorchester, MA, lived Derry, in 1970's when mother died

James W., b VT & _____ Mansfield, b St Louis, MO,
1. Louis M., d S Portland, ME, Feb 1, 1928, b St Louis, MO, ae 60

James C., b Boston, m Martha Rawson, b Cincinnati, OH
1. James C., b June 27, 1878, d Portland, ME, 1943, wife Harriet

James, b Ireland m Jane McCartney, b Fredericktown, NB
1. James H., b Portland, ME, ae 57, m Ann Hawkins of St
Johnsbury, VT, b Derby, VT, Jan 7, 1931, Portland, ME, dau
Edward Hawkins & Philandia Warbey

James, b Eng, ae 43, Essex Co VT, 1860 Census
Barbara, ae 41
Amee, ae 3]
Caroline, ae 1

James, son Patrick & Bridget, she of Southboro, MA, d July 3,
1873, ae 32, b Ireland, d Fall River, MA

James & Mary (Conroy), both b Ireland
1. Male stillborn, Jan 22, 1896, at Fall River, MA

James & Sarah, both b Ireland
1. Mary, d May 8, 1886, ae 22, b Eng, d Fall River, MA

James, d Dec 19, 1866, ae 2 mos, at Tewksbury, MA

James, son Mark W. & Ann Smith, d Dec 27, 1935, ae 58, wife
was Annie McGovern

James T., a musician, son of John, b Boston & Ann McCarthy, b
Manchester, NH, d Aug 17, 1900, ae 34, b & d Boston

James , b Ireland & June McCarthy
1. John F., 22, b Frederickton, NB, m Sylvia Montell of
Meredith, ae 18, b Greensboro, VT at Laconia, NH, June 30,
1913

James P. , Southboro, MA. 51 & Jennie Johnson, 43, b Nov
Scotia
1. John Francis of Suffolk, MA, 24, single & Judith
Harrington, ae 19, dau James & Sadie Freeney at Seabrook, NH,
Jan 23, 1948

James P., b Southboro m Jennie Johnson, b St John's NB
1. Russell, d Oct 28, 1919, ae 1 yr, b & d Boston
2. Female, d Boston, Jan 28, 1920, ae 7 dys
3. Female, d Feb 12, 1933, ae 1 mos, b & d Boston
Jennie Johnson, d Aug 26, 1941, ae 45, b NS, d Boston; husband
James, son John & Ada Uhlman, both b NS

James, d W Windsor, VT, ae 78, Nov 1, 1908

James, Census of 1790, Hillsdale, NY

James, m Madeline Beaupre, dau Edward J. & Josephine
Robillard. She d Mar 5, 1959, VT R says buried Pittsford, VT

James, son John & Margaret (Welch), b NY and lived there, see
brother of John Walton

James R. & Theresa of <u>Providence, RI</u>, m Feb 9, 1895

James, son Henry of <u>Green, PA</u>, ae 9, 1880

James , ae 30, b <u>Carroll, Camboia Co PA</u>
Agness, ae 26, wife, b PA
Annie S., ae 1, dau, b PA

James M. bt land of Ames Palmer & Martha, his wife and Horace
Newton & Mary in <u>Albany, NY</u>, May 18, 1857

Rev James, grad Harvard Colleg, 1719 (Savage)

James, ae 48, b <u>Upper Prospect, Camboia Co, PA Census of 1880,</u>
<u>for PA</u>
Elizabeth, wife ae 44, b PA
James McC, son ae 16, b PA
Osey Marella, dau, ae 14, b PA
Wm Henry, son ae 12, b PA
Charles Elmer, son, ae 10, b PA
Araminda Minerva, dau ae 8, b PA
Effie Laura, dau, ae 6, b PA
Hearry Calven ?, son, ae 1, b PA

James McC. ae 16, son James, b <u>Camboia Co, PA</u> (probably
Cambria Co)

James, ae 25, farmer, b <u>OH, Census of 1850 for Brown Co, Pike</u>
Rebecca, ae 27, b OH
John1/12, b OH

James, b Ireland & Mary Roach, b Ireland
1. James of <u>Woburn, MA</u>, ae 33, m Ellen C. O'Brien of Veasie,
ME, ae 29, dau Dennis O'Brien & Mary Buckley , June 16, 1897,
at <u>Bangor, ME</u>

James, son Joshua & Mary, b Mar 4, 1780, <u>Marlboro, MA,   m</u> Mar
30, 1808, at Marlboro, Elizabeth Gleason, b Oct 5, 1788, dau
John & Experience (Snow)

James B., b Ireland & Jane MacCardivey, b Canada
1. John Edward, b May 12, 1o954, d Mar 31, 1951, in <u>VT</u> .

James W. of <u>Dayton, OH, b Fayetteville, TN</u>, m Agnes Stevens
1. Lucy W., who m Charles Tinker, May 4, 1949, in <u>VT</u>

James & Lena Bigelow, of <u>Newbury, VT</u>, m Jan 12, 1815

James Bagguley m Barbara Gunn of <u>Burlington, VT</u>, Mar 28, 1846

James Francis, b <u>S Boston</u>, 26, m Daisy Cavanaugh, b Newton,
MA, 29
1. John Ronald, b <u>Rochester, NH</u>, Dec 23, 1941

James, b Boston m Daisy L, b Newtonville
1. James F., b <u>Newtonville, MA</u>., d <u>Monson, MA</u>, Aug 9, 1958,

James, son James & Joanna of Wethersfield, VT, both b Ireland,
b Oct 14, 1869, at Athens, VT

James, son Elisha & Louise Daniel, b 1841, at Pittsfield, IL,
family probably came from VA.   Supplied by Thomas Jones,
cousin, 1977

James & Minnie Baldinger
1.   James m Madeline Beaupre, lived Pittsford, VT
James of Pittsford, VT, wife Madeline B., d Mar 5, 1959, at
Rutland. She lived at Burlington, a school teacher, b Jan 28,
1900, ae 59, father Edward Beaupre, mother, Josephine
Robillard.   Informant Madleine Bagley.   They were m at
Burlington, Jan 9, 1937, he ae 31, given as of Hoboken, NJ,
son of James Bagley and Minnie Baldinger, b Switzerland.
Father, b Swanton, VT, mother, b Burlington, VT

James & Mary Spellman
1.   William James, m Ellen Blanche Haight at Montpelier, Vt.
Sept 14, 1880, ae 26.   He d Berlin, VT, ae 36, July 5, 1898.
2.   Jennie M., m Paul Yancey at Berlin, VT, Dec 7, 1891, ae 27

James & Mary, both b Ireland
1.   Thomas, d Boston, Apr 17, 1887, ae 1 dy

James H. & Margaret Snow, both b Chicoppe, MA
1.   James, d Jan 22, 1925, ae 3 mos, Chicoppe, MA

James, son Nelson, on Census of 1870 for New Baltimore, NY, ae
22, b NY

James, b Ireland & Julia, b Boston
1.   John, Jr., d Sept 7, 1884, ae 3 b & d Boston
2.   David, d Sept 8, 1885, ae 2mos, Boston
3.   Annie, d Dec 29, 1887 , ae 7 dys, Boston
4.   Joseph, d Nov 30, 1886, ae 1 dy, Boston.   His death
certificate gives both parents as b Boston

James & Anna (Keyon), both b Boston
1.   Annie, d July 28, 1897, ae 1, b & d Boston

James & Annie Kehoe, both b Boston
1.   Arthur, d July 23, 1899, ae 6 mos, Boston

James & Mary Walsh, both b Ireland
1.   Ellen A., d Mar 27, 1896, b & d Boston

James & Mary Fitzgerald, both b Ireland
1.   Maggie, b & d Springfield, MA, Nov 10, 1865
2.   Maurice, d Feb 27, 1872, ae, Springfield, MA
3.   Thomas, b & d Springfield, MA, Feb 24, 1872, ae 2
4.   Dennis, b & d Springfield, MA, Oct 27, 1873, ae 1

James m Bertha Dubuque, divorced, she d Aug 13, 1928, ae 35, b

& d <u>Chicopee</u>, dau Alphonse F. & Malvina Fortier, b Canada

James Edward, d Mar 9, 1934, ae 76, b <u>Zanesville, OH, d Watertown, MA</u>, son William W., b Redford, NY & Agnes Richmond, b Scotland

James E., b <u>Hillsdale</u>, NY & ME, Granville, VT
1.   Jane or Jennie, b Feb 14, 1864, at <u>Rutland, VT</u>

James, Apr 21, 1778, served 11 mos 10 dys in Capt Simeon Steven's Co, in regt raised for the defense of the frontier and adjacent and on to Conn River whereof Timothy Bedell, Esq is colonel, <u>Vermont Rev War Rolls</u>

James, son of John of <u>Watertown, MA</u>, b Mar 25, 1687 (?).   Was this the James who was grad of Harvard and a minister 1719?

James, 2-2-5, <u>Minisink Town, Orange Co, NY</u>, Census of 1790

James m Elsie. He d June 7, 1843, ae 51-5-21, Buried Enfield Center, Tompkins Co, NY
1.   Almira, d June 7, 1847, ae 21-1
2.   Pamelia, d Mar 22, 1846, ae 17
3.   Juliana, d Apr 22, 1845, ae 11

James m Ann Jone, Apr 2, 1809, <u>NYC</u>

James, b June 6, 1706, at <u>Groton, CT</u> son Thomas & Ruth

James, son Joshua, bapt May 5, 1795, <u>Marlboro, MA</u>

James Edward, b Hartford, (death certificate says <u>New Haven, CT</u>), d Dec 24, 1937, ae 45, at <u>Rutland, MA</u>, son James & Margaret Lynch, both b Ireland. His wife was Laura Bennett, b Boston, d Feb 12, 1948, ae 54, a Brookline, MA, dau Frank R. , b New Haven, CT & Mary O'Rourke, b NS
1.   Robert, d Feb 1, 1930, ae 11, b & d Boston

James & Johanna, both b Ireland
1.   Thomas, d Jan 1, 1886, ae 36, b & d <u>Lowell, MA</u>

James, d <u>Lowell, MA</u>, b Ireland, June 5, 1858, ae 46

James Edwin, d Mar 1, 1899, ae 31, clergyman, b <u>Craftsbury, VT</u>, son Henry F. & Olive Anice

James A., b <u>Marseille, NY</u> m Amanda Colby, b W Springfield, MA, who d June 14, 1954, ae 70, b & d Springfield, dau Frank Cherboneau & Aurelia Minot, both b Canada. He d Aug 14, 1931, ae 48, at <u>Springfield</u>, son James & Margaret Oakley, both b Rochester, NY

James & Bridget (Keegan), both b Ireland
1.   James, d Aug 15, 1871, 1 dy b & d <u>Salem, MA</u>
2.   Infant stillborn, July 23, 1880, Salem
3.   Annie, d Apr 18, 1890, ae 34, b Ireland, d Boston, given

as dau James & Bridget
4.   James H., d Mar 24, 1882, ae 1, b Salem
5.   James H., d Dec 26, 1894, ae 4, b & d Salem, MA.,
definitely given as son of James & Bridgett Keegan

James & Bridget, both b Ireland
1.   Thomas J., d Oct 10, 1887, ae 32, b Canada, d Malden, MA

James C. & Doris of Montpelier, VT
1.   Sally Anne, b June 6, 1939

James, d Lancaster, NH, ae 69, widower, Dec 30, 1942

James A. & Agnes Carney, both b Ireland
1.   Jane A., d Dec 16, 1953, ae 23, b & d Boston

James M. & Anna Edson Pierce, who d July 17, 1948, b N Truro,
MA, d Wellfleet, MA, dau David E. of Wellfleet & Ann O.
Grozier, b N Truro

James m Honora Lopuay, Apr 7, 1;863, in Douglas, NE

James, d Nov 13, 1908, published in Lincoln NE Star

James m Margery Black, Apr 2,   1795,   Swedish   Church,
Philadelphia

J. V. m Alice Marie O'Connell, who d Nov 8, 1943, b & d
Boston, dau Albert & Cecilia Reppetto, both b Boston

Jane of Newbury, VTR, m Joseph Fuller, Jan 8, 1861, at
Bradford, VT

Jane of Hillsboro, NH, m Elise Stevens of Hillsboro
1.   Mariah m Leon Lord, 1897, at Portsmouth, NH

Jane D. & Benaiah Titcomb of South Hampton, NH, m Apr 15,
1832, Salis, MA R). No children on Salis or Ames, MA r; nor
any record of deaths

Jane, b Feb 3, 1812, d July 16, 1887, m Orlando Howard
Sargent, son Edmund & Sally Sargent, dau of Moses Sargent who
was b Amesbury, MA, Aug 22, 1809; m Nov 27, 1834. He d July
13, 1884, lived Merrimac, MA, car manufacturer
1.   Arthur, b June 7, 1845, d Nov 9, 1847
2.   Edmund Howard, b July 29, 1849
3.   William Howard, b Nov 15, 1851
4.   Augustus H., b Feb 9, 1856; d Mar 11, 1891, unm (Sargent
Genealogy)

Mrs Jane Ragley, d Aug 28, 1847, Hartford Times, ae 34, CT

Jane, d Sept 4, 1847, Hartford, CT

Jane E., dau William H. & Jane E., b Feb 18, 1845

Jane E., ae 48, b <u>Hillsdale, NY</u>, dau James E., bridgebuilder, d June 2, 1874, <u>Rutland, VT</u>

Jane or Jennie, b Feb 14, 1865, at <u>Rutland, VT</u>, dau James E., b <u>Hillsdale, NY</u>, and M. E., b Granville, VT

Jane, ae 7, dau Frederick & Almira of <u>St Johnsbury, VT</u>, Census of 1860, b 1853

Jane E., dau William H. & Jane E., b Feb 18, 1845.   On same record with George W., b 1843 and Nelson, son of Moses & Abigail, but may be no relation

Jane, ae 15, b OH in household of John Miller, ae 23, & Mary Fuller, ae 21, b OH. Census of <u>Brown Co., OH, Lewis Twp</u>

Jane, mother of Joseph of <u>Philadelphia</u>, 1880

Joneva Alice, b Jonesboro, had an illegitimate child, Leslie LaVaughan, b May 23, 1927, <u>Whitneyville, ME</u>, father was William Kenneth LaVaughan.   Leslie LaVaughan, ae 21, b Whitneyville, ME., m Martha M. Paul, ae 20, b Pensacola, Fla and had (1), Pamela Jean, b Belfast, ME, res Searsmont, Feb 14, 1949; (2) June Alice, b Culter, ME, June 17, 1950; (3) Jeanine Marcie, b Lubec, June 11, 1951; (4) Betty , b Lubec, Oct 7, 1943

Jenette m Benjamin F. Hemstreet, Aug 26, 1863, <u>NY marriages</u>

Jenette, 1833, <u>Naugatuck</u>

Jennie, ae 3, <u>Tioga, Tioga Co., PA</u>, adopted dau of Joseph

Jennie, wife of William, d <u>Ludlow, ME</u>, Nov 7, 1909, ae 47, b NB, dau Robert McCarbindale, b NB & Kate Murphy, b NB

Jennie M, dau James & Mary Spellman m Paul Yancy at <u>Berlin, VT</u>, Dec 7, 1891, ae 27

Jennie E. Coutermarsh, d Aug 16, 1902, ae 18, <u>Chelsea, VT,</u> cem, near family lot of Charles W. Bagley

Jennie, b May 1, 1881, dau Elisha & Sarah, m Charles Deming, son Marion S., b Apr 21, 1877, in Lawrence, PA; resides <u>Auburn, NY,</u> trainman
1. Harry, b Sept 26, 1898
2. Francis Edward, b Dec 28, 1902, d July 18, 1903

Jennie, wife of Edward Hinman, 1848-1882, <u>Middleburgh, NY Cem.</u> See Jones Bagley

Jennie, wife of Edward M., 1848-1882, <u>Scholarie Co., NY</u>

Jerdiah, b Apr 23, 1708, <u>Groton, CT</u>, son Thomas & Ruth

Jerry & Joanna of Wethersfield, VT, both b Ireland

1.   John, d Aug 8, 1859, ae 6 dys want of care
2.   John, b Oct 14, 1860, Athens, VT
3.   Mary, b Aug 11, 1962, Wethersfield, VT

Jesse F., b Topsfield m Alice Thibideau, b St Dunces
1.   Samuel B., b Mar 19, 1902, Kingman, ME, 1st ch

Jesse & Sarah, his wife, Corinth, VT
1.   Permeley, b Aug 12, 1801

Jessie May Ayers of Brandon, OH, dau Edward, b 1810, &
Elizabeth Bennett of Bradford, PA

Joan, dau Francis P. & Ruth of Dorchester, MA, m -----Davis and
lived at Derry, NH, in early 1970's when mother died

Joanne of Hopkinton, NH, m Noah Persons of Hopkinton, June 18,
1778, at Warner, H (could be Bayley)

Job had wife Lydia Adams Oliver who d Feb 15, 1904, ae 82, b
Malden, MA; d Georgetown, MA, dau William Oliver, b Malden &
Lydia Neggles, b Boston

Job of Groton, NH, m Miss B. Taylor of Campton, Apr 12, 1806,
at Campton, NH (given under Bayley)

John, son John & Susan, both b Ireland, d Aug 29, 1885, ae 62,
b Ireland, d Peabody, MA

John, b NY & Mary Sullivan, b Ireland
1.   John, b Riverton, RI., d Fall River, MA, July 19, 1890, ae
3 hrs

John J., b South Hadley, MA & Susan Cuff, b Springfield, MA
1.   Mary, d July 3, 1913, ae 15 min at Springfield, MA

John m Lydia Adams Oliver, who d Feb 15, 1904, ae 82, b
Malden, d Georgetown, MA, dau William, b Malden & Lydia
Neggles, b Boston (See Job above)

John, b Ireland, d Cambridge, MA, Apr 16, 1879, ae 45, son
Andrew & Margaret, both b Ireland, m Mary, b Eng
1.   Margaret, b Somerville, d Cambridge, MA, Jan 3, 1872, ae 3
2.   John, b & d Cambridge, MA, ae 11 mos, Apr 6, 1873
3.   Catherine, d May 19, 1878, ae 4, Cambridge, MA
4.   Alice, d Cambridge, MA, Mar 18, 1877, ae 1
5.   Anna L., d Apr 28, 1880, ae 2
6.   Edward, d Apr 17, 1886, ae 18, b & d Cambridge, MA

John & Mary (Flynn), both b Ireland
1.   John, d Mar 7, 1892, b & d Cambridge, MA, ae 4
2.   Margaret, d June 6, 1887, ae 1 Hr, at Cambridge, MA

John, son Thomas & Letitia, both b Ireland, d Aug 11, 1882, ae
70, at Malden, MA

John, b Boston & Mary, b Erie, PA
1.   John, d Dec 10, 1888, ae 4 mos, b & d Malden, MA

John F. & Ann (MacDonald, both b Cambridge, MA
1.   Virginia, d Mar 12, 1935, ae 9, b & d Cambridge, MA

John B., d June 23, 1951, Milton, VT

John, b Harmony, Chautauqua Co, NY, d Jan 16, 1881; m Oct, 4,
1866, Rebecca Rowe. He was b about 1815; she b Apr 7, 1813,
d Jan 27, 1893, Chandler Valley, Warren, PA. She m (2) Oct
26, 1834, Vilus Morley, given as first husband.

John of Hooksett, NH, m Eliza Phelps of Allenstown at
Pembroke, Dec 21, 1823

John B., b Mar 21, 1828, d Aug 2, 1893, buried Aug 4, 1893,
Jackson Co, OH, Civil War

John, son Daniel, Census of Jackson, Union Co, OH, 1850

John m Sally Dearborn of Chester, NH, Dec 25, 1823

John George, son Zebedee Bagerly & Elizabeth Seneca, MI

John Ronald, b Rochester, NH, Dec 23, 1941, son James Francis,
b S Boston, 26, & Daisy Cavanaugh, b Newton, MA, 29

John of Topsham, VT,
1.   Sarah, b Dec 6, 1822

John G. & Ellen, who d Sept 18, 1896, ae 51, b Ireland, d
Chicopee, MA, dau Jeremiah Ferris & Abbie Moyahan, both b
Ireland

John & May, both b Ireland
1.   Johanna, d May 1, 1866, ae 1, Chicopee, MA

John & Delia, both b ME
1.   Mary G., d Oct 12, 1882, ae 3, b Boston, d Somerville, MA

John, son Cornelius & Joanna, both b Ireland, d May 11, 1868,
ae 65, b Ireland, d Boston

John, son Cornelius & Ellen (Calleghan), both b Ireland, d Jan
13, 1890, ae 50, at Salem, MA

John & Susan, both b Ireland
1.   John, d Aug 29, 1885, ae 62, b Ireland, d Peabody, MA

John, b MA, & Mary Warner, b CT
1.   Female, b Mar 5, 1874, Burlington, VT
2.   Male, d Mar 5, 1874, ae 1 dy, Burlington, VT

John Edward, b May 12, 1844, d Mar 31, 1951, in VT, son James,
b Ireland & Jane MacCardivey, b Canada

John, d Whitefield, NH, Sept 18, 1892, ae 54, b Ireland

John, b 1738, son of John from Mongomery, Eng, NY

John & Sally Hilbert, m Dec 10, 1809, Gloucester, M

John, b Canada, & Mary Melarvey, b Canada
Infant son John, d Whitefield, NH, Dec 24, 1890, ae 1 dy

John Bagley of Saybrook, CT, supposed to come from Orlando 3, branch, NY, 46, Vol 4V

John & Catherine, both b Ireland
1. Richard, d Feb 7, 1868, ae 2, b & d Holyoke, MA
2. Agnes, d July 17, 1874, ae 6 dys

John of Hopkinton, NH, m Harriet Webster of Hopkinton, Aug 26, 1826

John m Lucy Huntoon, July 3, 1857 (other source gives July 4, 1858, at Salisbury, NH). She d Franklin, NH, lived there 12 years, prev res, Nashua, d Sept 29, 1904, ae 96, widow John, b Feb 29, 1808, dau John Baker of Salisbury & Mary Wyman, b Chatham. First husband was David Huntoon of Unity, NH

John & Dolly Bagley, m Mar 8, 1812, had a dau Dolly who m Thomas Colby, son of John. A dau of John Colby, Dolly, m Alfred Bailey of Amesbury, son Thomas & Betsey of Ames. Children of John Colby and Dolly Bagley (Notice these are Colbys)
1. Hannah Edwards, b Jan 2, 1831
2. Charles Abraham, b Nov 9, 1820
3. Edwin John, b July 31, 1812
4. Elizabeth Ann, b Aug 15, 1817
5. John Bagley, b July 28, 1828
6. Lorentz Spitzenfield, b May 10, 1815
7. Patrick Henry,, b Jan 27, 1826
8. Sarah Bagley, b June 3, 1823, m Alfred Bailey, Nov 13, 1844
9. Ebenezer Thompson, b Sept 19, 1833

John Bigelow Bagley, a Watertown, MA, proprietor in 1642, m Aug 30, 1643, Mary, dau John Warren. She d Oct 19, 1691.   He m (2) Oct 2, 1694, Sarah, dau or widow of Joseph Bennett? This may be Bigelow.
1. John, b Aug 27, 1643
2. Judith, b Oct 11, 1646
3. Mary, b Mar 18, 1648, m June 3, 1674, Michael Flagg
4. Daniel, b Dec 1, 1650
5. Samuel, b Oct 28, 1653
6. Joshua, b Nov 5, 1655
7. Elizabeth, b June 18, 1657; m John Stearns, Jr.
8. Sarah, b Sept 29, 1659; m July 23, 1879, Isaac Learned
9. James, b Mar 25, 1687 (?)
10. Martha, b Apr 1, 1662,. m Woods

11. Abigail, b Feb 4, 1663/64, m Dec 10, 1684, Benjamin Harrington
12. Hannah, b & d 1665
13. Son, b & d 1667
John d July 14, 1703, ae 86. Will, dated Jan 4, 1702/03. Probated July 23, 1703, mentions wife Sarah; children: John, Judith, Daniel, Samuel, Joshua, James and daus M. Flagg, Elizabeth Stearns, Sarah Learned, Martha Wood, her children and Abigail Harrington

John came from Wiltshire, Eng to New England, cast away in terrible storm Aug, 1635, at Pemaquid, Bristol, ME. Was in Newbury, MA, in 1639. Will of his wife mentions John, Jr., and dau in Eng.

John, priv, Capt D. Elwell's Co, Lt Col Appleton' s regt from Sept 19 to Oct 12, 1814, Service at Gloucester in battle Sept 19, with barges of enemey, MA Vol Militia

John & Mary
1. Mary J., b Feb 12, 1828, VT

John Bagley served in Capt George's Co, War of 1812, Pension Certificate, No 17507, VT

John & Mary
1. Betsey Norge, b Dec 5, 1812, Orange, VT, d Dec 15, 1815

John, his child, d Aug 27, 1845, ae 2, VT

John Augustus, an illegitimate child under 14, mother Elizabeth M. Davis, formerly Elizabeth M. Bagley, adopted by George W. Wilson of Haverhill, MA and Alice J. Wilson, his wife, Nov 20, 1878, Essex Co MA Probate

John of Seabrook, shoemaker & Elizabeth, his wife, b Seabrook Male child, b Jan 25, 1878, at Seabrook, 1st ch

John, 1908-1909, Waterbury, CT

John, a seaman in Rev, Feb, 1777

John F., adm of estate of Elizabeth A. of Lynn, Sept 18, 1941, Essex Co R. Also adm of estate of Nellie T. Bagley of Lynn, June 6, 1941

John, Hillsdale, NY, Census of 1890

John Francis of Suffolk, MA, 25, single, son James P. & Jennie Johnson, m Judith Harrington, ae 19, dau James & Sadie Freeney at Seabrook, Jan 23, 1948

John F., son James, b Ireland & June McCarthy, ae 22, b Frederickton, NB., m Sylvia Montell of Meredith, NH, ae 18, b Greensboro, VT, at Laconia, NH, June 30, 1913, NHR

John A., d about 1933, when Nellie Bagley of W Newbury, MA was granted adm of estate, Feb 24, 1933, Essex Co MA R

John F., d 1851, ae 3 mos at Boston, son Benjamin & Rebecca

John, son Bernard & Phoebe, see John Bagley & Prudence Wesley

John, son John of Watertown, mentioned in father's will in 1703, b Aug 27, 1643

John Walton, son of John & Margaret, b NY, June 21, 1825, went to San Francisco, 1848
1. Mabel, b SR, 1870

John & Margaret (Welch)
1. John Walton, b NY, June 21, 1825
2. Two brothers James remained in NY
John & William came to CA 1848, John to San Francisco and William to Santa Rose where he was a judge; John's dau Mabel, b San Francisco, 1870; her dau was Mrs Tom (Katherine) Pangle, 963, E Rosewood Ct, Ontario, CA, 91764

John Burnham, b June 5, 1807, son William & Susanna, Dunbarton, NH

John, one of Lyon Gardiner's men at Saybrook, CT, 1637

John of Logan, OH, (Bureau of Pensions), 39th OH Vol infantry, corporal of William C. Newman's Co, enl, 10 July, 1861 for 3 yrs; re-enlisted Dec 26, 1863. Engaged in siege of Atlanta and wounded there; disch July 9, 1865, b Nov 26, 1843, at Muskingum Co, OH, lived at Nelsonville, OH, Athens, Co. Father was Samuel Bagley, He d Aug 12, 1927; m Jane Rhodes, Sept 10, 1856, at Zanesville, OH; m (2) Oct 18, 1921, Miss Anna Elizabeth Grigsby
1. Charles N., b Sept 9, 1867, given as of Nelsonville, OH; living 1927
2. Alta, b Mar 4, 1879

John H., b 1835, son Josiah & Elizabeth, Census of 1850, OH, family came from VA

John, b June 4, 1843, Muskingum, OH, d Oct 12, 1926, Newton twp. Civil War vet admitted to bar; m Isabella Tipton, Mar 15, 1877. Mrs B. has a note, Mrs Fenton Bagley, Zanesville, OH Hospital (don't know what it means)

John, d Jan 19, 1851, Charlestown, MA, father Edward

John F. & Maria, b b Newburyport, MA
1. Alice G., d Dec 7, 1887, ae 7, b & d Newburyport, MA

John & Caroline
1. Elizabeth, b Sept 9, 1826; m Hiram Tuttle, Smith Mills, Chautauqua Co, NY

John Bagley, m Annie Johnson, b Houlton, ME, d Jan 4, 1944, ae
93, dau Albert Johnson

John, b Oct, 1821, Pittsfield, MA, son David & Ann Hannah

John, soldier in Rev from Salisbury, NH. History of
Salisbury, by Dearborn. John is said to have lived on South
Road, was with Stark at Bennington. (We have searched
carefully and think this is a Bayley)

John Hazen, b Oct 10, 1868, Gardiner, ME

John C., supposed to have been b VA, 1805, m 1834, Grace
Frances Dugan in Zanesville, OH
1. Selina Elizabeth, m Bernard Callahan in 1858-60. They
lived Milwaukee and the John C. & wife grace lived nearby as
late as 1879 (Joan Beisle, a granddaughter)

Census of 1850, OH, Muskumgum Co, Perry, gives the following,
which seems to go with John C. above
John, ae 45, blacksmith, b VA
Grace, ae 34, b PA
Frances, ae 14, b OH
Selina, ae 12, b OH
William E., ae 10, b OH
Hannah R., ae 8, b OH
Louis, ae 6, b OH
Mary, ae 4, b OH

Census of 1850, OH, Belmont, Co Pultney,
John, carpenter, ae 48, b PA
Rebecca, ae 43, b OH
James, 18, laborer, b OH
Sarah, ae 16, b OH
William, ae 16, b OH
Luther, ae 12, b OH
Angel, ae 10, b OH
Isabella, ae 7, b OH

John Bagly, ae 29, b VA, farmer
Ann, ae 27, b OH
Frederick, ae 1, b OH

Joanne Bagly, ae 19, b OH
Census of 1850, Muskingum Co, Salem, see David, Catherine and
Gilman (OH)

John, ae 48, farmer, b PA. Census of 1850, Belmont Co, OH,
Pultney
Rachel, ae 37, b OH
Delila, ae 16, b OH
Dorcus, ae 13, b OH
George W., ae 11, b OH
Mary, ae 7, b OH
James, ae 3, b OH
Samuel, ae 4/12, b OH

John A. & Caroline, his wife, Apr 8, 1835, of the town of
Rensselaerville, County of Albany, sold land in manor or
Renssaler, subject to annual rent of Stephen Van Rensselaer

John B. with William Bagley, witness, bt land in Athens, NY,
Mar 24, 1837
John B. and wife Priscilla sold land in Athens, NY, Oct 14,
1830

John Bagley who I had supposed one of Lyon Gardiner's men at
Saybrook, in 1637, should be found in Watertown, 1643, but
Bondin in his all-embracing vol has not appointed him a place
there. Genalogical Dictionary of First Settlers of New
England by James Savage

John Bagley, one of first fire wardens, in Niagara Co, NY Feb
9, 1835

John F. b Peabody & Agnes Crowley, b NB, had dau Elizabeth M,
d Sept 1, 1897, ae 2 mos, b & d Lynn, MA
2. Mary, d Dec 31, 1902, b Peabody, d Lynn, ae 1 dy
Agnes, d Lynn, MA, Mar 19, 1960, ae 86, b NB, dau Michael &
Felinda

John of W Topsham, VT, Census of 1830; 1M under 5-10, 1M 15
under 20, 1M 40 under 50, 1F, under 5, 1F, 30 under 40

John M. d County Farm, Rockingham Co, Brentwood, NH, Dec 8,
1884, ae 93, a farmer

Jonathan J., 4th Reg NH Vol Co K, b Haverhill, ae 23, res
Salisbury, NH, enl July 27, 1861 in Sept 18, 1861 as priv;
killed July 6, 1864, near Petersburg, VA

Jonathan of Ayer Village, near Haverhill, MA, m Addie or
Abigail S. Eastman, dau Melvin Chamberlain Eastman & Eliza
Sargent, b June 23, 1858. She d New Haven, CT, Nov 14, 1882
1. Fred Eastman, b Concord, NH, Jan 21, 1885; d Nashua, NH
Aug 14, 1945

Jonathan of Bradford, VT, 4 males 1 female, 1800 Census

Jonathan Bagley, printer, d Aug 13, 1835, ae 67, from Rield
Co, VT, probably Jonathan of Philadelphia, VT, and Brandon,
VT, Rev War soldier. We could not find in Hatfield, MA,
Brandon, VT

Jonathan of Merrimac, MA, wife Helen F.
1. Irene G
2. Fred E., d 1921

Jonathan, b Canada, d July 5, 1928, ae 72, wife was Helen. He
was son of William, b Ireland and Jane McNeally, b Scotland.
She probably d Stoneham, MA, July 8, 1963, ae 102, b Concord,
NH, husband, Jonathan, dau Edwin Miller, b Concord, NH &
Emaline Varney, b Alton, NH

John, b Alna, ME, m Rachel Hazen, b Alna, ME
1. John Hazen, d Gardiner, ME, Aug 10, 1906, ae 37-10-12, b
Whiting, ME, Oct 10, 1868

John P. of Belfast ME, drowned in San Francisco Bay, ae 46, in
1862; m Mrs Sarah Cotterhill, intentions, Oct 1, 1844, dau
Martin Rogers & Sarah Grinnell. He m Myra Rogers, Dec 12,
1848, sister of late wife
1. Norma, child J. P. & S. P, d Sept 1, 1848
Sarah, wife J. P. d Aug 16, 1846

John C., b Arlington, IN, m Leona Lail, b Falmouth, IN
1. Elizabeth Lail, b Portland, ME, May 31, 1929

John, ae 43, farmer of Searsmont, m Sophronia Swett, dau D.
Norton Swett, Esq., who d Nov 9, 1853, ae 34, and is buried
all by herself at Montville, ME. In 1850, she is given as 30,
b Brookfield, ME
Leonard, ae 17,
Ralph, ae 16
Nelson, ae 12
Ceylon, ae 8
Charles, ae 2   Children from Census of 1850, all Searsmont,
ME

John of Searsmont, m Sophia Swett of Montville, ME, Oct 27,
1844 (probably the John above)

John of Worcester, MA & Hattie E. of Worcester
1. George, b Milford, MA, Aug 27, 1896; d Fort William, Cape
Elizabeth, ME, Feb 27, 1917

John, b Machias, ME & Rachel Andrews, b NB. She d
Machiasport, ME, Oct 4, 1908, ae 67-10, dau Ashbard Andrews
and Mary Ward
1. John H., ae 26, b 1868 of Gardiner, E, m Mrs Kate Vlair,
ae 32, b 1862, dau ____ Gambrel, b Scotland, m Dec 24, 1894, at
Gardiner, ME
2. Miriam Franklin, d Whiting, ME, b Whiting, Nov 10, 1864,
ae 1
3. Arthur W., ae 31, b Whiting, father deceased, b NB, m Eva
Ackley, ae 34, dau Corung Andrews & Edna Cook, Sept 7, 1910,
at E Machias, ME. He d E Machias, ME, Apr 9, 1922, ae 43, b
Whiting, ME

John Bagly, HMMI, p 64, Census of 1850, for OH

John Bagley, STWS, p 371, Census of 1850, for OH

John R. Bagley, CBLV, p 116, Census of 1850, for OH

John , 1-1-1, Freehold town, Albany Co, NY, Census of 1790

John, ae 1, son John & Susan, Census of 1880, for PA

John L., b Nov 26, 1842, <u>Muskingum Co, OH</u>, d Aug 12, 1927, <u>Hocking, Logan Co, OH</u>, widow Elizabeth Bagley; enl July 11, 1861; disch July 9, 1865, army, private Co C, 39th Regt

John Bagley, ae 53, b <u>Green, Ind Co, PA</u>, Census of 1880
Elizabeth (NR), ae 47, b PA
Jacob, ae 21, b PA
Almina, ae 13, b PA
Effue (?) Bill (NR), ae 12, b PA
Nora, ae 10, (NR), b PA
Elmeda (NR) ae 7   I think that NR means no blood relation.
Nora is given as separate entry and is listed as dau of John
Bagley, <u>Green, Ind Co, PA</u>

John on tax list of <u>Falmouth, ME</u>, 1776, 1 poll, see Benjamin

John Bagley, ae 35, b <u>NY</u>, Census of 1880, for <u>PA</u>
Susan, ae 33, wife, b PA
Susie, dau, ae 13, b PA
Isaac, son, ae 8, b PA
Caroline, dau, ae 6, b PA
Emma, dau, ae 4, b PA
John, son, ae 1, b PA
Richard (listed as female), ae 64, b Ireland

John P. Bagley, ae 30, estate valued at $1500
Myra E., ae 25
Sarah J., ae 24
Francis E, ae 2 Census of 1850 for <u>Belfast, ME</u>
(Edwina says his wife's name was Elenora, probably the E in
Myra E.)

John & Bridgett, both b Ireland
1. Thomas, d <u>Lowell, MA</u>, May 28, 1868, ae 29

John, b Boston & Ann McCarthy, b Manchester, NH. She d Feb 6,
1886, ae 36, at Boston, dau Patrick & Bridget McCarthy, both
b Ireland
1. Thomas, d Feb 28, 1959, ae 80, b & d Boston
2. James T., d Aug 17, 1900, ae 34, b & d <u>Boston</u>, musician

John H, m Beatrice M. Burnham, who d May 18, 1961, ae 73, b
<u>Essex, d Boston</u>, dau Xephonefon & Maria W, both b Rowley, MA

John & Anna M. Panit. He d <u>Boston, b Boston</u>, Mar 16, 1951, ae
62, son John, b Eng & Ellen Ford, b Ireland

John, b <u>Chelsea, d Boston</u>, Sept 12, 1951, ae 33, son Daniel &
Catherine McDonald, both b Chelsea, MA

John J., m Lillian Swenson, He d <u>Chelsea, b Boston</u>, June 30,
1947, ae 56, son Michael & Elizabeth McGilvary, both b Nova
Scotia. She d ae 82, at Plymouth, NH, b Boston, a summer
resident of <u>Dorchester, NH.</u> Mentions son, Robert L, of
Dorchester; two daus Norma Bagley and Mrs. Jean Good, of
Dorchester, NH

John J. m Josephine T. O'Hearn, who d Apr 11, 1945, ae 51, at Lowell, MA, dau Michael & Margaret Sullivan

John and Jane, both b Eng
1. Emmanuel, d Apr 28, 1899, ae 43, b Eng, d Fall River, MA; wife was Clara A., b Eng
a. Annie, d Dec 14, 1881, Fall River, MA, ae 8 mos

John, b Ireland & Ann Dalton, b Crampton, RI
1. Elizabeth, d Oct 10, 1899, ae 20, b Crampton, RI; d Fall River, MA

John & Sarah, both b Ireland
1. Mary, b Eng, d New Bedford, MA, May 8, 1866, ae 22

John & Ellen, b Ireland, lived Lowell, MA, where she d Mar 24, 1891, ae 80, b Ireland, d Lowell, MA
1. Catherine, d May 24, 1859, b Ireland, d Lowell, ae 35
2. Peter, d Mar 14, 1868, ae 30, b Ireland, d Lowell

John, b Ireland
1. John, d Lowell, MA, Jan 18, 1846, ae 19

John T. & Rosanna, both b Ireland, she d Mar 11, 1897, ae 79, dau Garnick & Rosanna Rafferty, both b Ireland
1. Hugh, b & d Boston, Nov 8, 1874, ae 8
2. John, b Ireland, d Boston, Jan 1, 1884, ae 34

John & Katie Sullivan, both b Ireland
1. Marienne, d Sept 22, 1899, ae 70, b Ireland, d Lowell, MA

John, b Ireland
1. John, b Ireland, d Lowell, MA, Jan 18, 1864, ae 19

John, b Ireland
1. Dennis, d May 17, 1882, ae 30, d Boston, b Ireland

John & Joanna, both b Ireland
1. Patrick, d Feb 26, 1883, ae 96, at Easthampton, MA

John, of Newburyport, MA, m Mary, she d Jan 5, 1890, ae 65, dau William & Mary, both b Ireland

John Joseph, d Oct 27, 1941, ae 45, b & d Cambridge, MA, wife was Mary Agnes Lang, who d Mar 2, 1956, ae 62, b & d Boston, dau John Lang of Boston. John Joseph was son of Michael Joseph, b Ireland & Honora Woodford, b NFL.

John E., d Nov 28, 1942, ae 23, b Blackstone, MA, d Boston, son George of Blackstone & Elizabeth Nichols, of Boston; wife was Olive W.

John & Julia Mac Neill, who d Mar 15, 1934, ae 75, b Cape Breton, d Boston, dau Angus & Catherine Johnson, b both Scotland

John & Mary, both b Ireland
1. George, d July 1, 1887, ae 24, mariner, b & d Boston
John F., m Margaret Winifred Fraser, who d Sept 3, 1921, ae
48, b Feb 20, 1873, b Hampton, NB, d Arlington, MA, dau James
M & Joan Pangborn, both b Pictou, Nova Scotia

John & Mary, both b Ireland. He d Cambridge, MA, Apr 16,
1879, ae 45, son Andrew & Margaret, b Ireland. Some death
records give her as b Eng.
1. Margaret, b Somerville, d Cambridge, MA, Jan 3, 1872, ae 2
2. John, b & d Cambridge, MA, Apr 6, 1873, ae 11 mos
3. Catherine, d May 19, 1878, ae 4, Cambridge
4. Alice, d Cambridge, MA, Mar 18, 1877, ae 1
5. Anna, d Apr 28, 1880, ae 2
6. Edward, d Apr 17, 1886, ae 18, b & d Cambridge

John, ae 41, of Belfast, Waldo Co. ME, Census of 1860
Elmeira, ae 36
Frances Anna, ae 12
Carrie E., ae 2

John of Baltimore & Lucy Strout, intentions, June 27, 1813,
Portland, ME

John, m Mary, widow of Joseph Lyon & dau Joseph Jackson of
Fairfield, CT
1. Joseph, christened June 2, 1700
2. Joseph, christened, July 12, 1702, removed to NYC and m
Anna Lockwood, dau John
3. James, b July 16, 1704, m Bethia Moore
4. Mary, b Apr 13, 1707
5. Sarah, b July 3, 1709
6. Ann, b Aug 20, 1711

Capt John of Belfast, ME, d Aug 15, 1848

Tax list of Falmouth, ME, 1766
John, 1 poll
Taxpayers in First Parish in 1760 as it appears in list in
posession of Mr Nathan Gould, not found in preceding list:
David, James, Joseph, Joseph, Jr., and William

John & Rosanna (Magee), both b Ireland
1. Edward, d Sept 29, 1900, ae 43, b & d Boston

John, b Ireland, and Mary Ryan, b VT
1. Patrick Francis, d July 18, 1899, ae 1 yr, b & d
Lawrence, MA

John & Margaret (Madden), both b Ireland
1. Michael, d Oct 13, 1893, ae 22

John & Catherine, both b Ireland
1. Thomas, d Nov 2, 1886, ae 70, b Ireland, d Boston

John, son Aaron of <u>Erie Co, PA</u>, ae 32, 1880

John S., son William, B <u>CT</u>, ae 14, on Census of 1880 for PA

<u>Hillsdale, NY</u>, Census of 1790
John Edward Christopher, b NYC
James
Stephen
David

John Bagley from England, settled in <u>Montgomery Co, NY</u>, m
1738, 10 children, 1st 6 not known
John, 1738
Daniel, 1741
Charles, 1746
Henry, 1748, in Rev War

John A., b <u>NY</u>, ae 48, Census of 1850, <u>Spring Twp, Crawford Co,
PA</u>
Prudence, b PA, ae 48
Marietta, b PA, ae 17
George W., ae 7, b PA
David, b PA, ae 16

John, 2-1-5, <u>Hillsdale Town, Columbia Co, NY</u>, Census of 1790

John Bright Bagley, b June 14, 1785, NY Census, m Jan 7, 1809,
Hannah, probably Genesee Co, NY, appear for first time 1810
Census of <u>Northampton, Genesee Co</u> NY. He d Apr 16, 1861, at
Marengo, IL, at home of son John Heman Bagley
Seven known children
Martha, 1812
Delilah, 1815
Julia, 1817
Emilene, 1820
John Heman, 1824
James Harlow, 1827, grandfather Lt Col Bagley
Frances, 1831
<u>McHenry County IL</u> Historical sketches say he came from early
Puritan settler, family

John J., son Michael & Bridget Bagley of <u>Providence, RI</u>, b
MNov 14, 1893

John of Amesbury, MA, 1810 Census 1M 5, 1M 5-10, 1M 15-20, 1F
5, 1F, 5-10, 1F, 10-15, 1F 15-20

John & Dolly had son John who d Feb 23, 1830, <u>Salis MA R</u>. He
had dau Annah Elizabethb at Ferry, Aug 30, 1847 (Ames)

John of <u>Salisbury, MA</u>, d Oct 14, 1889, ae 88, b <u>Newburyport,
MA</u>; m

John A. of W Topsham, VT, Census of 1830, 1M under 20, 1M
under 5, 1F under 5, 1F 20-30

Jonathan, b Ireland & Anna Smith, b Ireland
1.   Joshua, b Standon, QUE, d Augusta, ME, May 26, 1934

Jonathan & Martha Clark of Salem
1.   Amos, b Mar 9, 1756 NHR

Jones & wife Hannah Kniffen, 1824-1894
1.   Maria, who d 1853, Scholarie, NY
Middleburgh, NY cemetery
Jones S., 1884-1921
Bagley, Jennie, 1848-1882, wife Edward M. Hinman
Jones S., 1821-1884
Maria L. dau Jones & Hannah, 1852-1853
Stone next to Jones S. is overturned and can't be read

Jose Higgins, b Jan 28, 1923, dau Charles F. & Jemima M.
Higgins, Nashville, TN

Joseph R., Sr., son Thomas of Charleton & Mary Lane, d Oct 15,
1963, ae 63, b Southboro, d Framingham, MA

Joseph & Lydia, both b Withorn, RI
1.   William Henry, d Nov 5, 1920, b Sept 1, 1855, at Richmond,
RI, d Lowell, MA

Joseph W., son James & Margaret, b Ireland, given as of
Peabody, MA, m Mar 30, 1937, Helen Locke, b Salem, MA, 20, at
Nashua, dau Thomas Locke & Grace Pesse, he 36

Joseph & Mary of Portsmouth, NH
1. Eliabeth, b Portsmouth, m Frank Varney of Portsmouth, Jan
17, 1867

Joseph, m Rebecca True of Kensington, MA, int Oct 11, 1812,
called, Jr., Rebecca, wife of Joseph, d Mar 20, 1816, Salis MA
R, m Nov 12, 1812

Joseph of Humpreville, CT, m Jane Northup of Sherman, CT, Apr
19, 1840, at Derby, Conn.

Joseph, 1800 Census of Schenectady, NY, 1M 20-45, 2M 10, 1F
10, 1F 26

Joseph K., ae 33, miller, b NY, Census of 1850, Medina Co,
Medina Twp, OH
Mary, ae 32, b NY
Louisa A., ae 8, b OH
George V., ae 7, b OH
Sarah E., ae 5, b OH
Frank, ae 1, b OH
Emily Hall, ae 16, b OH (not a Bagley)

Joseph, ae 14, shipped to VA on Bonaventure

Joseph & Marey

1. Betsey Chase, b <u>Sandown, NH</u>, Aug 27, 1788

Joseph W., d July 13, 1941, ae 3 mos, at <u>Leominster, MA</u>, son
Earl, b <u>Lubec, ME</u> & Lona or Iona Sauvageau, b Leon, ME

Joseph,. d July 16, 1955, ae 42, b & d <u>Boston</u>, wife Catherine
Mollous, son Frank, b <u>Barre, VT</u> & Mary Wilson

Joseph
His wife Lydia, relict of Joseph bt land in <u>Gilmanton, CT</u>, Mar
18, 1774

Joseph, PURY, p 86, Census of 1850, <u>OH</u>

Joseph, b <u>Amesbury</u> & Mary Mitchell, son
1. Frank E., d July 26, 1929, ae 78, b <u>Brunswick, ME</u>, d
<u>Gloucester, MA</u>, wife Maria Jameson

Joseph & Mary
Aaron, b Nov 10, 1791, at <u>Dublin, NH</u>

Joseph, ae 32, b Ireland, living <u>Philadelphia PA</u>, Census of
1880
Bridget, ae 24, wife, b PA
Mary, ae 1, dau, b PA
Jane, 50, mother, b Ireland
Sarah, sister, ae 15, b Ireland
William, ae 19, brother, b Ireland
Maggie, ae 12, sister, b Ireland

Joseph, son John & Mary of <u>Fairfield, CT</u>, christened Jne 2,
1700

Joseph, taxpayer First Parish, <u>Falmouth, ME</u>, 1760, see David,
James, Joseph, Jr., William

Joseph, d Mar 19, 1883, ae 77, b abt 1806; Mehitable, his
wife, d Nov 6, 1847, ae 47, <u>Durham, ME</u> Cemetery

Joseph & Deborah of <u>Falmouth, ME</u>
1. Deborah, b Falmouth, Dec 13, 1735

Joseph of <u>Falmouth, ME</u> for transporting to Boston the French
interpreter and instructor, June 27, 1781 (ME Historical &
Genealogical Record)

Joseph, <u>North Providence, RI</u>, 2 males over 16, 2 females over
16, Census of 1774

Joseph, <u>North Providence, RI</u>, 1 male over 16, 2 females,
Census 1790

Joseph, ae 32, b <u>Tioga, Tioga Co, PA</u>, 1880 Census
Ida, wife, ae 23, b PA
Jennie, adopted dau, ae 3 or 3 mos

Joseph, Jr., tax list for First Parish, Falmouth, ME, 1760, see Davbid, James, William & Joseph

Joseph F., d Sept 31, 1944, at Worcester, b Southbridge, son Charles, b Northampton & Jacquelin Pelletier, b Southbridge, MA

Joshua & Mary had son James, b Mar 4, 1780, Marlboro, MA, who m at Marboro, Elizabeth Gleason, b Oct 5, 1788, dau John & Elizabeth (Snow)

Joshua & Anna
Dau, Anna, b Mar 4, 1774, at Hopkinton, NH

Joshua, son of John of Watertown, MA, Nov 5, 1655, mentioned in father's will in 1703

Joshua bt land in Cohoes, NY, May 21, 1857

Joshua and Sylvia had son Benjamin, b Jan 3, 1806, Windsor, Co, VT, m Hannah Worthley, b c 1816, W Windsor, VT, who had son Benjamin Horr, b Dec 28, 1828, W Windsor, VT

Josiah, b 1800, wife Elizabeth, b 1796, from Census of Bucsyks Co, VA, 1850
Luke A., b 1824, OH
Arthur C., b 1827
Nancy G., b 1828
Charles, b 1832
John H., b 1835
Eliza E., b 1835
Judith, b 1838
May T., b 1842
Josiah, (Marsha Twin or Town, b 1844)
Lucy, b 1847

Josiah 1830, Alleghany Co, Byardstown, PA 2M under 10, 1F 30-40, 1F under 5

Josiah 1840, Liverpool, Columbiana Co, OH, 1M 5-10, 2 M 15-20, 1M 20-30, 1M 50-60, 2F under 5, 2F 10-15, 1F 20-30, 1F 40-50

Josiah, ae 60, b NJ, Census of 1850, OH, Hamilton Co, Cincinnati, Ward 1
Jane, ae 57, born at sea
Phoebe E., b PA
Elizabeth, ae 24, b OH
John, ae 23, b PA (given as Bagley as is Sarah, probably a son of Josiah who had m and lived in same household with his wife?)
Sarah, ae 22, b PA
Thomas, ae 20, b PA
George, ae 12, b PA

Josiah, christened July 12, 1702, Fairfield, CT, moved to NYC and m Anna Lockwood, dau John. He was appt adm of her estate;

son John & Mary

Josiah W., m Lettie Decker, July 30, 1887, Gardiner, ME

Josiah (Marsha Twin or Town, b 1844), son Josiah & Elizabeth, Census of 1850 for OH, family from VA

Josiah, son Josiah & Martha, b Nov 13, 1754, NYC

Josiah of Hillsdale, NY, 1800, Census, 1M 45, 1M 5-10, 1M 10-16, 1M 26, 1F 10-16, 1F 26, 1F 45

Josiah, Lt Col Goose Van Scharck's 1st NY Regt; muster roll for Jan-Mar 1781; app Mar, 1780, reported on command at Fort Edward; also return dated West Point, Mar 22 and Mar 29, 1781; reported in command at Fort Edward; also return dated West Point, May1, May 11, May 24, and June 1, 1781; reported in command at Saratoga

Judah of Harford, VT, m Phoebe Converse of Randolph, VT, Sept 9, 1824

Judith, dau John of Watertown, MA, b Oct 11, 1646; mentioned in father's will in 1703

Judith & Samuel Swett, m, int Oct 3, 1795, Ames MA. A Widow Swett d Aug 1, 1813, No children on Ames or Salis. MA R

Judith, b 1838, dau Josiah & Elizabeth, Census of 1850, OH, family from VA

Julia M, dau Michael & Bridget, Providence, RI, b May 1, 1891

Julia Joseph., d June 10, 1871, ae 28, b Boston, d Cambridge, MA, HBC, b ME & Elvith Greene, b ME

Julia A., d Manchester, NH, Dec 30, 1856, ae 20

Junius R., b Luenenburg, VA & Elizabeth Adams of Luenenburg
1. John, ae 26, b Luenenburg, VA, m Laura Howard of Portland, ME, ae 24, b Warrenton, NC, dau Walter Howard & Minerva Boyd, m July 10, 1910, Portland, ME

Kate, b Scotland, m ____ List, b Scotland
1. Kate List, d Jan 16, 1914, ae 58, Danvers, MA, b Scotland

Katherine Calderwood, wife John Bagley, b Scotland, Oct 13, 1851, d Augusta, ME, Feb 6, 1939, dau Malcolm Gamble and Mary Jane Hood

Kent Watts, son Harry Watts Bagley, Jr., & Lois Bashaw, b June 29, 1942, Burlington, VT. This was NJ family

L. N. CBLV, p 110, Census of 1850, OH

Larkin, b 1798, Mt Sterling, KY, d 1865, father was Naty, who m Todd Hart, b 1800, d about 1806, at <u>Mt Sterling, KY</u>

Laura, m Leonard G. Blakeman, Dec 28, 1838, <u>NY</u> marriages

Laura Ann, dau Royal Anderson Bagley & Iris Goodwin, b <u>Logan,
UT</u>, June 18, 1949

Laura, dau Thomas of <u>Bedford, PA</u>
1. Rena, ae 11/12, b PA, Census 1880

Laura, dau George of <u>Philadelphia</u>, ae 4, 1880

Laurence Roberts (See Charles Frederick), m Oct 12, 1928, St
Stephens, NB. Helen Bartlett of Stetson, ME, b Nashua, NH, dau
Langley Bartlett & Ourida (Simpson)
1. Joan Bartlett, b Feb 11, 1929, <u>Bangor, ME</u>
2. Stephen Bartlett, b Dexter, ME, Oct 14, 1941
3. Frederick Charles, b Bangor, ME, Feb 14, 1931, 2nd ch
4. Sarah Jane, b Bangor, ME, Mar, 1940

Lavisa, ae 11, b 1859, Census of 1870 for <u>New Baltimore, NY</u>,
dau Nathan

Lawrence Brooks, b Aug 5, 1950, <u>Nashua, NH</u>, son Alexnader, b
<u>MA</u> & Annie McClinton, b Tenn

Ledric Selton, b <u>Ithica, NY</u>, m Minnie Boyle, b Ithica, NY
1. Raymond Ledric of Waldeboro, ME, ae 19, b Ithica, NY, m
Shirley Skay of Somerville, MA, ae 19, b Waldeboro, dau Robert
Skay & Estelle Green, m July 29, 1922, at <u>Waldeboro, ME</u>
a. Everett M., b July 10, 1924, Waldeboro, 2nd ch
b. Robert Warren, b Sept 18, 1925, 3rd ch

Leon Paul, Jr., b <u>Seabrook</u>, July 20, 1953, son Leon Paul, 22,
& Clara Emily Eaton, 16

Leon & Ella J. Campbell, b Bedford, NH
1. Emma, d <u>Plymouth, ME</u>, Oct 30, 1919, b there June 10, 1888

Leonard, d Oct, 1852, Petition of adm of his estate at Probate
Court, Waldo Co, <u>Belfast, ME</u>

Lesette, m Sidney C. Page, Jan 22, 1850, <u>Pawlett, VT</u>

Lester A., Sr. b <u>CT</u>, m Vera Caswell, b CT
1. Lester Albert, Jr., 20, b <u>New Britain, CT</u>, m Patricia
Glidden, dau Fred & Bessie Cole, about 1955

Levi, in Capt William Sharpe's Co, Col John Abbnott's Regt of
fortification of VT from 1st of Aug until 4th Aug, Sept 1781,
<u>VT Rev War Rolls</u>

Levi S., letters of adm on his estate issued Oct 31, 1826, to
Andrew Bagley, rough docket A, at page 9, probate records of
<u>Crawford Co, PA, town of Meadville</u>

Levi, priv Capt James Wallace's Co, Lt Col J. Cummings Regt
from Sept 5, to Sept 20, 1814, raised South Montville, service
at Belfast MA Vol Militia

Levi & Abbie of Nottingham, ME
1. Alice , b Bangor, ME, m Flagg Mitchell of Nottingham, Apr
18, 1891

Levi m Lucinda Hill, Jan 13, 1842, NY marriages

Lewis, d ae 5 yrs, Feb 28, 1843, Greensboro, ME

Lewis, b NH & Jean Connors, b Cambridge, MA
1. Male who d Aug 22, 1958, ae 3, b & d Winchester, MA

Lewis Badgerly, ae 77, b OH, Census of 1850, Belmont Co,
McKuaria Twp

Lewis of Pembroke, NY, m Laura A. Corser, b July 19, 1828, dau
Gardiner & Mercy Ann Thomas of Gates, NY

Lewis, d July 28, 1847, ae 7 mos, Hartford, CT Time
Lewis, d Sept 1, 1847, Hartford, CT Courant

Lewis or Bayler, 50, M, blacksmith, b NY, Census of 1850
Maria, ae 50
Hannah, ae 28
Henry, ae 20
Jackson, ae 15
Elizabeth, ae 14
Margaret, ae 11

Lila Margaret, b Jan 6, 1909, East Rochester, NH, dau Charles
H. & Anna Trafton

Lillian A., dau Thomas F. & Mary A., b Nov 10, 1893,
Providence, RI

Lilly Brush, ae 90, b Feb 18, 1859, d Aug 8, 18__, dau
Jonathan Brush & Cornelia Tuck (Mrs Helen Bagley, informant,
South Woodstock, VT

Lizzie, dau Michael of Philadelphia, ae 4, 1880

Lizzie A. of Sanbornton, NH, m Melvin LeBarron of Sanbornton,
June 3, 1897. She m (2) a Bagley, being dau of Turser &
Lavinia (Clemants) Young

Lodoiska Ashley Bagley, b Milton or Wilton, VT, dau Solon B. &
Beulah Woodruff Bagley, b Sept 23, 1834, m John A. Perley, b
Livermore, ME, Oct 15, 1833, son Nathaniel & Eliza Lane, at
Rutland, VT, Aug 15, 1860. In 1905 they lived at Wibaux, Mont
1. Howard King, b Aug 24, 1866, Prov RI, cow rancher, unm,
Wibaux, MT.
Solon's wife was living in Colchester, VT in 1888, given as
widow in Gazeteer. Solon d June 22, 1856, ae 51, at Milton,

VT. She d Mar 4, 1893, at Colchester, ae 87, dau Jesse &
Sally Ashley Woodruff.

Loise E., m Elvin R. Meader, July 16, 1879, at Montpelier, VT

Loren of Bethel, VT, m Lydia Davenport, of Haverhill, NH, Sept
9, 1817. Samuel of Washington, VT named a son Loren.   It
would appear that this is another of the sons of David &
brother to Samuel

Lorhama Bagley (Badeley), b NY, Nov 20, 1799, m Ziba Davis,
Jan 1, 1814 (Zachariah), b VT, Apr 24, 1798. Both d Jackson
Township, Randolph Co. IN having moved there Apr 1836.   Found
on 1820 Census of Coshocton, OH, once part of Washington Co.
Eight children, one of whom was her grandmother Lucinda.

Louis C., b Norwood and Dorothy Sutpher, b Newark, NJ
1. Glen Arthur, d Aug 31, 1942, ae 3mos, b Norwood, d
Tewskbury, MA

Louis Quinton, b Nov 13, 1921, Garland, UT, son Louis , b abt
1896, m Aug 13, at Brigham, UT, Blanche Ann Manning

Louis, b abt 1896, m Aug 13, 1921, at Brigham, UT, Blanche Ann
Manning, b Oct 19, 1904, Mendon, UT, other husband was Jack H.
Smith, whom she m July 29, 1928
1. Louis Quinton, b Nov 13, 1921, Garland, UT

Louisa Ella, dau Orlando and Mary Ann Bagley, d at Fairhaven,
MA, July 17, 1863, ae 39, She m Joseph Palmer Nye, son Ansel
& Harriet Palmer Nye. He was b Cincinnati, OH, d at
Nantucket, MA, Feb 21, 1894. He m (2) at Nantucket, MA, Oct
30, 1864, Mary H. Riddell.
1. Richmond Watson, b Nov 5, 1858
2. Orlando P., b July 1, 1860, d Oct 2, 1860 Nye Genealogy

Louisa of St. Johnsbury, VT, m Frederick Kendall of
Brattleboro, VT at Laconia, NH
1. Carl, b 1897
2, Roy, b 1900
3. Walter A., b 1891

Louisa of Troy, ME, m Aug 23, 1863, Francis Uhlman or Hulman,
She d Mar 3, 1882, ae 37, tombstone.

Loisa or Louisa, dau Benj & Hannah Harding, d Oct 18, 1877, ae
16, b ME, d Lowell, MA

Louise of Manchester, NH, m Daniel Emerson, Feb 4, 1856, at
Manchester, NH

Lott, b Eng, res Hamden, Conn, d June 13, 1856, ae 41, Hamden,
CT

Lucille Marvin, b Nov 30, 1923, dau Roy, b Decateur, IL and
Lottie Gokey, at Burlington, VT

Lucinda m Isreal Drew, Feb 1, 1820, Woodbury, VT

Lucy Murphy Bagley, d July 4, 1962, ae 63, b Amesbury, MA, d
Topsfield, MA, wife Astrid L. Arneberg (should this be
husband?), might be widow of Clarence of Merrmiac

Lucy H., Bath, ME, m Edward Ripley of Calais, ME, son Martha
Hortense Bagley and Fred Phelps, 1900, at Laconia, NH

Lucy A., ae 29, d Moretown, VT, Nov 24, 1894, b abt 1865 at
Northfield, VT

Lucy Frances, divorced, d Laconia, NH, b Aug 15, 1865, a Apr
22, 1943, maiden name was McManus

Lucy W., m Charles Tinker, May 4, 1949, b Dayton, OH, father
James W. Bagley, b Fayetteville, TN & Agnes Stevens, b Peoria,
IL, VT R

Luella Agnes on June 21, 1920, a minor under 16, res
Newburyport, MA, prayed for order allowing her to marry
Francis B. Cosgrove of Newburyport. It appears that
petitioner resides in said county of Essex and that her
father has deserted his family and her mother consents
thereto, and that the said marriage is proper under the
circumstances of the case. It is ordered that the petitioner
be allowed to marry the said Francis B. Cosgrove, Essex Co MA

Luisetta ? m James Pixley Dec 15, 1868, Bolton, VT

Luke A, son Josiah & Elizabeth from VA, b 1824, OH

Luna F., d Apr 6, 1895, ae 38, b Boothbay, ME, d Weymouth, MA,
dau Timothy & Rosa (Reed)

Luther Bagley, Col Samuel Ashley's Regt, Capt Cole's Co,
marched from Westmoreland NH, on alarm June 28, 1777. Listes
in National Archives as private. Went to Ticonderoga. Pay
roll of Capt John Cole's Co, Col Ashley's regt of militia
which company marched from Westmoreland on the alarm of June
28, 1777, within five miles of Otter Creek, where they were
met by an express from Col Bellows advising that the enemy had
retired and that it was best for the Milkitia to return, whcih
we did as far as the lower part of Number 4, where we were
overtaken by an express from the General forwarded by Col
Bellows requiring us to come forward immediately which we did
and marched three miles beyond Co Meade's where we met the
army on their retreat. Time of engagement, June 29. Time of
engagement July 4, to July 11 days. Amt of wages 1-4. Travel
twice to Otter Creek, 70, total 2 Lbs 13-2

Luzerne Bagley, Scholarie Co, NY
Polly Ann, his wife b 1843, d 1868
Carrie, infant dau
Alberta L., dau 1865-1928

On the same sheet of Mrs B's as above but note dates if she is
a dau
Alicew E. Bagley, b June 14, 1858, d Feb 5, 1916, m Peter   H.
Smith, b Aug 28, 1854, d July 16, 1895 (Is she a sister of
Luzerne?)

Lydia of Candia m Elisha Towle of Candia, June 14, 1801, at
Candia, NH

Lydia m William McMaster June 7, 1812, Montville, ME R

Lydia m William Swett, Jr. He b Oct 12, 1764, son Capt William
& Ann Morgridge, m at Salem, MA, Nov 14, 1785. He probably d
July 23, 1803. Children all on Salis MA R
1. Benjamin, b July 4, 1786
2. William, b July 17, 1788
3. Joseph, b Nov 24, 1793
4. Sally, b Feb 18, 1796
5. Lydia, b Mar 27, 1798
6. Bela M., b Sept 21, 1800
7. Mary, b 1789, not on Salis R but on Mrs B's list
8. Mary Ann, b Feb 11, 1804

Lydia Ellen, b Sept 13, 1863, Fowler, IL, dau George Rodney &
Ellen Chase, m William Kramer

Lydia Adams Oliver, d Feb 15, 1904, ae 82, b Malden, MA, d
Georgetown, husband Job, dau William Oliver, b Malden, MA, &
Lydia Neggles, b Boston

Lydia De Luce, d June 27, 1918, ae 69, b Boston, d Norwood,
dau Reuben G. & Sarah (Taylor), (wife of George F?)

Mabel, dau John Walton, of San Francisco, b 1870

Mabel, m William H. Margeson. They had son b Aug 29, 1900,
Carl E. Father's occupation RR section hand, b N Reading, MA,
mother's birthplace Salem, MA

Madeline m Castle Roy, June 9, 1945, Bennington, VT, father
Albert Connell, b Center Brunswick, NJ and Ann Dennessey, b
Ireland

Mae Tilton, d Oct 17, 1957, ae 80, b Groveton, MA, d
Haverhill, husband Elmen J., dau Newton & Harriet (Carleton)

Maggie, ae 12, sister of Joseph of Philadelphia, 1880

Maggie or Marguerite of Berlin, NH, m James Pickford, of
Berlin
1. Mary m John Geaves of Berlin, 1899
2. Sarah, m W. T. Kelly, 1899

Maggie Dow, dau George & Lucy Dow, m Leon Sawyer of Bradford,
VT, July 21, 1900, ae 21

Male, d Aug 22, 1958, ae 3, b & d <u>Winchester, MA</u>, son Lewis, b NH & Jean Connors, b Cambridge, MA

Mans, b Ireland, d <u>Tewksbury, MA</u>, Feb 14, 1871, ae 30

Manuel, who m Clara A. Normand, who d Aug 21, 1902, ae 50, b Eng, dau Matthew & Sarah, both b Eng. She d <u>Fall River, MA</u>

Margaret, b <u>Malden</u>
1. Male, d May 9, 1903, ae 1 dy at Boston

Margaret, b Boston
1. Elizabeth, b & d <u>Boston</u>, Aug 3, 1866, ae 5 mos
2. Katie, d Feb 23, 1870, ae 11, d Tewksbury, b Chicopee, MA

Margaret Annette, dau Alfred Howard & Marie Annette

Margaret, given on Census of 1880 as of <u>Bangor, ME</u>, no age given

Margaret, m Mason Handy, Providence, RI, Sept 1, 1858

Marie May, b Apr 28, 1881, d Sept 26, 1889, Mrs B says <u>Albany, VT</u>, father Gideon Bagley

Maria, dau Edward & Mary, b <u>Providence, RI</u>, Oct 4, 1855

Maria of <u>Newbury, NH</u>, m Elbridge Bailey, July 17, 1851, at Warner, NH, son Frank, m 1878, at Nashua, NH

Maria, dau Jones & Hannah, 1853, <u>Scholarie Co., NY</u> deaths, Hannah Kniffen, wife of Jones, 1824-1894

Maria C. Morse, d June 9, 1948, ae 88, b Grand Manan Island, d <u>Leominster, MA</u>, dau William, b Millbridge, MA & Alice Chanet, b NB

Marietta, b PA, ae 17, dau John A. & Prudence, <u>Spring Twp, Crawford Co, PA</u>, 1850 Census

Marion Warner, d Feb 18, 1902, at <u>Somerville, MA</u>, ae 60, b <u>Waterbury, CT</u>, dau Charles Warner & Mary Thomas, both b Waterbury, CT

Marion F., d July 23, 1882, ae 5 mos, b & d <u>Boston</u>, dau Charles H., b Boston & Mary C., b Turner, ME

Mark Wilkes, d July 14, 1923, ae 75, b <u>Eng, d Bedford, MA</u>, wife Ann M., son Benj & Elizabeth, both b Eng. His wife Ann M. Smith, d Mar 1, 1922, ae 72, b Apr 21, 1849, Stanford, Eng, d Bedford, MA, dau John & Abigail (Frost), both b Eng
1. James, d Dec 27, 1935, ae 58, wife Annie McGovern

Census of 1850, <u>Meigs Co, Bedford Twp, OH</u>
Martha, ae 35, b PA
Elijah, ae 10, b VA

James, ae 7, b VA
Walton, ae 5, b IL

Martha, dau John of <u>Watertown, MA.</u>, m ___Wood, her father's
will in 1703, mentions her child

Martha, ae 6, dau Daniel, Census of 1850, <u>Jackson, Union Co.</u>
<u>OH</u>

~~Mrs Martha~~ Bagley, of <u>Pawtucket, RI.</u> d in 79th yr, Nov 13,
~~1817~~

Martha Bagly HIJK, p 273, Census of 1850 for <u>OH</u>

Martha A., b Apr 23, 1918, <u>E Rochester, NH</u>, dau Charles H. &
Anna Trafton

Martin, son Michael of <u>Carbondale, PA</u>, ae 7, 1880

Martin & Margaret, both b Ireland. He d Feb 29, 1892, ae 46,
teamster, d Lowell, MA, son Peter and Hannah Griffin, both b
Ireland. She probably the Margaret, b <u>Ireland, d Lowell, MA,</u>
Oct 24, 1887, ae 41, dau John & Ann Whelan, both n Ireland
1. Marin, d Sept 9, 1883, ae 1 dy, at Lowell, MA

Martin, b Ireland & Mary Corrigan, b Bristol, RI
1. Timothy, d Feb 5, 1888, ae 1/8 dy at <u>Fall River, MA</u>
2. George, d Aug 10, 1897, ae 1 mo
3. Owen J., d Jan 24, 1889, ae 11 mos, Fall River, MA
4. Martin, d Oct 9, 1894, ae 4, b & d Fall River
5. Loretta, d Dec 5, 1893, ae 2, Fall River, MA
6. Annie L., d Sept 22, 1900, ae 7 mos, Fall River
7. Francis, d Apr 3, 1900 , ae 2 mos, Fall River, MA

Martin & Bridget, both b Ireland
1. Mary, d May 18, 1879, ae 9, b & d <u>Dedham, MA</u>

Mary, b July 1, 1909, <u>Manchester, NH</u>, illegitimate child of
Alice, b <u>Lowell, MA</u>, ae 22

Mary C., dau George A. & Mary R. m John Knowlton, Dec 12,
1867, at <u>Springfield, VT</u>

Mary of <u>Rockland, ME</u>, m Anthony Hosmer, Oct 4, 1794; he d Aug
1855
1. Frederick A., b Feb 21, 1826
2. Mary, m William E. Perr, d in NY
3. Lucy, d June 15, 1858
4. Louisa E., b Jan 5, 1830, m Capt Elijah Hall of Rockland,
ME
5. Etta
6. Elvira Speare, b Feb 21, 1832
7. Augustus, USNavy
8. Josiah Haskell, b Jan 22, 1834, d Nov 18, 1847, Rockland,
ME

Mary L. m William Baker of Brunswick, ME, Oct 19, 1842, Newburyport, MA, no children on Newburyport, MA R

Mary, b Berwick, ME, Dec 9, 1770, d Shapleigh, ME, Jan 4, 1849, m Douglas Baker, son Charles, b Jan 18, 1762, d Shapleigh, ME, Apr 26, 1844, m at Shapleigh, Feb 4, 1798.
1. Sarah, b Apr 5, 1800, m Sept 13, 1823, Samuel Roberts of Alfred, ME
2. Ahira, b Dec 23, 1801, m (1) Nov 13, 1825, Aphra Bean of Alfred, ME, who d Jan 20, 1848, m (2) Sept 3, 1848, Rhoda W. Ross of Shapleigh, ME
3. Samuel, b Oct 6, 1803; d Apr 20, 1815
4. Mary, b May 24, 1806, d May, 1849
5. Theodate, b Sept 13, 1809, m Nov 13, 1842, James Blaisdell of Sanford, ME where she now lives
6. John, b Mar 3, 1813, d Apr 12, 1815
Theodate suggests John & Lovey Bagley

Mary E., m William E. Cummings, Mar 8, 1879, at E Machias, ME

Mary T., of Clinton, m Dec 9, 1857, Edmund C. Ward of Troy, ME, at Clinton, ME. She d Feb 5, 1860 at Troy, ME

Mary Theresa, b Eastport, ME, m George Philip, b Biddeford, ME, Sept 18, 1745

Mary, ae 22
1. Frances Louise, b Portland, ME, Apr 21, 1951, b Berlin, NB or NH

Mary, a widow d Pittsfield, ME, July 13, 1913, ae 86, b Lincolnsville, ME, dau John Knowles

Mary or Polly, m Abraham Merrill, Jr., Mar 30, 1802, (Salis, MA). She d Dec 9, 1847, ae 69, wife of Abraham on death records, Salis MA
1. Abigail, b Sept 29, 1818, d Mar 18, 1820--
2. Amos, b Aug 25, 1809
3. Edmund, b May 29, 1807
4. Eliza, b June 14, 1802
5. John, b Feb 5, 1805
6. Mary Ann, b Nov 25, 1812

Mary, dau Jerry & Joanna of Wetherfield, VT, both b Ireland, b Wethersfield, VT, Aug 11, 1862

Mary Annette, d May 23, 1879, ae 31, dau P Bagley & Mary Green, at Bethel, VT

Mary of Amesbury, MA, a single woman, estate adm by John B. Sargent, June 8, 1847, Essex Co Probate R

Mary, d Apr 1845, at Salisbury, MA

Mary m Greeley Putney. Their dau, May M., b Washington, NH, Aug 31, 1859, m Newport, NH, Mar, 1878, Myron M. Tenney, b

Newport, NH, June 16, 1857. (Tenney Family). Their dau, Maria J., b Washington, NH, Sept 26, 1849, m Albert O. Codman, b Sept 12, 1842, m Oct 5, 1863. She d Feb 10, 1872.

Mary A., m Joel H. Wickwire, Dec 23, 1837, <u>NY</u> marriages

Mary, m George F. Putney, Nov 4, 1848, <u>Worcester, MA</u>

Mary K., m Hanford Smith. Their dau Prudence Borges Smith, m Feb 11, 1836, at Newfield, NY, Charles Treat, MD, NY, b 1852, son Mary & Aaron Lynn Treat, b Feb 5, 1822, living <u>Waverly, NY</u>, 1907, d Aug 3, 1907, at Waverly (New Eng Gen Register).

Mary B., wife of Capt Nicholas French, d Oct 9, 1871, ae 90, <u>Salis MA Cem</u>

Mary, m William Bearch, Oct 18, 1772, <u>NY</u> marriages

Mary A., widow of <u>Lebanon, NH</u>, June 28, 1920, Grafton Co R

Mary, ae 24, b NY, dau William & Sarah, <u>Portage, OH</u>, Census 1850

Mary Ann, b <u>W Topsham, VT</u>, ae 30, m Dec 24, 1839, James H. Coffin of Groton, VT, ae 30, b W Topsham
1. David B., ae 5, W Topsham
2. Sarah F., ae 2, W Topsham, VT, Census of 1850

Mary Adaline, died <u>Dover, NH</u>, Dec 26, 1945, ae 88, returned for burial to <u>Montpelier, VT</u>. He husband was Henry. She b Oct 31, 1857, Warren, VT, dau Edwin Dame & Sarah Benton

Mary, m Nathan Huse of South Hampton, NH, Dec 2, 1830, Salis MA. Children on <u>Amesbury, MA R</u>
1. Mary Alice, b Apr 1, 1838, d Mar 26, 1839
2. Nathan Challis, b Apr 23, 1835
3. George Washington, b Jan 28, 1832

Mary Alice, ae 21, d Feb 18, 1897, m dau Ira Hammond & Ellen Kendall at <u>Windsor, VT</u>

Mary D., of Meredith, m William Horne, July 1, 1829, <u>Meredith, NH</u> (Nathan & Rhoda Whitam?)

Mary of Troy, VT, m James House of <u>Bethel, VT</u>
1. Sarah House, m Sylvestre Lamprey, 1892, at <u>Laconia, NH</u>

Mary of Campton, m John Dearborn of Chester, NH, Oct 28, 1829, at <u>Campton, NH</u>
1. Martina Rogers, m David Perceval, 1865, NH R

Mary, m Charles York of <u>Raymond, NH</u>, July 23, 1829, NHR

Mary of <u>Newbury, VT or NH</u>, m Elisha Harrington
1. Sarah Stetson m Elijah Piper 1867, at <u>Bradford, NH</u>

Mary A. m ae 30, d Feb 12, 1875, in child bed, dau Thomas & Sophia

Mary, ae 72, d Mar 31, 1856, ae 72, Heath Cem, Hartland, VT

Mary E., m C. Morrison, Nov 11, 1849, VT

Mary, STWS, p 379, Census of 1850, OH

Mary A., CMMM, p 249, Census of 1850, OH

Mary, MUSP, p 8, Census of 1850, OH

Mary S., m Silas Undewood, July 15, 1844, Hardwick, VT

Mary, m William F. Law, Apr 12, 1824, W Topsham, VT

Mary, m William F. Lane, Feb 12, 1824, W Topsham, VT

Mary P., m Marsina Hallet, Feb 21, 1849, Newbury, VT

Mary C., d Dec 13, 1842, Hartford, CT Times

Mary A., d Sept 18, 1866, Canaan, CT

Mary E., 1865-1888, Naugatuck, CT

Mary Murphy Bagley, b 1835, d 1914, Bloomfield, CT

Mary N., b Oct 1836, d Oct 11, 1914, Southington, CT

Mary W, d ae 3 mos, Sept 5, 1843, Hartford, CT Times

Mary Conant Bagley, m George Simons, son Christopher & Nancy Locke Simons, b Weare, NH, May 13, 1828. Mary d June 3, 1870. He m (2) Elsie G. Dearborn, dau Moses & Bestey.   Children by Mary
1. George Fred, b Aug 3, 1856, m Marianna Govel; he d, and she m (2) Frank Eaton
2. Lewis, b July 11, 1858, d Feb 23, 1861
3. Frank Norman, b Dec 10, 1866, m Oct 27, 1891, Mable A. Colby of Weare, NH, b May 16, 1869, dau Stephen & Josephine Simons Colby

Mary Polly Bagley, m Stephen Jones, Mar 28, 1797, South Hampton, NH
1. Sarah, b Feb 12, 1798, Springfield, NH
2. Nabby, b Sept 7, 1799
3. Robert, b Sept 9, 1801
4. Bagley, b Jan 22, 1804
5. Mary, b Dec 24, 1805 NHR

Mary, d 1900, b Ireland

Mary E., Norton R. Smith, son Roswell of Windsor, VT, b E Middlebury, VT in 1831, on July 10, 1853. He d Denver, CO in

1886. She probably d La Crosse, WI
1. Egbert N, d infancy, LaCrosse, WI. Record of Family of
Roswell Smith

Mary of Newburyport, MA, single, insane, John A. & Rebecca
Chaffee Guardians, 1881, Essex Co MA R

Mary, dau William of Green, PA, 1880, ae 9

Mary E. m Charles H. Adams, both of Bangor, ME, Oct 21, 1851,
Bangor, ME R

Mary M. & John Mason, both of Providence, RI, m at Cranston,
June 27, 1823

Mary of Greenesville, NY sold land there 12 Aug 1895

Mary, widow of Providence, RI, d in 92nd yr, Jan 6, 1791
(Might be widow Joseph of Providence)

Mary V., dau Patrick & Ellen, b Aug 28, 1895, Providence, RI

Mary, dau John & Mary, Fairfield, CT, b Apr 13, 1707

Mary A. of Fitchburg, MA. Will filed Oct 9, 1912; mentions
dau Cecilia Margaret O'Brien; Mary C. Parker; Annie M. Murphy
Worcester Co MA Probate

Mary E. of Southboro, MA, will filed Sept 6, 1928
dau Angeline
son William
husband Dennis (see Thomas of Southboro, MA)
son Charles (Worcester Co, MA R)

Mary, dau John & Mary, d Feb 12, 1828, VT

Mary Katherine, b Warren, VT, Oct 28, 1839, dau Russell
Remember & Mary (Stagg) m Rochester, IL, Oct 28, 1857, Julius
Munson Carter, b Vergennes, VT, Sept 11, 1836, merchant &
postmaster, St John's, MI. 1867-1875. Lt Capt & Brevet Major,
4th MI Cavalry, 1862-1862. Res Rochester, ILL, 1853-1859,
Elsie Ovid & St John's, MI, 1859-1876, Los Angeles, 1876-1893,
Pasadena, CA, from 1893. Son Munson Carter & Evaline (Beach)
Carter, personal friend of Abraham Lincoln.
1. Van, b Sept 27, 1859, Rochester, IL, d Mar 1, 1862, at
Ovid, MI
2. Nell (Helen), b Aug 2, 1861, Elsie, MI

Mary, dau John of Watertown, MA, b Mar 18, 1648, m June 3,
1674, Michael Flagg. Her father's will in 1703 mentions dau
of Michael Flagg but does not mention Mary

Mary, dau George of Philadelphia, ae 4, 1880

Mary, d Oct 10, 1857, ae 26, d Milford, b Hopkinton, MA, dau
Adam

Mary C., d Dec 15, 1909, ae 60, b Searsport, ME, d Boston, wife Charles H.

Mary R. Hoage, d Jan 18, 1885, ae 50, b Newmarket, NH, d Newburyport, MA (Is this Hodge?)

Mary Ann, d July 31, 1858, ae 52, b & d Longmeadow, MA, dau Stephen & Mary Ashley

Mary, dau Edward & Amarilla, ae 23, Census of 1860 (see Edward)

Mary, dau Frederick & Almira of St Johnsbury, VT, Census of 1860, b 1845

Mary, dau Daniel, Census of Jackson, Union Co, OH, 1850

Mary, ae 28, b Belmont St, Carbondale, Lack, Co, PA, Census of 1880. Also gives Effie, ae 7, b PA, but under relationship gives only "at school"

Mary, dau Michael, b Ireland, living Carbondale, PA, ae 12, 1880

Mary, dau Joseph of Philadelphia, 1880

Mary Ann, b May 20, 1816, dau David of IL

Mary J., of Pittsfield, NH, m Charles Green of Pittsfield, Dec 10, 1892, dau Abner & Sarah Whittier

Mary, dau ae 2 of Ralph of Pittsburg, PA, 1880

Mary C., dau William Bagley of CT, ae 10, Census 1880, PA

Mary, b Ireland, d Chicopee, MA, Aug 24, 1856, ae 48

Mary, b Blanchard, ME, d Lowell, June 4, 1896, ae 64, dau Josiah Webster & Elizabeth (Brick) (think this is Lowell, MA)

Mary (oram), d Nov 23, 1984, ae 84, b Ireland, d Boston, dau William & Fanny, both b Ireland

Mary, b Boston
1. Joseph, d Aug 7, 1960, ae 72, b Boston, d Wrentham, MA

Mary Bell Geddes, d Mar 17, 1920, ae 82, b Scotland, d Pittsfield, MA, dau Robert Geddes & Agnes Bell, both b Scotland

Mary Walsh, dau Michael & Catherine Nugent, both b Ireland, d Boston, Nov 26, 1900, ae 36, b Ireland

Mary Emmons Clark, d Mar 21, 1918, ae 32, b Stockport, Eng, d New Bedford, MA, dau William Clark, b Stockport, Eng & Mary

Rooney, b Manchester, Eng

Mattie Emma Pease, d Dec 25, 1960, ae 71, b Merrimac, MA, d Amesbury, husband Howard G., dau John, b Merrimac & Mattie Perry, b Sherman Mills, ME

Maude Baker, granddaughter Henry of Green, PA, ae 5, 1880

Maureen, b Apr, 1938, Manchester, NH, given as dau of Doris Evelyn Bagley, b Cape Elizabeth, ME; no father given

Mavis Ann, b Dec 15, 1910, dau William Scott & Ellen Stone, DeKalb, Co, NY

May T., b 1842, dau Josiah & Elizabeth, Census of 1850, OH, family from VA

May, dau Henry of Green, PA, ae 6, 1880

May, dau Elisha, ae 3, PA, 1880

May E. of Littleton, NH., and Grace M. of Littleton, sold land May 25, 1931. Mae made will Oct 4, 1932

Mehitable of Castine, ME, m Jeremiah Maxwell of Bangor, ME. Apr 29, 1834

Melissa, child Charles & Catherine, b Oct 16, 1836

Melville S. of Bangor, ME, m Annie F. Milliken, Feb 17, 1861, at Belfast, ME

Melville, minor heir of Sewell D., late of Dixmont, ME, deceased. His guardian was Eli Whitcomb of Dixmont who obtained license to sell real estate Jan 3, 1843

Meriam J., dau Moses of Rollingsford, NH, m August S. Hazelton of Rollingsford, Dec 6, 1858

Michael Joseph, b Ireland & Honora Woodford had son John Joseph who d Oct 27, 1941, ae 45, b & d Cambridge, MA, wife Mary Agnes Lang, who d Mar 2, 1956, ae 62, b & d Boston, father John Lang of Boston

Michael J., b Ireland & Honora Woodford, who d Mar 22, 1908, ae 36, b NFL, d Cambridge, MA, dau Edward Woodford & Ellen Wall, b NFL
1. Mary, d Aug 13, 1908, ae 5 mos, Cambridge, MA
2. Richard T., d Jan 13, 1920, ae 16, b Boston, d Cambridge
3. Male, d Cambridge, MA, July 24, 1896, ae 1 1/2

Michael & Mary (Olonnon), both b Ireland
1. Brandon, d Nov 12, 1881, ae 21, b Ireland, d Holyoke, MA

Michael Joseph, wife Mary F. Higgins, b St Brazil, GUE, d Somerville, MA, son James & Ann E. McCarthy, both b Canada, d

Feb 24, 1943, ae 52

Michael, b Berlin, NH, m Mary Higgins, Eastport, ME
1. Michael Joseph, of Baileyville, ME, ae 30, b Portland m
Alice M. Haley of Baileyville, ae 26, b Baileyville, dau Edwin
J. Haley & Mary Lawler, m Dec 29, 1949, Bangor, ME

Michael & Mary Malone, both b NFL had son Michael who d Nov
23, 1936, ae 73, b NFL, d Danvers, MA, wife Elizabeth
MacGillivary

Michael m Elizabeth Harding, who d Aug 31, 1900, ae 50, b & d
Medford, MA, dau Stephen & Mary Carroll, both b Ireland

Michael, son John & Margaret M. Madden, both b Ireland, d Oct
13, 1893, ae 22, Boston

Michael & Elizabeth, b NS
1. Catherine, d Boston, Dec 25, 1887, ae 4

Michael J., b NS & Elizabeth McGilvery, b Halifax, NS had son
Thomas who d Boston, Dec 3, 1961, ae 67
They had another son John J., who m Lillian Swenson, who d
June 30, 1947, ae 56, b Boston, d Chelsea

Michael & Nanora (Cantittie), both b Ireland
1. Philip T., d Dec 24, 1899, ae 44, b Needham, d Lowell, MA

Michael & Margaret, both b Ireland
1. William, b & d Boston, Jan 2, 1879

Michael & Catherine (Nugent), both b Ireland
1. Mary W., d Nov 26, 1900, ae 36, b Ireland, d Boston

Michael A. & Bridget, Providence, RI
1. Helen M., b Nov 14, 1893
2. John J., b Nov 14, 1893
3. Julia M., b May, 1891

Michael, ae 50, b Ireland, living Carbonville, PA, Census of
1880
Sarah, ae 41, b Ireland
James, ae 15, b PA
Mary, ae 12, b PA
Michael, ae 10, b PA
Martin, ae 7, b PA

Michael m Ann Maher, Apr 7, 1861, Lincoln, NE

Michael, ae 33, b Eng, living Philadelphia, Census of 1880
Sallie, wife, ae 26, b PA
Lizzie, dau, ae 4, b PA
Clara, dau, ae 5/12, b PA

Milo Darwin, son Francis Marion & Ellen Thompson, b Sept 19,
1874, given as married

Milts of Boston, MA, mortgage, Nov 1, 1883, <u>Grafton Co NH</u> R

Milton Wilson, ae 22, b Great Manan, NB, m Patricia Ann Harris, b Yarmouth, NS
1. Barbara Dianne, b <u>Presque Isle, ME</u>, Jan 19, 1954

Molly, m Leoman Herrick at <u>Beverley, MA</u>, Apr 26, 1905

Morris, b Irland, d Apr 11, 1881, ae 85, d <u>Springfield, MA</u>

Moses, b Apr 27, 1842, supposedly son John Bagley and ___Bailey <u>(Albany, VT line)</u>

Moses , Sergt C. Gordon's guard from Lt Col Col P. Merrill's regt of <u>Newburyport</u> from July 26-Aug 2, 1814, Service at Plum Island, musician

Moses, b 1829, at <u>Athol, MA</u>

Moses of <u>Vinal Haven, ME</u>

Moses of <u>Deerfield, NH</u>. George Turner of <u>Salisbury, MA</u>, adm of estate, Sept 9, 1857, Rockingham Co NH

Moses of Rollingford, NH
1. Meriam H., m Augustus Hazelton of <u>Rollingford</u>, Dec 6, 1858

Moses and Abigail had son Nelson who d Mar 3, 1844, ae 5 dys
On same record with George W., b 1843 and Jane E., dau William H & Jane E., but may be no relation

Moses & Polly Favour had dau Nancy, b Apr 17, 1806, at <u>Newton, MA</u>

Moses of Newton, NH, 1810, Census, 1M 15-20, 1M 20-30, 1F 20-30

Nelson, son Moses & Abigail d Mar 3, 1844, ae 5, dys <u>Chelsea, MA</u>

Myra E., ae 25, Census of <u>Belfast, ME</u> 1850, household of John P.

Myrtie, dau Clarence, son Rev Daniel m Earle Jenner

N. H., PURY, p 86, Census of 1850, <u>OH</u>

Nancy of Candia m George Dustin, Aug 12, 1809, at <u>Candia, NH</u>, suggests Stanstead, QUE line

Nancy , Josiah Brown, Feb 4, 1827, <u>Hartland, VT</u>

Nancy, ae 5, dau Daniel, Census of 1860, <u>Jackson, Union Co, OH</u>

Nancy of Montville, ME, Census of 1810, 2M 15-20, 1F 50-60, 1F

Nancy of Newton, NH,. m Isaac Hoit at Newton, Nov 22, 1829, Plaistow, NH R. Son Joseph & Sally, b May 1, 1808.
1. Martin Van Buren, b 1831
2. Lewis Cass, b 1834 (Hoyt Genealogy)

Nancy Hoit Bagley, b Apr 17, 1806, at Newton, NH, dau Moses & Polly Favour

Nancy S., 1828, dau Josiah & Elizabeth, Census of 1850, OH, family from VA

Nancy m Isaac Fitts of South Hampton, NH. He is given as of Kensington,, Aug, 1814. No children on Salis & Ames, MA R

Nancy of Newton, NH. d Sept 7, 1841, married

Nancy m John Jay Garland, son Benjamin & Mary, b July 21, 1800, m Dec 21, 1831. Four children all died. He d Sept 4, 1845; resided Joliet, IL

Nathan, Census of 1870 for <u>New Baltimore, NY</u>, given as carpenter, b Ny 1831
Aleda, ae 37, b 1833
Emma, ae 18, servant, b 1852
Lavisa, ae 11, b 1859

Nathan, b c 1751, <u>Randolph Co, NC</u>, m Sept 18, 1776, Mary Lowe

Nathan of <u>New Ipswich, NH</u>, June 25, 1771, ad granted to James Spalding of Ashburnham in county of Worcester, MA, July 22, 1773

Nathaniel of <u>Braintree, MA</u>, Ensign, Crown Point expedition, 1756

Naty of Mt Sterling, KY had son Larkin, b 1798, d 1865, m Todd Hart, b 1800, d abt 1866, at <u>Mt Sterling, KY</u>

Nellie Wood, d Oct 6, 1951, ae 85, b 1866, at <u>Upton, MA, d Milford</u>, dau Gilespie, b Upton & Sarah Holmes, b Hopkinton, MA

Nellie of <u>W Newbury, MA</u>, adm of estate of John A. Bagley, Feb 24, 1933, Essex Co R

Nelson, Census of 1870 for New Baltimore, NY, given as laborer, b NY 1820
Elisabeth, ae 49, b NY, 1821
James, ae 22, b NY, b 1848
Rachel, ae 15, b 1855
Anna, ae 13, b 1857
George, ae 9, b 1861
Caroline, ae 19, b 1851

Nellie, <u>Washington, VT</u>, will, Oct 1929

Nettie L. Wright, d Oct 9, 1931, ae 78, b <u>Troy, ME, d Boston</u>, husband Eric, father Isaac, b Geryin, ME, and Abigail, b Troy, ME

Bettie M., dau Frank of <u>Gloucester, MA</u>, m Chester Andrews

Nora, ae 10, b PA, dau John, <u>Green, Indiana Co, PA</u>, Census 1880

Norma m Alfred Riggs, May 8, 1850, <u>Springfield, MA, but on Vt R</u>

Ode, son Cephas & Maggie Paris, <u>PA</u>

Olin H., Co M, 1st regt, New Eng Vol Cavalry, b <u>Peacham, VT, ae 23, res Warren, VT</u>, enl, Dec 20, 1861, mustered in Dec 24, 1861, as priv, appt corp Jan 28, 1862, captured Aug 22, 1862, at Carlett's Station, VA, released; des Jan 21, 1863, Falmouth, VA, Ayling's Civil War

Olive, m Charles Aldrich, b Dec 18, 1820, son Mercy Smith & Asa Aldrich, he b Northwest, NY & d Saugatuck, MI, July 2, 1902. He m Sept 6, 1845, as of Northwest, NY

1. Charles A., d Sept 4, 1846; d Oct, 1877
2. Frances M., b June 16, 1851; m (1) Myron Munson, m (2) J. E. Cohenour (Jesse Smith his ancestors and Descendants)

Olive m Richard Gave, Mar 7, 1813, Montville, ME

Olive, dau Abigail, d Dec 19, 1851, ae 19, Berwick, ME Cem

Olive m Reuben Nott. Their son Sylvestre Gilbert Nott, b Summerville, St Lawrence Co, NY, Feb 2, 1836, m Emma P. Cleveland, b Dec 29, 1845, at Adams, d Oct 11, 1864 (Cleveland Genealogy)

Opal Marve, dau Roy, b Decateur, IL & Lottie Gokey, b VT, m Feb 26, 1922

Orlando M. intentions, Jan 10, 1791, Newburyport, R, m Lucretia Green

Orlando Filander, b 1816, Dutchess Co, NY, see David

Orlando F., m Melissa M. (Mrs), at Belfast, ME, June 17, 1875

Orlando J., m Mary O. He b Mar 14, 1817; she Mar 22, 1819, Vital R of Greenbush, ME
1. George W., b May, 1835
2. Samuel M., b Apr 18, 1860
3. William H., b Dec 18, 1861

Orlando & Mary Ann had dau Louise who d at Fairhaven, MA, June 17, 1863, ae 29, wife Joseph Palmer Nye, b abt 1834

Orlando J. of Dixmont, ME, m Mary E. Johnson at Dixmont, May 25, 1868, by Arnold Palmer, Bangor, ME. Apparently she divorced him about 1877

Orvilla m Francis Stillman, Mar 19, 1829, Brandon, VT, m (2) Seneca Ellis, Dec 30, 1830, Brandon, VT

Osey Marella, dau James of PA, b VA, ae 14, 1880

Osias & Lydia of Lebanon, NH
1. Nellie F., of Lebanon, NH, m Charles K. Presby, June 5, 1883

Owen, d Cambridge, MA, Mar 20, 1863, ae 52, b Ireland, son John & Catherine. Ellen his wife, d Quincy, MA, b Ireland, July 29, 1868, ae 52, dau Daniel & Julia Coney, both b Ireland
1. Mary, b & d Cambridge, MA, Apr 7, 1854, ae 1 yr
2. Andrew, d Oct 23, 1865, ae 26, b Ireland, d Quincy, son Owen
3. Owen, son Owen & Ellen, d June 6, 1865, ae 22, b Ireland,

d Cambridge, MA

Owen & Joahnna, both b Ireland. She d Mar 3, 188, b Ireland,
d Cambridge, dau Dennis Sullivan & Brigett, both b Ireland

P. Bagley & Mary Green had dau Mary Annette, d May 23, 1879,
ae 31, Bethel, VT

Patrick & Hannah (Hines) both b Ireland
1. John, d Lowell, MA, May 22, 1882, ae 4
2. Frank, d June 1, 1891, ae 1, b & d Lowell, MA

Patrick & Bridgett, who d Southboro, MA, Dec 25, 1876, ae 46,
b Ireland, dau Patrick & Ellen Cosgrove
1. James, d July 23, 1873, ae 32, b Ireland, d Fall River, MA
2. Timothy, d Mar 1, 1893, ae 62, d Fall River MA

Patrick & Mary, both b Ireland
1. Mary, d May 5, 1887, ae 23, b Ireland, d Lowell, MA

Patrick & Mary, both b Ireland
1. Mary, b Ireland, d Holyoke, MA, May 3, 1886, ae 31

Patrick, b Ireland & Elizabeth Dunlap, b Eng, had son William,
who d Dec 5, 1908, ae 74, b Ireland, d Chelsea, MA

Patrick & Bridget, both b Ireland
1. Thomas, d Oct 9, 1895, ae 32, b Portland, ME., d Montague,
MA

Patrick, a carpenter, d Boston, b Ireland, son Patrick &
Helen, b Ireland, d Feb 12, 1875, ae 23

Patrick & Mary, both b Ireland
1. Cecilia, d Aug, 1866, ae 10 mos, at Springfield, MA
2. Stillborn, Springfield, 1869
3. Annie, d Mar 14, 1885, ae 2, Springfield, MA

Patrick & Sarah Fenner, b Ireland
1. Sarah E., d Oct 31, 1870, ae 11, b & d Fall River, MA
2. John T., d July 9, 1888, ae 77, b Eng, d Fall River
3. James F., d July 11, 1883, ae 23, Fall River, MA

Patrick & Margaret Cassidy of Lowell, MA
1. Walter, ae 40, m Mary Josephine of Lowell, dau John Deeney
& Theresa Wheeler, Aug 26, 1956, at Nashua, NH
2. Edward Francis, ae 43, 2nd m, m Hazel LaCourt, 34, 2nd m,
dau William Boyle & Cecilia Van Court, Apr 14

Patrick & Margaret M. Cassidy, who d June 25, 1955, ae 75, b &
d Lowell, MA, dau John & Catherine Dailey, both b Lowell.
1. Joseph, d Sept 10, 1902, ae 2 dys, d Lowell
2. Mary, d May 13, 1905, stillborn, Lowell
3. Female, stillborn, June 19, 1914, Lowell
4. Lillian, d Oct 24, 1913, ae 1, b & d Lowell, MA
(Probably same as above)

Patrick, d June 9, 1899, ae 27, b Ireland, d Leominster, MA, son of Patrick & Margaret, both b Ireland

Patrick
1. Abner, b & d Dover, MA, Feb 23, 1855

Patrick & Ellen of Providence, RI, had dau Mary V. b Aug 28, 1895

Paul, d July 13, 1958, ae 57, d Sioux Falls, SD, wife Helen, d July 13, 1958; they were m Lake Co, SD, he was son of Alick & Theresa Miller

Paul, son William & Elizabeth, d Jan 4, 1956, ae 57, b Somerville, MA, d Fall River, MA

Pauline, d Manchester, NH, Aug 19, 1897, ae 3 mos, dau Edward & Della Ashley of Concord, NH

Penelope, wife George W., Ellsworth, ME, Mar 9, 1897, ae 54, widow, dau Frank & Harriet Little

Parmely, child Jesse & Sarah, his wife, b Corinth, VT, Aug 12, 1801

Peter & Hannah Leahy, both b Ireland
1. Male stillborn, d Sept 3, 1898, b & d Lowell, MA

Peter, son John & Ellen, both b Ireland, d Mar 14, 1868, ae 30, b Ireland, d Lowell, MA

Peter L. of Fulton, Scholarie Co, NY, bt land in Rensalaerville, Dec 21, 1861. He and his wife Maria and John Kline and Matilda, his wife sold land in Renssalersville

Peter in Bracken, KY
Phebe, wife Robert, b Exeter, m 1735, d E Greenwich, RI

Philena F. of Waldo, ME, deceased, adm Bertha Pease, money left in Gloucester of Edward J. Geary's heirs (widow of Luther?)

Philip, ae 19, shipped to VA on Paule from London, Eng

Philip T, son Michael and Nanora, both b Ireland, b Needham, MA, d Lowell, Dec 24, 1899, ae 44

Philip, b 1616, Manchester, Eng, went to VA, 1637.
He had son Edward, who had son Joseph who m Ann Champion. Their dau Betsey, b 1740, in VA, m (2) Thomas Traylor. Mrs Thelma (Gillum) Harris is a great great great grandaughter of Betsey
Rte 2 Box 318
Frankston, TX, 75763

Phoebe of Plymouth, NH, m Charles Flanders of Ply, NH, Jan 28, 1839, at Plymouth

Polly, m John Harding Apr 23, 1801, China, ME

Polly m Dustin Nutt
Their son Valentine Nutt, d Apr 3, 1915
His son m a Bagley

Mrs or Miss Polly of Candia, m Ebenezer Brown of Raymond, Aug 20, 1857 NHR

Polly of Candia, b June 10, 1775, m Aug 28, 1794, at Candia, Thomas Dearborn, b Mar 21, 1774. Marriage record gives her as Mrs.
1. David, b Dec 10, 1794
2. John, b Jan 8, 1797

Polly Bagley, child of Polly Colby, b May 11, 1780, Corinth, VT

Polly, m Stephen Putney of Boscawen, NH, Oct 11, 1804

Polly m John Pillsbury, Sept 27, 1801, at Bridgewater, NH

Polly m Dudley Perkins of Dunbarton, NH, May 2, 1797, at Dunbarton, NH

Polly m John Hilbert, Brookfield, VT, Sept 27, 1793

Polly Ann of Scholarie Co, NY, m Luzerne Driggs, her dates 1843-1868, on Jones Bagley lot, Middelburgh Cem
Carrie, infant dau of Luzerne and Polly Ann Driggs

R. DeCharmes, ae 22, b PA, son Samuel of Bedford, PA, 1880

R. C. Bagley, sex female, ae 36, Census of 1880 for Newburgh, ME, see Blanche in same household

Rachel, dau Horatio, Census of 1870 for New Baltimore, NY, ae 6

Rachel, ae 15, b NY, 1855, dau Nelson, on Census of 1870 for New Baltimore, NY

Ralph W., ae 17, son Ralph of Shaler, PA, 1880

Ralph, b Grand Lake Stream, ME, m Alice Carson, b Robbinston, ME
1. Darrell Ralph , b July 10, 1912, 2nd ch (associated with Dover-Foxcroft), m Phyllis McInter of St Stephen, NB, dau Bernard McInter and Vina Webber, Mar 11, 1934, Calais, ME
a. Gary Carson, d Mar 23, 1953, Bangor, ME

Ralph, b England, ae 62, Shaler, Alleghany Co, PA, Census of 1880

Caroline, wife, ae 43, b PA
Sarah B., dau, ae 19, b PA
Ralph W., son, ae 17, b PA
Caroline, dau, ae 14, b PA
Richard, son ae 9, b PA

Ralph, ae 33, b PA, living Pittsburgh, PA, Census of 1880
Mary A., wife, ae 26, b PA
 Robert A., son, ae 4, b PA
Mary, dau ae 2, b PA

Ray F. on lot with Frank P. of Detroit Lakes, MI, cem

Raymond Ludwig, b Ithica, NY, and Shirley V. Skay, b
Waldeboro, ME
1. Robert Warren of Waldeboro, ME, ae 23, b Waldeboro, m July
4, 1949, at Washington, Dorothy Helen Eugley of Nobleboro, ME,
ae 19, b Waldeboro, dau Osgood Eugley & Mildred Hall
a. Michael Robert, b Damariscotta, ME, Apr 5, 1952
2. Everett Montagne, b Waldeboro, ME, ae 33, m Constance
Simmons, ae 33, Friendship, ME, 2nd m divorced, dau Stacy
Simmons and Mildred Burns, July 14, 1955, at Newcastle, ME

Raymond Charles Bagley, b c 1929; d Feb 17, 1952, ae 23 NHR

Rebecca Hollis, b abt 1807, d May 8, 1880, ae 73, b & d
Braintree, MA, dau John, b Braintree and Lydia Hobart, b
Quincy, MA

Rebecca m Levi Fuller, VT, Oct 17, 1825

Rebecca, b Nov 28, 1811, d Feb 15, 1880, East Haven, CT

Rebecca m Leonard Shorey, St Johnsbury, VT, Oct 19, 1829

Rebecca m Barack Snell, St Johnsbury, VT, Nov 27, 1834

Reginald S., d Sept 13, 1913, ae 14, b Greenwood, SC, d
Worcester, MA, son Charles E., b Lebanon, NH, and Achasa L.
Allen, b Hyde Park, VT

Reuben, 62, b NY, listed in Cairo, NY Census of 1850 in same
house with family of Asa Finch, 51, farmer, NY

Rhoda W., of Lowell, MA, ae 19, dau David & Dorothy m Isaac B.
Chaplin of Dracut, MA, ae 27, carpenter, son Samuel & Eliza,
May 31, 1846, Lowell, MA

Rhoda, m Henry Low, Apr 1845, Newburyport, MA. Nothing else
there

Rhoda, d Mar 26, 1922, ae 90, East Haven or Waterbury, CT

Richard and Marcia, both b Canada
1. Richard J., d July 15, 1883, ae 10 mos, b & d Somerville,
MA

Richard m Joanna C. Donovan, who d Oct 6, 1930, ae 29, Boston, dau Michael & Mary J. Harris, b & d Boston

Richard H., d Mar 29, 1888, ae 50, b Eng, d Lawrence, MA, parent James, b England

Richard, son ae 9, of Ralph, Shaler, PA, 1880

Richard P. son Richard & Sarah Webb, b Boston, England, d Boston Dec 24, 1939, ae 60. He m Eliza Entwistle who d Apr 18, 1952, ae 70, b Lancashire Eng, d Chelsea, dau Samuel, b Lancashire, Eng.
1. Their son Robert W., d Nov 24, 1959, ae 47, b & d Boston, wife Mary Noonan, US Army

Richard, b Eng, probably d Jan 7, 1910, ae 61, son Benjamin & Elizabeth Wilkes, both b Eng, who m Sarah Webb, b Eng. (See above)
1. Benjmain Gerald, d June 13, 1920, ae 31, b Eng, d Quincy, MA
2. Robert W.,d Mar 6, 1945, ae 50, b Boston, d Watertown, MA, wife Elizabeth Hargreaves (gives parents as William and Sarah Menns), both b Eng. Elizabeth d Jan 9, 1963, ae 75, at Lexington, MA, dau William & Esther Ann Brierly, both b Eng
3. Richard who m Eliza Entwistle, above)

Richard & Elizabeth, both b Ireland
1. Cornelius, d Jan 27, 1888, ae 3, b & d Peabody, MA
2. Richard, d Peabody, Oct 15, 1877, ae 4yrs

Richard, listed as female on Census of 1880 for PA, ae 64 living in home of John Bagley & Susan, b NY

Robert, b Jacksonville, ME. , Shular Watson, b Eng
1. John Robert, b Marshfield, ME, Jan 28, 1947, stillborn

Robert A., ae 4, b PA, son Ralph of Pittsburgh, PA, 1880

Robert and Ann Jane McAdoo Bagley, had son William Scott, b Canton, NY, Dec 27, 1874

Robert Field, b Apr 14, 1825, Bachaman, MD, d Jan 27, 1909, m Feb 24, 1854, Esther Sumner Perkins, b Dec 23, 1826, d Dec 1, 1914

Robert, b Eng., m Ruth Williams, b Eng
1. Robert L., b Chicago, IL, ae 40, m Freida Schrebber, b Fort Germay at Nashue, NH, June 17, 1918, dau of Carl Schrebber & Annie Mills of Mason, NH
1. Marchanne, d Nov 23, 1919, ae 3, b Worcester, d Fitchburg, MA

Robert W., son Richard & Sarah Webb, d Mar 6, 1945, ae 50, b Boston, d Watertown, MA, wife Elizabeth Hargreaves who d Jan 9, 1963, ae 75, at Lexington, MA, dau William & Esther Ann

Brierly, both b Eng

Robert W., son Richard & Eliza Entwistle, d Nov 24, 1959, ae 47, b & d Boston, wife Mary Noonan, US Army

Robert J., son of Francis P. & Ruth lived at Chester, NH, in 1970's when mother died

Rodea m John Ford, Jan 26, 1803, Corinth, VT

Roger Lewis, son Royal Anderson & Iris Goodwin, b Logan, UT, Dec 13, 1946

Rosa McHare Reed Bagley, d Sept 21, 1914, ae 79, b Wiscasset, ME, d Quincy, MA, parents both b ME. Does not give husband

Rosannah, b Canada, d Essex VT, ae 67, Feb 23, 1863

Rosanna, b Boston, m Thomas Subey, b NS
1. Mary E., b Cambridge, MA, d Nov 30, 1910, ae 34

Rose M., of Lebanon, NH, always wife of Charles, d Lebanon, NH, May 17, 1917, ae 57, b Minnesota, 1860, Feb 11, dau Jerry Dyer & Lucy Colby

Roy Edmond, b June 23, 1920, VT, son Roy, b Decateur, IL and Lottie Gokey

Roy, b Decateur, IL, son Sidney, b IN & Harriet Powers, b IN, ae 28, m Lottie Gokey at Burlington, VT, Aug 23, 1919
1. Ipal Marve, b Feb 26, 1922
2. LeRoy Edmond, b June 23, 1920
3. Lucille Marvin, b Nov 30, 1923

Roy Curtis, b Apr 22, 1895, farmer, b Purdin, Linn, MO, d Nov 15, 1957; m May 19, 1918, Purdin, Edna Ann Foster, b Jan 16, 1895, Browning, MO, dau George Fletcher Foster & Mary Ann Knifong.
1. Margaret Elaine b May 10, 1920, Purdin, m June 2, 1940, Clyde Russell McCollum
2. Charles Fletcher, b Aug 17, 1922, Purdin; d Jan 14, 1932
3. Clarice LaVina, b Apr 1, 1925, m May 11, 1947, Ruppert Milton Lavern
4. Wilma Carlyn, b Aug 25, 1926, Purdin, MO, m Aug 18, 1946, Curt Helms
Roy was son of Charles Stewart Bagley and Anna May Hedges

Roy E., d Aug 13, 1896, ae 7 mos, b & d Hopedale, MA., son Charles H. & Mary E. (Fletcher), both b Milford, MA

Royal Anderson, b Aug 26, 1922, at Moroni, UT, father Royal and mother, Mary Anderson,, m Sept 24, 1934, Iris Mary Ellen Goodwin, b Feb 21, 1922, at Bicknell, UT, dau Lewis & Thisbe (Hanks)
1. Roger Lewis, b Dec 13, 1946, Logan, UT
2. Laura Ann, b June 18, 1949, Logan, UT

Royal Bagley & Mary Anderson had son Royal Anderson who m Iris Goodwin, Bicknell, UT, 1934

Russell Remember Bagley m Mary Stagg and had dau b Warren, VT, Mary Katherine, Oct 28, 1839, m Julius Munson Carter

Russell, d Warren, VT, Jan 28, 1840, ae 37-7, b 1807 tombstone

Russell D., d Feb 13, 1890, ae 2 dys, b Wakefield, MA, son William H., b Newbury, VT & Ruth T. Blackman, b Minneapolis

Russell Bagley, farmer, ae 41, Census of 1850, OH, Cuyaga Co. Brecksville, all born NY
Hatasak, ae 41
Theodore, ae 19
Harriet, ae 15
Savresse, ae 12
Brigham, ae 9
Enfils, ae 6
Ann, ae 5
Selah, ae 3
David 3/12

Ruth m Charles Smith, May 12, 1805, Salis, MA R
1. Caroline, b Mar 1, 1808
2. Charles, b Mar 1, 1806
3. Nelson, b Feb 28, 1810, son Charles F. & Ruthy, d July 9, 1811, ae 16 mos
4. Nelson, b Aug 5, 1814

Ruth of Nova Scotia m Elijah Saben
1. Mattie m Feb 24, 1866, George H. Tenney, son Jacob B. & Caroline (Cram) Tenney of Ipswich, MA

Ruth E., b Oct 31, 1864, d Sept 28, 1928, either East Haven or Waterbury, CT

Ruth, m Nathan Eaton
1. Joseph F., b E Kingston, NH, Dec 14, 1831, painter, came to Milford from Lynn, m (1) Mary L., dau John & Abigail Mace Holmes of E Redfield, ME, b Apr 19, 1832, d there May 22, 1863. He m (2) Mary F., dau Charles P. & Jane Drew Barry, b Sept 21, 1833. He d Merrimac, MA, Apr 3, 1895

Ruth m David Osgood, Oct 1, 1772, Gen Reg

Ryth Tyndale, d July 25, 1901, ae 5, b Amesbury, might be dau of Clarence, d Feb 6, 1908

Ruth, dau T. K. & Carrie Aiken of Bedford, NH, b Jan 11, 1890

S. R., of Newton, NH, d Jan 2, 1849

Saley m John Johnson Reade, int Jan 30, 1796, Salis MA R

Sallie, dau Henry of Bedford, PA, ae 10, 1880

Sallie B., granddaughter of Thomas of Bedford, PA, 1880, ae 10

Sally of Sutton, NH, m Abner Ward, son Abner & Polly Davis, b
1800. Resided at Sutton. No children. She d Feb 16, 1857,
ae 63, gravestone. Ward Genealogy

Sally Ann, dau James C. & Doris of Montpelier, VT, b June 6,
1939

Sally m John Brown, Dec 24, 1812, at Salis MA. She d Apr 19,
1833 (Salis R). Children on Salis MA R
1. Alexander Bayley, b Aug 26, 1822
2. Clarissa, b Dec 3, 1823
3. Eliza, b Aug 24, 1826
4. Mehitable M., b June 13, 1819
5. Polly T., b Mar 12, 1817
5. Polly T., b Mar 12, 1817
6. Sarah Ann, b Nov 28, 1821 (try Franklin of Seabrook)

Sally of Salisbury & John Gale, m Jan 1, 1797, Ames MA. She d
Jan 10, 1841, ae 66. He probably d May 1813, ae 45, son of
Eli & Dorothy. Children on Ames MA R
1. Adams, b June 15, 1806
2. Edmund, b Feb 15, 1797, d Aug 31, 1840, ae 42
3. Jacob, b Sept 16, 1803
4. John, b Sept 13, 1801
5. Sally, b May 15, 1799
6. William B., b Sept 21, 1809

Sally & George Brown, Jr., m June 29, 1837, Salis MA, no
death dates , nor in Ames
1. Abiagil, b Dec 7, 1839, Salis MA
2. George W., b June 24, 1844, Amesbury
3. Henry M., b Apr 6, 1846, Amesbury
George was a carpenter and he and his wife, Sarah lived at the
Ferry, Amesbury, MA

Sally of Strafford, VT, m Isaac Chamberlain, Mar 31, 1814

Sally m James Miner, b 1772, son Anna Champlin & Capt Benj
Miner, Cheeseborough Genealogy

Sally Elaine, 2 Mar 1930, Detroit, MI dau Harmon & Josephine
of Berne, IN

Samantha, dau Henry of Green, PA, ae 18, 1880

Samuel & Sarah A., Oliver, both b Eng
1. Mabel, d July 26, 1901, ae 1, b Fall River, MA

Samuel m Cynthia Meach, b at Preston, CT, Nov 26, 1789

Samuel, priv in Sgt Young's guard from June 28, to July 5,
1814, raised at Newburyport. Service at Newburyport, MA. MA

vol militia

Samuel of Hudson, NH, 4 males 2 females, 1800, Census

Samuel, Co B, 5th Regt NH Vol inf., substitute, b NH, ae 19, b
Thornton, enl, Aug 19, 1863, mustered in Aug 19, 1863, as
priv, wounded Apr 7, 1865, Farmsville, VA, d July 10, 1865,
Washington, DC, Res given as Manchester, NH

Samuel B., late of Hampton, NH, Dec 5, 1867, Stephen Smith,
adm, Rock Co NH

Samuel L. of Portsmouth, NH, 1M under 9, 1M under 62, 1F under
83, 1800 Census

Samuel, son John of Watertown, MA, b Oct 28, 1653, mentioned
in father's will in 1703

Samuel, b Aug 28, 1792, W Newbury, MA. son Jacob ae 27 or 77,
& Betsey Woodman, at Weare, NH

Samuel G. & Christina Thomas, both of Boston
1. Caroline C., d Jan 17, 1914, ae 84, don't know if maiden
name was Thomas and she m a Bagley, no husband given

Samuel MGYK, p 80, Census of 1850, OH

Samuel & Hannah, b Scotland
1. Jane E., d Mar 29, 1862, ae 6, b & d Andover, MA

Samuel & Elizabeth Steeves, both b NB had a son William H., d
Chelsea, MA, b NB, d Sept 3, 1929, ae 63, wife was Bertha B.
Bishop

Samuel of Muskigum Co, OH had son John of Logan, OH, Civil War
vet, John, b 1842

Samuel ae 46, Bedford, Bedford Co, PA, Census of 1880
Rebecca, wife, ae 46, b PA
Thomas E., son ae 23, b PA
R DeCharmes, son, ae 22, b PA
George H., son, ae 9, b PA

Samuel of Smithfield, RI, d suddenly May 22, 1773. Phebe, wid
of Samuel d at Smithfield, ae 70, Sept 15, 1787

Samuel R., d July 16, 1890, ae 6 mos, b & d Norwood, MA, son
George & Lydia, both b Boston

Samuel K., b abt 1813, VT, m Euretta Hawks, b abt 1827
1. David, b 1847, NY
2. Nancy, b 1851, NY, m William Smith
3. Magy M., b 1850, NY
4. Lyman, b 1852, NY
5. Mary E, b 1854, NY
6. Jessie Ruth, b 1857, NY, m William Lelzar Coulter in

Antrim Co, MI

Sarah White Bagley, d Oct 12, 1913, ae 69, b Weymouth, MA, d
Taunton, dau Edward White b Weymouth & Sarah P. Lovell, b MA

Sarah C. Briggs, d Sept 8, 1918, ae 94, b Wareham, MA, d
Fairhaven, da Israel Briggs & Nancy Clark, both b Wareham, MA

Sarah J., d Oct 16, 1899, ae 64, d New Bedford, MA, b Eng,
single

Sarah E, given on Census of Medway, ME for 1880, see Alexander

Sarah, ae 7, dau George of Philadelphia, 1880

Sarah G., widow Sewell D. was allowed 100 dollars out of his
estate, Mar, 1840, Bangor, ME Court

Sarah, sister of Joseph of Philadelphia, 1880

Sarah A., of Liberty, ME, m Augustus J. Wilson of Liberty, Oct
23, 1862, at Belfast, ME

Sarah B., ae 19, dau Ralph of Shaler, PA, 1880

Sarah Louise, dau George A. & Mary Perkins, b Aug 22, 1861, VT

Sarah J., ae 24, Census of 1850 for Belfast, ME, household of
John P.

Sarah, ae 15, b NY, dau William & Sarah, Census of 1850 for
Sciot, Portage, OH

Sarah of Wilton, ME, m Eliah W. Badger, son of William &
Rebecca (Taylor), b July 3, 1835, Maine Genealogist

Sarah, dau John & Mary, Fairfield, CT, b July 3, 1709

Sarah, b Jan 29, 1774, dau William Bagley, Salem, NH

Sarah, dau John of Watertown, MA, b Sept 29, 1659, mentioned
in father's will in 1703 as wife of Isaac Learned whom she m
July 23, 1679

Sarah J. Cloon, d Mar 23, 1926, ae 76, at Peabody, b
Marblehead, husband Henry A., dau Thomas & Mary (Glass), both
b Marblehead

Sarah m John Nutt, Newbury, VT, Apr 2, 1791, VT R

Sarah of South Haven, Mich, m Edwin Jacob, b Sept 28, 1833,
son Marion (Scovill) and Jacob Lockwood, Survey of Scovils in
Eng & Am

Mrs Sarah m Isaac Wing, Jan 13, 1817, res St Johnsbury, VT

Sarah S., m D. W. Stevens of <u>Newbury, VT,</u> Dec 13, 1848, res Rockingham, VT

Sarah m Gilman Wheeler, 1835, at <u>Warren, VT</u>

Sarah E., 1855-1916, m Flynn H. MacDonald, 1865-1949, <u>Danville Village Cem, VT</u>

Sarah, b Nov 29, 1824, m John Taylor & d Sept 23, 1895, Family R

Sarah D., b Sept 4, 1820, d Oct 21, 1822, <u>Amesbury MA</u> tombstone

Sarah E., of <u>Hanover, NH</u>, spinster, estate to A. W. Guyer, July 26, 1921, b Oct 4, 1832

Sarah Bagley, wife of Ezekiel Hadley buried in same yard with Jonathan Bagley who m Goodwin. He d Aug 6, 1871, ae 82. Tombstone, <u>Bradford, NH.</u> Her stone cannot be read. An Ezekiel Hadley, b Feb 12, 1792, son Obediah & Ann Getchell, m Sarah Bagley, 1813
1. Infant Nancy, b Jan 13, 1826
2. Rachel, b Jan 2, 1817
3. Sally, b May 12, 1819
4. Jonathan Bagley, b May 10, 1821
5. Ezekiel, b July 15, 1823
6. Nancy G., b Jan 13, 1826
7. Harry, d y
8. Lucy A., b May 6, 1826. Children from Bradford, NH R. Ezekiel's birth from family Bible as is her marriage. Mrs B lists son Hadley, b 1813, d Oct 10, 1813, Nancy G., b 1815, d Mar 31, 1820, Rachel, b Jan 2, 1817, Sally, b May 12, 1819, Jonathan, b May 10, 1821, Ezekiel, b July 5, 1823, Nancy, b Jan 13, 1826, Lucy A., b May 6, 1836, all b Bradford, NH

Sarah of <u>Lowell, MA,</u> m Archibald Waugh of Lowell, Dec 25, 1843, at <u>Nashua, NH</u>

Sarah of Boston & Joel Richards, b Lyman, son Frank Richards m 1876, at <u>Orford, NH</u>

Sarah Badgerly, ae 18, b OH in household of Moses Rigger, Census of 1850, <u>OH, Brown Co, Pike</u>

Sarah Bagby, ae 20, b Ohio, in household of Otho Perry, Census of 1850, <u>OH, Brown Co, Pike</u>

Sarah with David & Nancy Morrison of <u>Salisbury,</u> sold land in Seabrook, NH, Jan 2, 1828, Rock Co Deeds

Sarah m Daniel Hazen Emerson of <u>Hampstead, NH</u>
1. Albert Hazen, b Sept 21, 1861, m Sept 26, 1893, Susie Holt, dau Emily Almira & Capt Thomas V. Stinson; b June 11, 1862, New Eng Gen Register

Sarah m Elmer Temple
1. Robert B., d Aug 19, 1890 ae 7 mos, <u>Bakersfield, VT</u> cem

Sarah, dau John, b Dec 6, 1822, at <u>W Topsham, VT</u>

Sarah, d <u>Tunbridge, VT</u>, June 21, 1885, married, recorded at <u>Boscawen, NH</u>

Sarah, published to Jonathan Hoit, Nov 16, 1784, <u>Amesbury, MA</u>

Sarah m James Potter, Feb 1, 1776, <u>Salisbury, MA</u>

Mrs Sarah, d Dec 19, 1953, in Berlin Twp, <u>Delaware Co, OH</u>
Three daus:
Mrs Leona Freeman of Westerly, OH
Mrs. Lodena McNamara of Marion, OH
Agnes Jaycox of Galena, OH

Sarah Emily, 1844-1927, wife of J. T. William, 1837-1914, <u>Craftsbury, VT</u> cem

Schyler, Census of 1870, <u>NY, New Baltimore</u>, not on Census of 1860
Schyler, ae 41, laborer, b NY, 1829
Jane, ae 38, b 1832
Connelly, ae 19, male laborer, b 1851
Hearne, ae 11m b 1859
Clarence, ae 7, b 1853
Borger?, ae 1, b 1869

Serene C., d Dec 31, 1890, ae 80, b <u>Plum Island, MA,</u> d Lynn, dau Bejamin & Ann Clifford, both b NH, no husband given

Estate of Seth, deceased, late of <u>Morristown, VT</u>, Nov 1, 1830, probate r of Orleans Co, VT

Seth of <u>Plainfield, NH,</u> m Sally Kimball of Cornish, NH, Feb 20, 1803

Sewell, had died by Mar 1840, when his widow, Sarah was allowed 100 dollars out of his estate, <u>Bangor, ME Court</u>

Sidney C., m Adelaide Lock. He d Jan 4, 1920, ae 57, b Aug 18, 1862,, b & d <u>Boston.</u> His parents given as Cullen & Adelaide Locke, birth RI. However on the death certificate of Adelaide Locke, she is given as d Jan 31, 1925, ae 60, b Warren, RI, d Melrose, MA, dau John Locke, b Rye, NH, and ----Mason, b Rehobeth, MA, wife of Sidney C.
1. Ralph H., b Boston, Sept 4, 1890, d China, ME. Aug 13, 1946, husband of Lottier Foster

Sidney, b <u>IN</u> m Harriet Powers, b IN
1. Roy, b <u>Decateur, IL</u>, ae 28, m Lottie Gokey at Burlington <u>VT,</u> Aug 23, 1919

Widow Silence, m Caleb, son Caleb Carpenter, published Sept

27, 1784. He b Dec 4, 1759, d Mar 31, 1833. She was an original member of the 1st Baptist Church of E Providence, RI, d Nov 17, 1799?

Solomon, early record of Providence, RI

Solon B. & Beulah Woodruff Bagley, had dau Lodoiska, who m John Perley. She was living in Colchester, VT, 1888, given as widow of Solon B. in Gazeteer. Solon d June 22, 1856, ae 51, at Milton, VT. She d Mar 4, 1893, at Colchester, ae 87, dau Jesse & Sally Ashley Woodruff

Sophia of Brookfield, VT, m Massena Greenslit Feb 24, 1821

Stanley J. of Athens, NY, a minor under 14, was placed under guardianship of Eva Spoor of Athens, Robert Wilkinson & Daniel Daley, town of Coxsackie, NY, Feb 9, 1912

Stephen m Ann Allen, b in Eng
1. Edward, b 1810, m Elizabeth Bennett in Bradford, PA
a. Alonzo, b Bradford, PA, 1837, d 1902, ae 65, Earlyville, IA
Armour W.
Harry A.
Mrs Ann Town
Jessie May Ayers of Brandon, OH
Benjamin M. Cedar Point
Charles H., North Dakota

Stephen of Bradford, MA & Judith Warren, m May 22, 1740, Ames MA

Stephen D., 1886-1931, Waterbury, CT

Stephen T., m Alice Read, Providence, RI., Dec 17, 1864

Stephen, 1 1 2, Stephentown, Albany Co. NY, Census of 1790

Stephen, on Census of 1870 for Catskill, NY
Stephen M, ae 26, buther, b NY, b 1844
Ella, wife, ae 23, b NY, 1847
Not on Census of 1860, probably son Horatio

Stephen, Census of 1790, for Hillsdale, NY

Stephen, m Mary Ashley
1. Mary Ann, d July 31, 1858, ae 52, b & d Longmeadow, MA

Stephen T. son William V., b Providence and ____ Tabor, b RI, d Mar 12, 1920, ae 27, b Providence, d N Attleboro, MA

Sturlin, CMWS, p 46, Census of 1850, Ohio

Mrs Summer Bagley (Antoinette), ae 75, d Laconia, early 1970's. Born Winthrop, MA, husband Summer of Meredith, Burial in Canton, MA. Manchester Union

Sumner of Argyle, ME m Liddia Fernald, Argyle ME, b June 1,
1837
1. Alfred Morton, of Foreston, MN, ae 22, b Argyle, m Flora
Estella Vinal, ae 22, b Orano, dau Martin J. Vinal and S.
Patten, m July 7, 1896, at Orano, ME
a. Florence M., m ----Larson, b 1900
b. Catherine J., deceased by 1869
2. James F., d Augusta, Oct 9, 1922, b Argyle, ME, Apr 24,
1873, m ae 34, Winfred Stubbs of Wollaston, MA, ae 35, dau
Samuel & Frances Blatch, m Feb 12, 1908, Concord, MA
a. Fernald Stubbs, Bagley, d National Soldiers Home. Dec 1,
1909
A Sumner m Gertrude Nelson, 1897, at Bagley, MN.   He d July
27, 1914. This Sumner was in lumber busines at Bagley, MN
which is named for him.

Surkey, d Dec 22, 1853, at Hingham, MA, ae 87, b Boston

Susan may have been living with granddaughter and Henry
Patterson in 1860 Census. This goes with Thomas of Troy, ME
line

Susan H., m James Kimball of Rutland, VT, Oct 17, 1830

Susan Ann, m Shepard
1. John Shepard of Boston
a. John Shepard, Jr., of Palm Beach, and Lenox, MA, former
owner of Shepard stores, b Boston, Jan 2, 1857, m Flora E.
Martin and Alice Maude Miller. Miller Genealogy (Try William
Richardson line of Duluth, MN)

Susan F. of Nashua, m Charles Robbins, b Concord, NH
1. William m 1889, at Concord, NH
2. Charles m 1885, at Concord, NH

Suzanna of Plymouth, NH, m James Stearns of Rumney, May 1,
1834, NHR

Susannah m Mar 14, 1802, Bailey Cross, son Jonathan Cross &
Polly (Bailey). Bailey Cross d Sept 28, 1813, Susannah m
sometime after 1817, Stephen Worth. History of Canaan, NH
1. Leonard, b Feb 14, 1803
2. Luther, b Sept 16, 1804
3. Lemira, b Aug 31, 1802
4. Susannah, b May 12, 1813

Susie, dau ae 11, of John Bagley & Susan, b PA, Census of 1880

Sybil M., d Wilmot, NH, Sept 8, 1898, ae 3, b Wilmot, dau
Fred, b Bradford, VT, & Isabelle Downes, b Andover, NH (This
is one who lived at Potter's Place)

Sylvester, entered May 2, 1779, Capt Burt's Co, in Col Warren
Regt of militia in voluntary service in guarding the frontier
of VT. Rev War Rolls

Y. D., captain, July 16, 1829, Weymouth, MA

Y. K. m Sept 23, 1887, Carrie Downing Aiken, b Sept 17, 1864, dau Charles of Cincinnati, OH, and Martha S. Merrill, History of Bedford, NH
1. Ruth, b Jan 11, 1890
2. Helen, b Feb 27, 1892

Terrance & Mary, both b Ireland, He d Jan 27, 1879, ae 49, b Ireland, d Worcester. I am not sure if this is his death date or her's.

Thomas, d Apr 13, 1865, ae 40, Bangor, ME

Thomas I, b Brownsville, JCT, ME, m Clara Little, b Melrose, MA
1. Donald Albert, b Portland, ME, July 15, 1932

Thomas of Bangor, ME., m Margaret E., b Ireland, dau Timothy & Ellen Dennison. She d Bangor, ME, Jan 16, 1905, ae 65, his widow

Thomas F., W Warwick, RI, d Boston, Feb 25, 1951, ae 72, son Thomas & Mary McQuire, both b Providence, RI

Thomas & Eleanor Harveley, both b Eng
1. George m Claudia, who d Aug 20, 1947, ae 64, b Providence, RI, d Boston

Thomas, d July 27, 1917, ae 60, b Eng, d Lowell, MA; m Alice, who d June 2, 1888, ae 25, b Ireland, d Lowell, dau Patrick & Alice Coyle, both b Ireland

Thomas of Boston & Elizabeth Ricks or Rocks, b Scotland
1. John, b & d Boston, Oct 4, 1914, ae 1

Thomas & Hannah (Johnson), both b Ireland
1. Rose, d Nov 23, 1882, ae 3, at Holyoke, MA

Thomas, b & d Boston, d Dec 3, 1961, ae 67, son Michael, b NS, and Elizabeth McGilvery, b Halifax

Thomas J., b Bronville, ME & Margaret Roche, b NFL
1. Male, d Aug 24, 1954, ae 1 dy, Winchester, MA

Thomas, son John & Bridgett, both b Ireland, d Lowell, MA, May 28, 1869, ae 29

Thomas, son James & Johanna, both b Ireland, d Jan 1, 1886, ae 36, b & d Lowell, MA

Thomas W. F., & Chasie T. Duren, who d Sept 2, 1950, b & d Lowell, dau Edwin, b Chelmsford & Christina Hady

Thomas F., m Ellen F. Mackin, who d Oct 24, 1932, ae 51, b & d Boston, dau Patrick, b Ireland & Ellen McGrath, b Boston

Thomas & Catherine (Launeau), both b Ireland
1. Catherine, d Jan 31, 1889, ae 45, b Ireland, d Newton, MA

Thomas, b Ireland, d Boston, Nov 2, 1886, ae 70, son John &
Catherine, both b Ireland

Thomas F., b Cranston, RI, m Bertha A. Turner, b Lynn
1. Thomas F. III, d Oct 19, 1940, ae 23, b Providence, RI, d
Newburyport, MA

Thomas & Hannah, both b Ireland
1. Doyle, d Tewksbury, MA, Dec 11, 1869, ae 1

Thomas H., d Jan 31, 1941, ae 54, b Boston, d Medford, MA,
wife Mary McDermott, son John b Eng & Ellen Ford, b Ireland

homas & Mary Horrigan, b Montague, MA
1. Graydon, d July 28, 1908, ae 15, b & d Montague
2. Thomas, d May 21, 1911, ae 16, b & d Montague

Thomas O., d Hopkinton, MA, Sept 19, 1852
Betsey, d Hopkinton, MA, b Haverhill, NH, d Sept 17, 1854, ae
82

Thomas , Emma Mayo, who d Apr 21, 1960, ae 98, b Malone, NY, d
Springfield, MA

Thomas, b NS & Catherine, b Roxbury, MA
1. Mary A., b & d Cambridge, MA, Feb 1, 1868, ae 2

Thomas J., son James & Bridget, both b Ireland, d Oct 10,
1887, ae 32, b Canada, d Malden, MA

Thomas m Letitia, both b Ireland
1. John, d Aug 11, 1882, ae 79, at Malden, MA
2. William, d Apr 11, 1887 ae 66, b Ireland, d Malden, MA

Thomas H., b Medford & Lillian Boostel, b Brooklyn, NY
1. Female, d July 8, 1914, ae 70, Boston
2. Henry, d Sept 24, 1915, stillborn, at Medford
3. Thomas Philip , d Oct 23, 1912, ae 6 dys at Medford, MA

Thomas, d Oct 9, 1899, ae 32, d Montague, b Portland, ME, son
Patrick & Bridget, both b Ireland

Thomas Baguley, d 1863, Concord, MA

Thomas S., b 1871, d Jan 10, 1936, ae 65, buried Lincoln
Memorial Park, NE

Thomas came from Eng and lived in Boston in summer; in winter
lived Fossum, MN. He was there before the railroad, in lumber
business floating logs down river. Now the town of Bagley.
He must have some connection with Sumner of Argyle, ME.

Thomas of <u>Amesbury</u>, Will, June 28, 1908, Sarah Bagley, widow
of my deceased son to be executrix of my will.   I have not
forgotten any of my children or grandchildren but I desire
Sarah to have all my property.

Thomas H., b May 13, 1834, d Jan 5, 1905, <u>Hartford, CT</u>

Thomas F. & Adelia Brown of <u>St Johnsbury, VT</u>
1. Mamie, ae 2, d Sept , 1876, b Danville, VT

Thomas m Margaret Donvan, residence, <u>Bangor, ME,</u> m there Feb
10, 1855

Thomas & wife Mary Jane of <u>Albany, NY,</u> sold land there Mar 29,
1876, NY deeds

Thomas, b Montral & Annie Campbell, b Providence, RI
1. Edward J., d Mar 28, 1901, ae 21, b & d <u>Malden, MA</u>

Thomas E., son Samuel of <u>Bedford, PA</u>, ae 23, 1880

Thomas, d Sept 9, 1858, ae 10 mos, b & d <u>Boston,</u> son William &
Mary

Thomas & Jane of Eng had in Eng
1. James m Elizabeth Anderson, Nov 7, 1866, 3rd m, at <u>Essex,</u>
<u>VT,</u> He d Dec 17, 1866

Thomas, ae 75, b PA, <u>Bedford, Bedford, Co</u>, Census of 1880
Sallie, wife, ae 72, b PA
Boher, Laura B., dau ae 23, b PA
Boher, Rena, dau Laura, ae 11/12, b PA
Sallie B. Bagley, dau ae 10, b PA

Thomas & Mary A. Kennedy
1. George, d Jan 12, 1903, ae 2 dys at <u>Leominster, MA</u>

Thomas C., ae 2, son Daniel, Census of 1850, <u>Jackson,   Union</u>
<u>Co, OH</u>

Thomas & Ellen Colville Bagley, had son b Nov 27, 1884,
<u>Lincoln Co, TN,</u> See Charles

Thomas had a dau, b <u>Providence, RI,</u> Oct 7, 1859. A dau d Oct
7, 1869, ae 10

Thomas of <u>Richmond, GA,</u> 1830, 3 males 1-5, 1M 15-20, 1M 20-30

Thomas, d May 20, 1930, ae 42, <u>Hartford, CT</u> Cem

Thomas of <u>Amesbury, MA</u>, 1810, Census 1M 10-15, 1M 20-30, 1F
30-40

Thomas & wife Ruth, at <u>Groton, CT,</u>
1. James, b June 7, 1706, at Groton
2. Jerediah, b Apr 23, 1708, at Groton (Try Thomas & Ruth in

Boston)

Thomas, 1913-1920, <u>Waterbury, CT</u>

Thomas Francis of <u>Lynn, MA IL</u>, estate to Russell Westerfer, Nov. 1940, Essex Co R

Thomas Lowell Bagley, b 1836, <u>IL</u>, d Apr 18, 1918, m Martha
Collumber
Lauina, b 1839, in IL, m (1) Tanner, m (2) Taylor
Christine, b 1844, IL, d Nov 30, 1898, m Boardman Mills
Orlando Aton, b Apr 28, 1846, IL, d Jan 4, 1909, m Eliza Jane
Banguess
Catherine, b 1849, Pottawatomil, IA, m McAdams
Joseph Hyrum, b 1852 in CA
This family were Mormons, William & Catherine were baptized
and endowed in church Jan 23, 1846 (Don't know where the
William comes in)

Thomas H., b Charleton, MA & Mary A. Carrigan, b Westboro, MA
1. Mary F., d Aug 4, 1891, ae 4 mos Hudson, MA
2. Ferdinand, d Nov 10, 1955, ae 50, b Southboro, MA, d
Marlboro, MA
3. Hannah G., d May 3, 1956, ae 69, b Southboro, d Marlboro
4. Joseph R., Sr., d Oct 15, 1963, ae 63, b Southboro, d
Framingham
5. Marie M., d Feb 12, 1956, ae 53, b <u>Southboro, d Marlboro,</u>
teacher
6. John Francis, d July 16, 1906, ae 20, b Southboro, d
Marlboro, MA

Thomas of <u>Southboro, MA</u>, will filed May 8, 1911
son Thomas of Southboro
son Dennis of Southboro
dau Mary S. Salmon of Southboro
son Patrick of NYC
dau, Hannah G.of Southboro
does not desire to leave his wife anything. Hannah was
Eexcutrix, Worcester Co, MA R

Thomas F. of <u>Leominster, MA</u>, will filed May 19, 1934
son T. Frank
wife Mary A. Worcester Co, MA R

Thomas F. & Mary A., had a dau Lillian A., b <u>Providence, RI,</u>
Nov 10, 1893

Thomas F. & Mary. <u>Providence, RI,</u> had a dau Genevieve, b
Providence, RI, Aug 17, 1899

Thomas, given as of <u>Albany, NY</u> bt land there Nov 1, 1867 (land
given as once part of Bethlehem) bt more land in Albany, Dec
10, 1874
Thomas & Mary Jane, his wife bt land in Albany, Apr 1, 1878
Thomas given as of Bethlehem, bt land in Albany, May 28, 1877

Thomas, b Malden, MA & Elizabeth, b Westford, MA
1. Minnie, d Oct 20, 1890, ae 46, Medford, MA
2. Michael, b Crampton, RI, d Medford, Mar 10, 1883, ae 36,
given as son of Thomas & Elizabeth, both b Ireland

Thomas, son of Daniel & Mary of Newton, b Ireland, d Newton,
MA, July 20, 1861, ae 32

Thomas, son John, b Boston & Ann McCarthy, b Manchester, NH, d
Feb 28, 1959, ae 80, b & d Boston

Thomas W. & Margaret Mullen, who d Aug 29, 1963, ae 82, b
Woburn, MA, d Medford, MA., dau Peter, b PEI & Mary Berine, b
Ireland

Timothy, son Patrick & Bridget, she b Southboro, MA., d Mar 1,
1893, ae 62, d Fall River, MA

Timothy, b c 1670 of Oyster Bay, NY, m Freelove Townsend, b
Dec 29, 1674 of Oyster Bay, dau Thomas & Mary (Aling).   Her
other husbands was Major Thomas Jones.   She d July, 1726

Timothy m Margaret A. Corbett, who d Sept 3, 1891, ae 34, b
Ireland, d Boston, dau John & Mary Madden, both b Ireland

Timothy, b Ireland, d Boston, Dec 24, 1893, ae 40

Timothy m Elizabeth Horrigan, who d Jan 15, 1900, ae 39, b
Ireland, d Malden, MA, dau Timothy & Mary Harding, both b
Ireland

Timothy, land grant in Herkimer & Oneida Co, NY, Jan 20, 1734
Timothy in Oneida, June 25, 1736, in Montgomery Co, June 17,
1737

Timothy, Concord, NH, 1800 Census, 2M 7, 1M 11, 1M 3, 3 F
under 35, 1F under 9, 1F under 12, 1F under 20 (Is this the
Timothy from Candia?)

Timothy, b Oct 1803, child Mr Bagley, June 7, 1827, twin inf
of Timothy d Sept 14, 1831, Child Mr Bagley June 19, 1833

Timothy of Salem, MA, estate granted to Lillian Bagley, wife,
June 22, 1922, Essex Co R

Timothy & Hannah had son John Clifford, b Franconia, NH, Mar
1, 1809, probably Bayley

Timothy & Rosa had son George D., d Apr 28, 1942, ae 70, b
Braintree, d Weymouth, MA

Timothy m Mary Elizabeth Sullivan, who d July 1, 1955, ae 77,
b Framingham, d Bourne, MA, dau Patrick & Mary Elizabeth Hall,
both b Framingham, MA

Timothy, son Timothy, b Boston & Rebecca Hollis, b Braintree, d May 7, 1901, ae 71, b Braintree, d Weymouth, MA

Timothy, b Boston, probably m Rebecca Hollis, b Braintree
1. Joseph, d Jan 19, 1903, ae 65, d Taunton, b Braintree, MA
2. Timothy, d May 7, 1901, ae 71, b Braintree, d Weymouth, MA

Tommy Earl, b June 24, 1937, Jefferson, TX, son Beryl E. &
Mildred Mickeroy

Tristan, ae 69, 1850, Census of NY, Greene Co

Tuna G., d Apr 6, 1895, ae 38, d Weymouth, MA, b Boothbay,
ME., dau Timothy, b Braintree, MA & Rosa Reed, b Boothbay, ME.
No husband given

Valentine & Elizabeth Fowler had son Charles H., who d Apr 15,
1900, ae 37 (probably Seabrook, NH)

Vespucines A., d Jan 1, 1843, Hartford, CT

Viola Hannah, dau Benjamin & Hannah Tuttle, d May 18, 1891, ae
34, at Montpelier, VT, b Dixmont, ME

W. W. of Hartland, VT & C
1. Male, b Mar 30, 1870

Walker, son Alfred, b Washington, DC, d Boston, Apr 24, 1892,
ae 39

Wallace D. of Randolph, VT, Will probated June 8, 1927

Walter, b Hyde Park, VT, m Cora Estelle Wilcox, dau Cryus of
Cambridge, VT & Augusta Bullam, b Hyde Park, VT. She d Sept
4, 1899, ae 29, b Hyde Park, d Milford, MA

Walter, b E Machias, ME, m Elizabeth, b E Machias
1. Arthur A., b E Machias, ME, Mar 23, 1853, d Lubec, ME,
June 23, 1918

Walter Royce, ae 20, b Lubec, ME, m Martha' Ann Richards, ae
18, b Roger's Bluff, ME
1. Ruth Ann, b Lubec, .ME, Jan 31, 1749
2. Sharon Philip, b June 18, 1950
3. Kim Michelle, b Sept 14, 1954
4. William Royce, b Aug 31, 1947 all Lubec, ME

Walter, son Patrick & Margaret Cassidy of Lowell, MA, m Mary
Josephine of Lowell, dau John Deeney & Theresa Wheeler. Aug
26, 1956, at Nashua, NH

Walter, b & d Sept 25, 1893, ae 6, b Springfield, MA, son
William, b NY & Mary Goodsuie), b Ireland

Widow Bagley, d Chester, NH, Aug 8, 1834

Wilfred m Grace Karl, who d Aug 31, 1936, ae 60, b Rockland,

William F. of Boston, MA, ae 37, b Boston, 2nd m, divorced, son John J., b Ireland & Ellen Ford, b Ireland, m Ellen Teresa Leary of Boston, ae 32, b S Boston, dau Cornelius Leary, b Ireland 7 Nora Grady, dead, m Jan 16, 1928, at Portland, ME

William, b Eng & Margaret Ann Tweedie, b Eng
1. Thomas of NY, ae 30, b Eng, m Cordella Sullivan of Bucksport, ME, ae 33, b Prospect, ME, dau Ephraim & Anice Dodge, July 29, 1912, at Bucksport, ME
1. Male, 1st ch, b Feb 28, 1915, Ashland, ME

William of Saco, ME, 31st Inf, 1864-1865, History of York Co, ME

William James, son of James & Mary Spellman m Ellen Blanche Haight at Montpelier, VT, Sept 14, 1880, ae 26. He d Berlin, VT, ae 36, July 5, 1898

William & Mary (Lawlor), both b Ireland
1. Fanny, d Jan 10, 1898, premature at Dedham, MA

William m Mary Freeman, in RI by Rev Joseph Snow, Apr 25, 1765
William Esq, d at Pawtucket, RI, in 177th yr, suddenly Apr 29, 1815
Mary , wife William d at Pawtucket, Mar 24, 1814

William, b 1832, Vinton Co, Ohio, wife Mary, Hamden, OH service Civil War, enl Feb 27, 1864, priv Co A. 62nd Regt OH Vol

William, d Cincinnati, OH, ae 57, d June 24, 1975, b Eng, a butcher

William of N Providence, RI, m Cerina Tabor of Seekonk, Feb 14, 1816

William N & Catherine had a dau Emma, b Taunton, MA, Nov 9, 1853, who d Providence, RI, ae 13 mos

William, trustee officer, 1827-1830, Hocking, OH. See John L. of Hocking

Command is given to sheriff of Prince George Co. Maryland. June court, 1696 that he return the panel of his grand inquest which is being returned the Juros thereof called by their names Likewise came (viz) William Bagley and others

William Lloyd, son Alfred Howard m Marie Annette

William, son John & Margaret (Welch) of NY came to Santa Rosa, CA, 1848, where he was a judge. brother of John Walton

William & Susanna had son John Burnham, June 5, 1807, at Dunbarton, NH

William, ae 54, farmer, b MA, Census of 1850, Sciota Co, OH, Wheelersburg
Sarah, ae 42, b ND
William ae 20, b ND
Mary, ae 18, b ND
Honora, ae 13, b ND
Charles, ae 10, b ND
Caroline, ae 8, b ND
Sarah, ae 6, b ND
Alice, ae 3, b OH (this sounds peculiar because ND wasn't settled until long after OH)

William, ae 50, farmer, b Eng, Census of 1850 for Summit Co, OH, town of Boston
Lucy, ae 50, b Eng
Ada, ae 14, b Eng
Robert Andrew, ae 11, b Eng
Ellen Andrew, ae 5, b OH

William of Salem, NH had dau Sarah, b Salem, Jan 29, 1774, NH
R

William m Sarah Nichols
1. Hannah Nichols Bagley, probably of Newton, MA, m James Francis Lovejoy, a mason & farmer. He was b Oct 19, 1833, of Dec 24, 1835 at Pepperell, MA, d there Dec 28, 1877. M Nov 7, 1859, son of James Bradley Lovejoy.
a. Nora Grace, b Sept 19, 1877, at Lawrence, MA. Lovejoy Gen.
Another record gives William's wife as Hannah Nichols. Says James Francis was son of James Bradley Lovejoy and Nancy Augusta Shattuck. Says Hannah (Bagley) Lovejoy m James Francis at Lawrence, MA, Nov 7, 1859. She b Feb 1, 1831

William H., d Sept 24, 1931, ae 49, b Westerly, RI, d Tyngsboro, MA, musician. His wife, Lura J. Dyer, d May 11, 1927, ae 71, b Westerley, RI, d Lowell, MA

William, b Lowell, MA & Margaret Preston, b N Andover, MA
1. Female stillborn, Apr 7, 1904, at Lowell, MA

William L. & Mary Flaherty, both b Boston
1. William d Apr 2, 1935, ae 22, at Monson, MA

William & Mary, both b Ireland
1. Catherine, b & d Boston, Feb 11, 1889, ae 13

William H. m Bertha B. Bishop, He d Sept 3, 1929, ae 63, b NB, d Chelsea, MA, son Samuel & Elizabeth Steeves, b NB

William, b Redfords, NY & Agnes Richmond, b Scotland, had son James Edward who d Mar 9, 1934, ae 74, b Zanesville, OH, d Watertown, MA

William & Katie, both b Boston

1.   Maggie, d July 17, 1872, ae 5 mos, b Boston, d
Charlestown, MA

William V., b Providence, RI & _____ Taber, b RI
1. Stephen T., d Mar 12, 1920, ae 77, b Providence, d N
Attleboro, MA

William, b Pawtucket, RI
1. Charles d Nov 26, 1863, b & d Boston

William & Elizabeth
1. Paul, d Jan 4, 1956, ae 57, b Somerville, GA, d Fall
River, MA

William, d Dec 5, 1908, ae 74, d Cheslea, MA, b Ireland, son
Patrick, b Ireland & Elizabeth Dunlap, b Eng

William of Malden, MA & Elizabeth McLaughlin of Boston
1. William, d Aug 6, 1914, ae 1, b & d Boston

William & Mary, both b Ireland,. Mary, d Sept 13, 1884, ae
37, d Boston, dau John & Conora Stuck, both b Ireland
1. William, Jr., d Mar 26, 1879, ae 12, b Boston, d Malden

William J. & Catherine, both b Boston
1. Stephen G., d Mar 29, 1880, ae 2, b & d Boston

William & Margaret, both b Ireland
1. Matthew, b Ireland, d Boston, Mar 12, 1861, ae 58

William in Bedford Co, PA, 1840
1M 50-60
1F 40-50

William Edward Garland Bagley m Elizabeth Wilson had son
Garland Grey Bagley, b July 9, 1890, Petersburg, VA, who d
Junew 8, 1950, and who m Jan 17, 1918, Mary Upton Garland, b c
1897, Alberne, Albermarle, VA, dau Eugene Stuart & Maggie
Shields Snead who d Feb 10, 1956

William & Catherine
1. Sarah, b PA, Sept 12, 1810, d Feb 5, 1879, ae 68-4-24. She
m William James, b Bedford Co, PA, a circuit rider and their
children were b in OH. William James d 1850 by lightening.
1. Norval Wilson, b Mar 16, 1833
2. Catherine, b Oct 29, 1834, m _____ Fuller
3. Cyrus M., b July 10, 1838
4. Elias H., b Sept 29, 1840
5. Alexander N., b June 18, 1843
6. Sarah A., b Sept 21, 1846
7. Matilda E., b May 10, 1849, m _____ Sweet. Sent by Mrs
Dorothy E. Miller, Box 99, Vincent, OH, 45784

William & Mary, both b Ireland
1. Rosanna, d dec 30, 1874, ae 33, b Eng, d Fall River, MA

William & Mary McCarthy who d May 13, 1874, ae 46, b Ireland

William & Birdsget Gilds, who d Oct 12, 1948, ae 81, b
Ireland, d Medford, MA. father Edward, b Ireland

Willim & Mary, who d Apr 2, 1872, ae 34, b Ireland, d Boston,
dau John & Catherine McGonagle
1. William, Jr., d Aug 7, 1859, ae 1, b & d Boston
2. Thomas, d Sept 9, 1858, ae 10 mos
3. Ann E., d Mar 29, 1872, ae 1 day
4. Catherine, d July 23, 1871, ae 1
5. Dominick, d Oct 11, 1894, ae 26, Boston

William m May McCarthy, who d May 13, 1874, ae 44, b Ireland

William & Betsey
1. Harriet, b & d Amesbury, MA, Jan 23, 1852, ae 16

William, b Boston m Catherine, b Charleton, MA
1. Hughy, d Aug 5, 1875, ae 4mos, b & d Boston, MA
2. Female stillborn, d Apr 23, 1878, at Malden, MA

William & Mary, both b Ireland
1. Thomas, b Ireland , d Dec 9, 1887, ae 7, at Malden, MA

William J., son Dennis & Mary Lane, d July 7, 1942, ae 55, b &
d Southboro, MA

William & Sylvia, he b Portland, ME, she b Lee, ME
1. Lilla A., d June 19, 1887, ae 26, b Lee, ME, d Fall River,
MA

William H., listed Census of 1880, Lee, ME, ae 21

William, son Thomas & Letitia, both b Ireland, d Apr 11, 1887,
ae 66, b Ireland, d Malden, MA

William & Catherine, both b Ireland
1. Loisa, d Sept 29, 1886, ae 3, at Malden, MA

William J., so, ae 8 of William A., b CT, Census of 1880, for
PA

William A., ae 36, b CT, Census of 1880 for PA
Mary, wife, ae 31, b PA
John S., son, ae 14, b PA
Elizabeth J., dau, ae 11, b PA
Mary C., dau, ae 10, b PA
William J., son, ae 8, b PA
Carrie, dau, ae 6, b PA
Charles N., son, ae 3, b PA

William, Rev soldier from Salisbury, NH, History of Salisbury
by Dearborn. think this must be Bayley

William, b Lowell, & Margaret Preston, b N Andover

1.   Female, d Apr 7, 1904, ae 7 dys, d Lowell, MA

William Vincent, b Dedham & Mary Ann Taylor, b Ireland
1.   Edward M., d Apr 19, 1947, ae 46, b Dedham, MA

William W., m Frances Jackson, who d Feb 2, 1929, ae 47, b
Salem, d Lynn, MA, dau John, b Salisbury & Mary Dupree, b
Salem, MA

William & Mary (Gousill), b NY and Ireland
1.   George , d July 17, 1892, ae 2, at Springfield, MA

William Thomas, son William & Mary Goodsill, d Nov 19, 1939,
ae 64, b Springfield,, d Agwam, MA, m Jennie Evelyn Mather,
who d July 2, 1958, ae 78, b Westfied, MA, d Agwam, MA, dau
George & Lizzie Bennett, both b Westfield, MA.   William is
given as son of William, b Cohoes, NY and Mary Goodsill, b
Ireland
1.   William, d Jan 21, 1903, stillborn, Springfield, MA
2.   Female, d Feb 27, 1904, ae 1 dy, d Springfield, MA

William H., b ME & Mary Lennen, b Ireland
1.   Edward M., who d Dec 25, 1948, ae 67, b & d Newton, MA,
wife Catherine Nugent

William, ae 19, brother of Joseph of PA, 1880

William on tax list of First Parish, Falmouth, ME, 1760; see
David, James, Joseph, Joseph Jr

Census of 1790, William Bagley, 2 males over 16, 3 females

William Bagley of N Providence, RI, Census of 1790, 1 male
over 16, 2 males under 16, 1 female over 16, 1 female under 16

William, early records of Providence, RI

William
1.   Francis M., b May 15, 1841, East Liverpool, OH, d Sept 4,
1901

William H. & Jane E.
1.   Jane E. , b Feb 18, 1845
On same record with George W., & Nelson, son Moses and
Abigail, but may be no relation

William B. b Bellows Falls, VT, & Mary Bush, b Todi, NY
1.   William V., d July 25, 1892, ae 2, b Providence, RI, d
Chicopee, MA

Willia, b NY or Canada, probably d Mar 13, 1912, ae 71, at
Springfield, MA, son of Thomas, b Ireland & Abigail, b Canada,
who m Mary (Goodsill), b Ireland
1.   George F., d July 17, 1892, ae 2 mos, Springfield, MA
2.   Walter, d Sept 25, 1893, ae 6, b & d Springfield, MA
3.   Mary, d May 12, 1883, ae 1, at Springfield, MA

4. Maggie, d Sept 8, 1866, ae 1, b & d Springfield, MA
5. Edward James, d Nov 14, 1937, ae 62, b & d Springfield, MA, wife Mary Conlin
6. Charles A., d June 22, 1936, ae 48, b Springfield, d Agwam, MA, wife Laura E. Kimache, son of William, b Plattsburg, NY & Mary Goodsill, b Cork, Ireland
7. William T., d Nov 9, 1939, b Springfield, d Agwam, MA, m Jennie Mather (see cards)

William J., d Nov 13, 1908, ae 69, b Merrimac, d Springfield, MA, son William & Annie Perry, b Merrimac, MA

William, Census of 1870 for Coxsakie, NY, given as 43, harness maker, b Conn, 1827
Janett, ae 43, b NY, 1827
Charles E., ae 17, dry goods clerk, b NY, 1853, Not on 1860 Census

William & Mary
1. Thomas, d Sept 9, 1858, ae 10 mos, b & d Boston

William C., d July 14, 1926, ae 46, b Haverhill, MA, d Newhampton, MA, wife was Pearl Hyde, son of Edward, b NH

William H., of Newbury, VT & Ruth T. Blackman, b Minneapolis
1. Russell, d Feb 13, 1890, ae 2 dys, b Wakefield, MA

William, son David of IL

William, son Daniel, Census of Jackson, Union Co, OH, 1850

William Henry, ae 12, son James of PA, b VA, 1880

William, ae 33, b PA, Green, Ind. Co. PA, Census of 1880
Sarah, wife, ae 33, b PA
Mary, dau, ae 9, b PA
George, son, ae 6, b PA

William, son of George W., b Eng & Jessie Williams, b Wales, b Claremont, NH, Oct 7, 1922

William Bagley of Salisbury was in Civil War, History of Salisbury, NH by Dearborn

William Scott, b Canton, NY, Dec 27, 1874, son Robert & Ann Jane McAdoo, m Sept 22, 1897, Ellen Amelia, b Oct 18, 1875, dau Newton Stone & Alice Walker of Oswegatchie, NY, farmer, De Kalb, NY
1. Gena L., b Jan 16, 1899
2. Harold Williams, b Sept 22, 1900
3. Mavis Ann, b Dec 15, 1910. Simon Stone Gen.

William A., of Boston, widower of Anna Bagley, late of Boston, who left property in Hillsboro, NH, Apr 23, 1956. She d intestate, leaving no direct lineal heirs and that no settlement was made upon him before marriage, releases homestead right in said real estate so he can receive whole of estate, value not to exceed $10,000 and one half of all real in excess of that valued at $10,000, provided that remains after debts, Oct 19, 1956. Other heirs of hers claimed shares.

William m Betsey, dau Enoch Colby & Catherine Tyler

William J. & Jane E.
1. Jane E., b Feb 18, 1845

William of Cohoes, NY, Albany Co, NY, soldier Co H, 4 NY Heavy Artillery

William of Portsmouth m Mary Sparks, Dec 20, 1785

William, d May 31, 1866, b VT, m, farmer, at Manchester, NH

William Vincent of Dedham, MA, ae 29, m Hilda Kennedy, ae 27, b NS
1. Helen Louise, b May 3, 1926, 1st ch

William H. of Tulsa, OK whose ancestors were Thomas, Thomas, Jr., Abijah, Thomas, Zebediah, Beulah (Ashley), Sallie (Woodruff), Beulah (Bagley), William. He was ae 65 in 1941

William A., m Anna May, dau Walter Wether and Effie Blanchard, she b Jan 28, 1898, d Milford, NH, Sept 13, 1954

William, BUMI, p 415, Census of OH, 1850

William A., HMMI, p 19, Census of 1850, OH

William on Census of 1790 for Providence, RI

William, 1727, Wills of Burlington Co, PA

Willie S. d Sept 8, 1894, ae 14, given as son William & Mary Olds

Willis, ae 26, Census of 1850, b NY, living in home of Jacob Ben

Willis of Middletown, NY, bt land of Elizabeth Wright in Durham, NY, Apr 15, 1868

Winthrop, m Sally, 1799, by Jedidiah Tucker, at Louden, NH

Zebedee Bagerly m Elizabeth, dau Joshua Foster and Sally Hopkins and lived Seneca, MN
1. John
2. George
3. Abby Ann
History of Hancock, NH

Following information from Bagley News Letter which Jane Bense was putting out. Got out a couple of issues and then to had cease because of illness in family. 1987

My mother Alice Bagley Butler and I visited cousins in Northern Ireland.

Linda, dau Alan & Connie, graduated from high school, Salem OR, May 29, 1987

Suzanne Bagley Freeland, dau John & Alice, graduated June 3, 1987, from Cypress College, Long Beach, CA

Father of Connoe Bagley, Mr Allen Weist, d PA, Mar 15, 1987

John Asher (Laura Bagley) changed residence from Salem OR to Redmond, OR

Jeff Freeland, son Ron & Sue spent summer with cousin Gary Bense, Arlington, WA.

John Heman & wife, Rita, of Nodesto, CA, took trip

Mary Chilton was first female that set foot on shore of New England at Plymouth. Her father and mother d in first winter, she she m the brother of Governor Edward Winslow. Five children of whom, Susannah m Robert Latham. James, son Robert & Susannah, m Deliverance Alger. Their son Joseph m Sarah Hayward in 1717. Their son Joseph m Mary Prior in 1748. Their son James m Esther Baker at Royalton, VT. Their son Isaac, m Jemima Poor, in 1792. Their son Alsup m Polly Cole. Their dau Almira Latham m Simeon Arvin Bagley. Eight children: William, Harry, George, James, Almira, John, Arvin, and Ellen. (Samuel of Orange, NH & IA

Addenda to Bagley Notes

John and Mary Bagley had seven children baptized in Fairfield, CT, between 1700 and 1711. One dau May, bpt, Apr 13, 1707 probably m Cornelius Dikeman. Another dau Anna, bpt Aug 20, 1711 may have married Cornelius' brother Frederick Dikeman. Another dau Bethia may have married into the Monroe family.

Lusetta Bagley, b Enosburg, Vermont, 1838-1840; d Sept 1884, Stowe, VT (may have been called Laura or Luretta); m James M. Pixley, Dec 15, 1856, Bolton, VT, b 1836/38, Middlesex, VT, d Jan 28, 1914, Eau Claire, WI; he m (2) Clara Ball in WIS.
1. Safford (Sanford E.
2. Edgar A.
3. Arthur J., ancestor of Barbara Pixley, 22351 De Grasse Dr Woodland Hills, CA, 91364

Charles Hutchinson, 750 Bodega Ave, Petaluma, CA, 94952 is interested in a James Bagley, who came to AK, when it was still part of MO territory in 1816. He is said to have been born about 1787 in NJ. He was interested in family of James

221

Bagley, listed in 1790 census of Orange Co, NY, with two males 16 plus, 2 females and five others. In 1772, a militia regt of ten companies was organized, Jeremiah Hogeboom, Colonel, and one of the officers was James Bagley. The James he is looking for would have been too young to be this James.

At the same time that James came to AK an Ashur Bagley also came. Asher enlisted in the Rev in 1781, and gave his address as Claverack, NY, was furloughed 1782 to Sussex Co, NJ, and he served in NJ troops. He gave his age as 19, in 1781, but late he claimed he was b 1753 instead of 1763. He d in 1840 in Saline Co, AK and gave his age as 88 in Census of that year. His children were Asher, Jr., Lewis and Esther, all born between 1801 and 1807 in St Clair Co, IL where he lived between 1798 and 1807. A large group led by a Rev Badgely settled at St Clair about 1800. A brother of Asher, Benjamin served in the same company, 1st NJ Regt Continental line and came to AK and settled in Pulaski Co, about 1820-30.